The
Alien Gene

The
Alien Gene

Interactions between Humanity and Visitors to planet Earth

Moira McGhee

Published by INUFOR – Independent Network of UFO Researchers

THE ALIEN GENE: Interactions between Humanity and Visitors to planet Earth

Copright © 2017 by Moira McGhee. All rights reserved. Printed in Australia. No part of this book may be reproduced in any manner whatsoever without written permission.
For information address INUFOR, P.O. Box 169, Katoomba NSW 2780, AUSTRALIA.

INUFOR books may be purchased for business, educational, or sales promotional use. For information please write: INUFOR, P.O. Box 169, Katoomba NSW 2780, AUSTRALIA.

INUFOR web sites:
 http://www.independentnetuforesearchers.com.au
  www.ind.net.ufo.res@bigpond.com
  www.FACEBOOK/INUFOR

FIRST INUFOR PAPERBACK EDITION PUBLISHED IN JUNE, 2017
ISBN: 978-0-9587045-3-3

The Alien Gene

Contents

	Introduction	1
1:	The Early Years	5
2:	Humanoid Visitors	20
3:	Rosemary and Millen	33
4:	Close Encounters	48
5:	The European Wars	52
6:	After World War 2	65
7:	Those in the Know	80
8:	Elizabeth	94
9:	Lydia, Vera, and Ronda	110
10:	The Wrekin and Isle of Man	122
11:	More British Cases	127
12:	Genetics	137
13:	Implants and Microchips	148
14:	Further Cases	158
15:	Leesa	176
16:	Alien Bases	198
17:	New Zealand	209
18:	More 'Generational' Cases	230
19:	Prophecies, Messages, Lessons to Learn	241
	Epilogue	253
	Index	255

Introduction

UFO research is very complex, and dedicated investigators produce countless books, articles and documentaries about it. Disputes and disagreements abound as to what is the 'truth'. Many different alien presences are reported on planet Earth and investigators can get lost in the numerous reports and conflicting viewpoints as they attempt to uncover the facts.

I am often asked if I 'believe' in UFOs or aliens, as if it were some kind of religion. Yes, I believe there is ample evidence for the existence of many different unidentified flying objects, with occupants. However, I have yet to ascertain their origin, motives and technology. Archaeological discoveries, such as ancient rock art, paintings, architecture and scrolls, record our interaction with strange craft and visitors over millennia. These occurrences are echoed in myths and legends of indigenous peoples across the world.

In this book I attempt to provide an overview of UFO phenomena in the 20th century, concentrating on some facets of the alien contact-abduction phenomenon itself – that of the humanoid visitors, who are physically real and present. These 'Visitors' seem to look like us – or is it we look like them? They impart essentially the same message; that we must improve how we care for this planet, and co-exist peacefully with one another. Not only have they been coming here for some time, they have infiltrated our society, and live, undetected amongst us.

(Other investigators, with impeccable credentials consider this possibility: Dr David Jacobs feels that 'human-alien hybrids' walk among us undetected. Russian professor Valery Burdakov studied UFOs for many years, and communicated with cosmonauts about their UFO sightings. Burdakov felt 3% were genuine contacts from extraterrestrial civilizations – and that we should listen to their messages!)

I mainly discuss a small portion of this category. In some cases extraterrestrials seem to affect three or more generations within one family. Each case includes one or more instances where a nuts-and-bolts UFO is sighted in the air or on the ground, and many contactees report physical effects such as an implant or damaged reproductive systems. In addition to superior advanced technology, many of my cases include an element of genetic manipulation, telepathic communication, psychic abilities, or 'synchronicity' between contactees and other phenomena. As I delved into details more consistencies became apparent. Most were of British birth or descent, with some connection to the Isle of Man, and male fathers or grandfathers in the military or secret service. Nearly all had a similar 'blood-line' or could trace their lineage back to the aristocracy.

My investigations have taken many years of liaison with family members. The contactees I worked with desperately needed the support of someone who not only believed them, but had also shared similar experiences. Unfortunately, I could not refer them to any support group, until I had determined their report was genuine, and their recall was not influenced by anyone else.

In most cases I use pseudonyms for the witnesses. While they asked me to write about their experiences and the messages received, they needed to get on with their lives without publicity. In a couple of instances some subjects, whom I have known for many years, requested pseudonyms because they experienced unwarranted harassment when their identities were disclosed by the original researchers. Others, for several reasons, asked me to wait for their passing before disclosing their experiences, activities and messages.

On visits back to Britain, I joined the British UFO Research Association (BUFORA), and became firm friends with the then secretary, Betty Woods, whom I stayed with on a couple of occasions. Through Betty, I communicated with other UFO organisations and researchers, including several abductee support groups. Due to the similarities between subjects such as Elizabeth, Lydia, Vera and Mary we were also able to combine some of our investigations.

At various times, I corresponded with or exchanged data with independent investigators in Ireland and Wales, besides these better-known groups.

Although Visitors were often mentioned in the 1950s and 60s, (to the point of being given saintly status), little is reported or discussed about them today. They do not seem to have ulterior motives, other than a desire for our wellbeing. Their message is simple – practice peace, love and harmony, and protect the ecology of the planet before our warlike and destructive ways annihilate planet Earth and all who live here. They regard us as a barbaric, arrogant and selfish species which tries to dominate everything. A more subtle communication has been that although humanity is now venturing into space, we will not be allowed to leave our planet to create havoc elsewhere in the Galaxy.

It is not known if they anticipated any ensuing problems and consequences from these pronouncements, which in themselves were benign and logical. Some contactees treated these Visitors and their message in a religious context, and others, like George Adamski, let ego and publicity overtake any meaningful progress. This had not been the intention of the Visitors, who have now become much more cautious and covert with their contacts and communications.

Further, Earth's authorities did not welcome these messages being relayed to the general population. They could not, and would not disarm; in fact the opposite, given current world politics. Most importantly, these Visitors and their vastly superior technology, were seen as an unknown quantity that constituted a threat.

Our past civilisations record multiple references to these Visitors from the skies, some producing unusual children. Their presence was usually benign, helpful and enlightened. They were teachers or masters to show us the right way of peace, love and harmony. Any religions arising from such contact were hijacked by power-hungry humans, who killed, brutalised, and suppressed their human beings in the name of their own particular God – this is still happening today! There are too many variables to predict our future collective behaviour.

The Visitors are <u>not here to rescue us</u>; they offer us <u>another chance</u> by warning and advising how we can save ourselves from our own stupidity. Human history is full of cruelty to our fellow beings and all other life-forms; continual warfare, slavery, slaughter and oppression. Millions of women are regarded as 'property' and sold into marriage or slavery. Trillions of dollars are spent on military pursuits, while hundreds of thousands of children die of malnutrition and preventable diseases. We show little concern for animals, and wipe out entire species for profit, expedience, or trophies. We justify their slaughter in abattoirs and laboratories, and the pollution and destruction of the natural environment as necessary for the economy and progress.

There is reason to suspect some Visitors had an initial 'Plan A' to aid a particular race or society, (such as the Nazis, or others later), to manage Earth as a de facto World Government. So far this has been unsuccessful; we still have competing powers of America, Russia, China and Islamic Fundamentalists.

'Plan B' seemed to be open contact, when it was safe to approach normal human beings away from the scrutiny of the military and authorities. This was only possible for a very short time, and nobody heeded the messages anyway. Some obviously blended in with our society; trying to make a difference and impart better technologies to replace our more damaging practices.

(In 1998 Dr. John Mack wrote about Jim Sparks, a businessman who recalled contacts a decade earlier. Jim suffered horrendous experiences at the hands of an unknown alien race, and was told 'They' were now concentrating on ordinary people because agreements with Earth's leaders to "correct the environmental condition of your planet" had been violated.)

This has had only partial success. Perhaps 'Plan C' is to genetically manipulate humans and instil more peaceful, caring and ecologically-aware attitudes. This apparently involves focusing on particular individuals, and an often unwanted, incursion into the lives and bodies of those who are 'chosen'.

Unless we radically change our attitudes and behaviour, why would any intelligent, advanced race want to see us let loose in the Galaxy? Possibly someone out there considers our planet, maybe not us, to be of value. There could be a 'Plan D' involving the control of our behaviour by micro-chipping the barbaric humans of planet Earth, but it may not be instigated by these more pleasant type beings.

During the 1950s, some experiencers reported their 'friends' advised *most* would be leaving soon, suggesting there was an urgency to publicise their messages. Only a few would remain. This may validate some contactee reports that the Visitors bid "farewell" around 1960. Their departure was qualified with a promise that they would return in about fifty years.

Why most of these Visitors left about 1960 can only be a matter of speculation. Had another alien race arrived, or was our technology now more able to detect them, their ships or bases, wherever they were located? While many landed UFOs were relatively small, some enormous discs were reported during the 1950s.

Since then there has been a huge increase in the incidence of crop circles. Some researchers believe these are messages sent by the humanoid Visitors during their absence. Unfortunately, they have left a vacuum in the human-alien interaction scenario; an opportunity which other, less ethical entities, have been quick to use.

One aspect of the departure of this particular race has rarely been addressed. We do not know what the relationship was, and indeed still is, between our friends and the less desirable entities reported soon after. Did they blend and integrate incognito into our population in order to conduct underground activities and campaigns against the opposition?

Most researchers concentrate on blond-haired 'Nordic' type humanoids, mainly because these alien beings are the ones reported in Western society. What of other races? The Chinese, certainly a modern super-power, must also be of interest to the Visitors, but like the Russians, the Chinese have been very reticent to publicise any contact or interaction with extraterrestrials.

A few years ago, at a conference in Australia, I had the opportunity to meet Sun Shili, President of the Beijing UFO Research Society. His lecture divulged little, except an abduction of a sexual nature, of a peasant from the north of his country. Pictures were shown of a gentleman grinning from ear to ear! We were left little wiser regarding UFOs in China.

More recently, Chinese researchers have been more forthcoming. Rosanne Lin reported in the *Shanghai Star* that rocket scientist Shen Shituan said all reports of alien encounters are worth investigating. Sun Shili does not rule out any possibility, including aliens living and working in Chinese society. (This indicates that some look oriental, and not necessarily the blond Nordics favoured by western authors!)

There is much talk of evil Greys and Reptilians and their gruesome experiments in underground bases and military laboratories (MiLabs). That is not what this book is about. Instead I wish to look at the situation during the 20th Century concerning contact with Visitors of human appearance, although other types of entity were starting to make an appearance.

Unfortunately, the subject is fraught with lies and manipulation, and it is difficult to determine what really is the truth.

Chapter One

The Early Years

Many types of Visitors are reported by contactees. I am most interested in the fair-haired, Caucasian-looking humanoids – as described by witnesses in this book – the information they impart, and the possibility of genetic manipulation or enhancement. My contactees insist these beings and their craft are as physically real as we are.

Much has been reported about crashed flying saucers during 1947. I am interested in the years before this. After many years of research I am convinced by the evidence of humanoid type visitation and influence upon many countries, during those earlier decades. A commonality in these accounts indicates fair-haired humanoids in charge, with smaller Greys performing assisting roles. I have always considered the possibility that these little entities are biological robots.

Some witnesses claim multiple meetings with extraterrestrials as human as we are – just more evolved and with advanced telepathic abilities. These witnesses report being told that Visitors had been coming to Earth since ancient times. There are many hypotheses, with really no way of knowing which, if any, are correct. Modern day reported contacts certainly go back 100 years or more.

Days gone by

There are many UFOs cases recorded well before the modern surge of reports which began in 1947. UFO reports from the early twentieth century are of great interest because we had little *known,* aerial technology at the time.

While I am unsure about many 'airships' sightings from the beginning of the 20th century, no conventional explanation can account for a report made in 1927, by Russian explorer and author Nicholas Roerich. Roerich was fascinated by reports about, and with finding, Shambhala (Shangri-la) – a mystical realm where powerful, spiritual lords were rumoured to reside.

During his August, 1927 expedition, Roerich and his party saw a fast-travelling metallic, disc-shaped object at high altitude over the Himalayas. He documented this in his book, *Altai Himalaya* in 1929. One of Roerich's companions, a Tibetan lama, put a spiritual connotation on the event, because at the time of sighting it was a clear day, and they'd been watching a large black eagle flying overhead.

Roerich described the UFO as a huge oval object, with a shiny surface, with one side brilliant from the Sun. It moved quickly north to south. When overhead it changed direction from south to southwest, and quickly travelled out of sight.

(I have also wondered about the myths regarding ancient Atlanteans retreating to little known parts of the Himalayas.)

Albert Coe

In his book *Alien Base*, Timothy Good describes the experiences of Albert Coe in Canada, from a chance meeting in 1920 with a possible humanoid alien, a blond-haired young man, whom he rescued from a fall down a cliff. Coe claimed he had seen the man's craft, a 20-foot round silver disc on a tripod, and had found a torn bandana with blood on it, indicating a physiology similar to ours. Later meetings revealed the young man's race – 'Norcans', had migrated to the Solar System after a natural disaster on their own planet, and interbred with humans. Some details (which are extensive) are suspect, and involve living on Venus and Mars.

Part of the information Coe received was that Norcans had infiltrated human society since 1904 to observe and evaluate our progress. (Coe claimed his 'friend' masqueraded as an engineering student – he had seen him later, in a suit and tie at a city restaurant.) Humanity was on the verge of discovering nuclear power, which could have disastrous consequences for our planet.

Unfortunately, Coe did not publicly disclose his encounters until 1977 – long after the atom was first split. Although healthy scepticism is required, we cannot dismiss Coe's claims out of hand. We know that the extensive use of nuclear energy carries the inherent danger of serious accidents, which could damage the Earth for tens of thousands of years.

Norman Massie

MUFON Colorado reported a US case from Wayne County Illinois. In June 1923 maths teacher Norman Massie was only 10 years old. He had just let his parents' horses out into pasture, and was closing the gate, when he saw a metallic object, standing on three legs in the field. It had lights all around, and a domed top that looked like melted glass. Massie approached to within 50 feet and watched five men who were inside. It may have been difficult to estimate, but he said they were at least four feet tall, with blond hair.

"I got close enough that I could hear them talk ... One guy sat in a chair and the others called him 'Commander'. Four others made trips back and forth in the ship. I didn't know what was going on until the end, when one of the men said that 'the repairs had been made'. In a minute, it came to a hovering position, and the tripod legs telescoped up into the belly. It went straight up about 200 feet, and whizzed off to the west like a bullet."

Obviously Norman could hear the men speaking to each other in the English language. If these beings were from Earth then someone had an advanced technology of which we knew nothing!

Ian Rogers

Some years ago, an elderly Australian man, Ian Rogers, rang me about an incident in 1924 when he was a boy. One morning he was checking their rabbit traps in the Lysterfield State Forest, south of Coolamon. He has lived on the family farm there all his life, and in the 'old days' rabbits and other game formed part of poorer residents' diets.

"I was behind a tree, when I heard a humming noise, looked up and saw this flying object which landed in a clearing about 100 yards away. I have never forgotten it, and as best as I can remember, it was a long cylindrical shape, rounded at both ends, with four square windows along the side. It was at least 30 feet long, and I remember lights of some kind."

"I hid behind a tree and watched it for about an hour. At one stage, some people got out – they just looked like 'people'. I don't know where they went; they didn't come my way. After about an hour it flew up and away into the sky."

The helicopter was invented in 1939, and asked him if anything else happened. "The ground was burnt black where it had been, and the trees were singed. There were dead birds all around, and nothing grew in that small area for a long time. After it had gone I saw something glinting on the ground. It was a small piece of metal. I kept it for a long time, as it was like magic. When I rubbed it with my hands it would 'move off' of its own accord. When I raced home to tell my mother, she scolded me for getting back so late. I don't remember being gone so long. She said not to tell anyone else what happened."

Ian had mislaid his 'magic' piece of metal, and it was pointless even looking for the landing site so many years later. As for any 'missing time', given his age, that was also futile.

Leo Dworshak

Leo waited until he was 83 before divulging his contact with the Visitors, in his 2003 book *UFOs Are With Us – Take My Word*. In 1932, Leo, then a twelve-year-old farm-boy in Killdeer, North Dakota, USA, saw a large spaceship land in a nearby valley on several occasions. The seamless craft, at least as big as their barn, was a light blue colour, which allowed it to blend-in with the sky. It had flashing coloured lights on the outer shell, and rotated in a complicated way, with the inner and outer bands going in opposite directions.

At first, they encountered what seemed like an invisible force which stopped them moving too close to the spaceship. After several trips to the landing spot, he and his seven-year-old brother got to know several men from the craft, which they were eventually allowed to enter. Inside it had living quarters, and what appeared to be a movie screen showing pictures "of a place or process we could not fathom."

The men were five to six feet tall, similar in appearance, with short light brown hair, light beige complexions, and blue eyes with dark pupils. They spoke fluent English and German and told him that they were from another galaxy. Their people had been visiting Earth for thousands of years, and at that time 12 of their group were living on the planet to monitor human activity – it was part of their 'responsibility'.

Leo observed: "They were so ordinary looking in one way – but so exotic in another. If you dressed them in ordinary clothing, you would pass one of them in a strange town without blinking an eye."

Leo had spasmodic contact with them. As the years went by Leo aged, but his 'friends' did not! (This is an interesting anomaly. Recent genetic research indicates that degeneration of our genes contributes to the aging process. Some Visitors indicate they undergo a 'regeneration' process from time to time, which may explain their increased longevity and youthful appearance.)

Leo entered the Navy in 1941, and his brother Mike was killed in Korea. In 1962, with his three daughters and two friends present, they all saw the ship land. He had wanted to take his companions over to meet the occupants, but they were so scared they just watched, at a distance, for about thirty minutes.

On 21 October 1963 Leo again visited his friends on the landed craft. Two welcomed him and explained their activities had become more difficult: "Your science and technology have advanced enough to pose a threat to our ships, as well as to the entire planet." They went on to explain that although provoked, they would only respond in self-defence if our military threatened their lives by trying to damage their ships.

Leo observed; "These great men willingly took the time to speak to two grubby little farm kids in North Dakota, and changed our lives forever."

Jean

Australian investigator John Pinkney detailed another British case which occurred in Essex in 1937. Jean, who was eight at the time, was picking bluebells in a meadow, and realised there was a large shining silver object, on stilts looming above her. She dropped her flowers, and was frozen in terror, not knowing where it had come from.

Jean recalled, "Then a platform descended and three tall, red-uniformed men stepped down. One of them picked me up and took me inside. I thought I would never see my parents again. In the 1930s no-one had heard of flying saucers, and I thought it was some form of house. When inside it seemed so vast you couldn't see the far wall. They made me sit in a raised chair, and shone a dazzling bright light on me. It filled my mind with thoughts and scenes I'd never imagined before."

They took Jean to what seemed like an enormous pyramid, and upon entering she wandered the corridors for what seemed like hours, until she found a door which opened back into the meadow.

From then on Jean was gifted with psychic powers, which disturbed her family as she predicted the deaths of friends and relatives, some of whom were in other countries. She had dreams of World War 2, and became very intuitive and clairvoyant the rest of her life.

Humanoid 'neighbours'

My friend and colleague Margaret Fry, a long-time Welsh ufologist, has documented early extraterrestrial incidents in the United Kingdom. While some do not directly relate to my special category of contactees, they record the activity of 'humanoids', during the 1930s and early 1940s. It then begs the question; were the authorities aware of, or complicit in these interactions?

Ruth's experiences mirror closely what seems to be a carefully constructed program involving many experiencers. In 1934, in a rural farming area of South Wales, young Ruth went to play with her friend who lived nearby. She saw 'soldiers', dressed in tight green-grey suits and armed with 'ray guns', pushing her friends with their 'rounded-up' family ahead. When Ruth tried to intervene she was pushed along with the others to a 'big silver caravan' behind the trees. She kept tugging one soldier's legs, saying: "Leave my friends alone!"

Ruth remembers being taken into a room with lots of people, and when her friend's family said she was not one of them, the soldiers put her outside. She went back home and told her parents, who naturally didn't believe her. Later that evening they went over to the neighbours' two houses and found them empty – both families had disappeared.

(About the same time, in Canada in 1932, after a huge UFO was seen in the sky, it was discovered that the entire Eskimo community at Lake Anjikuni had vanished without a trace. Everything was intact; rifles at the door, signs of meals being cooked over now long–dead fires. Their dogs were later found frozen to death under a snowdrift. None of the 20-30 residents was ever found. Were they connected to the Visitors? Every grave in their burial ground, was open and devoid of remains.)

By 1943, nine years later, Ruth had moved to an even more rural area. She used to talk to gypsy children who lived in caravans on the Common, and would take them food. One day she realised all the gypsies had gone, however she saw a much larger silver 'caravan', which was like a long silver disc. It was similar to a helmet with rows of windows and very bright lights. At first, she thought the owners must be very rich, and walked across the field to get a closer look.

As Ruth approached, a man and woman came towards her. They were wearing the same green-grey boiler suits and carrying ray guns as she had seen in 1934. Ruth was afraid, remembering what had happened to her neighbours before, but they took her into the caravan and shut the door behind her.

Ruth could see over 80 local people, many of whom she recognised. They stood like statues and were being guarded by more men with ray guns, wearing the green-grey uniform. These soldiers were small, about four feet tall, with grey-white skins, slanted diamond-looking eyes and thin mouths.

Ruth was taken to see a taller, good-looking 'man'. She could distinctly remember a very ornate ring he was wearing. She called him "Khan." He told her they were from another place or galaxy. He reminded her of the incident when she was a small child: "You were with your friend and her family who were 'ours'; we programmed you then for the first time."

They told Ruth they wouldn't harm her, but she wept as she recounted the procedures they performed. As with many other female abductees, contact did not stop there, and continued in later life.

When Ruth was 21 she went parking with her boyfriend in a field near the ocean. It was a clear night. Suddenly a mist began creeping up around the vehicle. They saw some bright lights, but thought these were from ships at sea. Ruth vaguely remembers being lifted from the car, and her boyfriend followed a little later. They 'lost' two hours and afterwards edged their way around the mist to find the road was clear. Ruth's boyfriend was not happy to find the duco on his brand-new car ruined, with many circular rings on the rear. They drifted apart soon afterwards …

Some recollections of this encounter are vague, but Ruth recalls other parts very clearly. There had been some form of examination, and she was then taken to see the Khan. She remembers him talking about anti-gravity, and telling her an 'anti-matter' world existed near his solar-system. One also existed alongside ours, and to interfere with it could destroy the whole universe.

Ruth mentions that after she married and had a baby daughter, she and her husband went for a walk one night, and experienced another abduction. Her husband is aware of what happened, but is still so scared he refuses to discuss it.

Scandinavia also reported 'Nordic' type encounters during World War 2. *Skandinavisk UFO Information* (SUFOI) reports from the summer of 1940 in central Jutland how a teenage boy saw three humanoids, wearing shiny one-piece suits, in a nearby field. As he walked towards them, they turned away, but he kept following. The beings disappeared a few feet from a windowless, dome-shaped craft, about the size of a plane, which then rose vertically and shot away.

The same year in Warwickshire England, a woman walking through fields saw a dome-shaped object on the ground. It emitted a powerful blue light, and several tall 'men' with tanned skins stood around it. She walked past, thinking foreigners were working on their craft; when she looked back the craft and beings had gone.

During the early 1940s a family living at Dover Beach saw a huge white craft hovering in the foggy night sky outside their home. It looked like two inverted saucers, separated by a broad band of bright blue. The top half was a transparent dome, and inside were the figures of two men with shoulder length, sandy hair. They were quite good looking and dressed in white jumpsuits with matching blue sashes. At the time the family never realised the significance of what they were witnessing, and thought they must be Russian, because of the hairstyle.

Udo Wartena

Australian investigator, Warren Aston, conducted excellent in-depth research into the case of Udo Wartena who, in May 1940, encountered a disc-shaped craft in Montana USA. It was a dull, stainless steel colour, 35 feet high with a diameter of 100 foot. It hovered just above the ground, and a man descended from a downward-extended part of the hull.

He was nice-looking, young and strong with white hair and clear, almost translucent skin, and wore a grey coverall. He was not a mirage or in any way ethereal as he shook Udo's hand firmly, and spoke in slow English.

After explaining he had stopped his craft to take on water, Udo was allowed on-board where there was another plainly-dressed, slightly older man. Both told him they were several hundred years old! They explained their ship had its own gravitational field, was powered by electromagnetic forces, and could travel faster than the speed of light.

Like other such incidents, the visitors said they came from a distant planet which had been monitoring our civilisation for some time; including living with us incognito. One of them told Udo: "As you have noticed, we look pretty much as you do, so we mingle with your people, gather information, leave instructions or give help where needed." They also qualified this with the comment that they cannot interfere in any way.

Before they left, Udo was invited to go with them. Sometimes he wondered why he declined. He later recalled that two years earlier a young man had gone missing, without trace, in that area. Perhaps he had met with the same Visitors and accepted their offer.

Germany

There is much speculation about 'official' alien contact with Germany prior to and during World War 2, but very few reports exist from citizen sources.

Gordon Creighton, Editor of *Flying Saucer Review*, documented an interesting case in the Sept-Oct 1969 edition. On 25 May 1948, Hans Klotzbach, a young German without a passport, was on a coal-train headed for Luxembourg, where he hoped to enter illegally.

Just before it reached the border control-station at Wasserbillig, Hans jumped out of the train onto the trackside embankment. He sustained terrible injuries to both legs, and could not walk. He lost blood, and eventually fainted.

On regaining consciousness, Hans found himself in a cabin bathed in an indescribable sort of opal-bluish light. He was inside a flying saucer. A disembodied voice spoke to him in German, saying they had chanced upon his body as he lay dying beside the railway line, and felt compassion for his plight.

The voice gave Hans much information about cataclysmic events which would affect this planet in future. Hans listened before eventually losing consciousness or drifting off into sleep.

Four days later he recovered consciousness. He found himself lying on a mossy bank, safe, six kilometres *inside* Luxembourg – ten kilometres from where he had made his jump.

His trousers and shoes were thickly encrusted with dried blood, but his injured legs were completely healed. (Were his rescuers the Nordic aliens? It is interesting that the disembodied voice that Hans heard is similar to that reported by Dan Fry, in 1949, on his first encounter with 'Alan', a Nordic alien.)

UFO-Nachrichten (Jan/Feb 2001) reports another German event from a Frankfurt UFO Research group. This was investigated by Helmut Chodan, who was contacted by the witness on 30 November 1989, whom he then met.

The man wished for anonymity. While 'A' was walking with his metal detector in a forest near Judenwiese, (Altenstadt area), he encountered a landed UFO and three human-looking crew members, dressed in silvery garments. Their craft was shaped like an airship. It was a silver-colour, about forty feet long and thirteen feet high, and he did not notice any windows.

'A' said they were very friendly. They spoke to him in German, and their conversation lasted about three hours. They claimed they had underground and underwater bases on Earth, and that to get here, they use cosmic energy-lines as our sailing ships use winds. They also told him that they could manipulate matter.

'A' was disappointed that during their discussions they did not invite him aboard their ship. He said that they later entered the craft, which rose rapidly into the sky, and "made off toward the Moon."

'Space' Romance

Although motives are debatable, the Visitors are essentially similar to us, both in physical form, emotions and psychology. Their paranormal powers seem to relate to humans on a fundamental level. If they have 'had their wicked way' with female abductees, I'm not sure if this is manipulation for scientific purposes, their own sexual needs, or perhaps genuine emotional attachment. I am aware of cases where 'love' seems to be an important factor.

The South African case involving Elizabeth Klarer remains controversial. Born in 1910, Elizabeth claims her first contact with a flying saucer occurred when she was seven. She was sent to Oxford, England for her education, but returned to South Africa and worked for the Air Force intelligence there during World War 2.

This case was investigated by researcher Cynthia Hind, who knew Klarer personally. In 1957 Elizabeth was staying with relatives on a farm in the Drakensberg Mountains near Durban. She was out riding in the hills and saw a strange craft overhead. Before it shot off, out of sight into the clouds, she noticed there was a man standing inside, watching her.

Sometime later, she felt compelled to go back to the area, and found the same man waiting for her beside the landed craft. He was tall, and extremely handsome with slightly slanting grey eyes. Elizabeth claimed his name was 'Akon', and although he was from another planetary system, they fell in love. Their relationship eventuated in her going to his planet and bearing him a son, 'Ayling'. Klarer was unable to adjust to the atmosphere there, and returned to Earth.

Elizabeth wrote two books *Beyond the Light Barrier* and *The Gravity Files* and addressed many prestigious gatherings. She spoke of Akon's craft more as a living entity, calling it 'she' and said it was constructed from natural cosmic energy. Elizabeth also mentioned a huge 'mother ship' about five miles in length that hovered some distance from the Earth. She described the occupants as "human, slightly taller, better looking, more considerate and gentle, and living far, far longer than us on planet Earth. They are more advanced, technically and spiritually."

Cynthia claimed that, despite publishing her love story, Elizabeth was not an attention seeker, and presented as an attractive, intelligent and softly spoken lady. She was, however, paranoid that the Russians were spying on her, possibly to seize Akon when he visited. Elizabeth also claimed ongoing contact with the South African Air Force (SAAF), a fact which had some limited verification from a witness, who said that when she was too elderly to go on horseback, the SAAF used to fly her to Flying Saucer Hill where she would meet Akon.

Elizabeth died in 1994, and although her story was treated with a great deal of scepticism, an interesting event in 1992 caused some to re-evaluate her story: Connor, the owner of a lodge below the mountains, told of how one day a tall, blond, handsome man came in looking for Elizabeth Klarer., whom he was supposed to meet there. He seemed a little strange, with "good features and high cheekbones" and spoke perfect English.

The landlord had never heard of her, and after the stranger walked out to the carpark, his wife urged him to follow, to see if they could do anything else to help. When he looked out the man had literally "vanished" which was not possible. A week later, when Elizabeth arrived and booked into the hotel, they told her of the man looking for her. She showed them a photo of a sculpted bust of Akon in her book. Connor and his wife immediately recognised him.

The injured visitor

Another interesting case from South Africa, from 1961, was reported by Juan Benitez and translated by Gordon Creighton. The witness, Englishman 'HM', was an engineer working on aircraft automated pilot systems for a Spanish company. HM was travelling 20 miles out of Cape Town when a man, who looked about 40, asked help to get some water. After taking him to a mountain stream, HM gave him a lift back to a rock face about 100 meters off the road.

There was a strange object, about four metres high and ten to fifteen metres in diameter, with steps leading up to an opening in the craft. HM was invited up to the entrance, but not allowed beyond the doorway. Inside he could see a circular room with square windows, beneath which there was a couch going all the way around. There seemed to be a white light, 'coming from everywhere', and in the centre were two rows of levers, set in a rectangle. On the other side of the room there appeared to be an instrument panel.

There were four other men inside. Three of them were attending the fourth, who appeared to have been burned in an accident, and was lying down. They looked completely normal, dressed in beige laboratory-type overalls, about five foot, to five foot three inches tall, of slim build with chestnut-coloured, short hair. HM asked the man he brought back if they needed a doctor. He was told 'No', but asked if HM had any questions. He spoke English, but with a strange, unidentifiable accent.

HM asked how their craft worked and was told that they nullified gravity using a heavy fluid, which circulated in a tube at infinite speed, and created a magnetic field. (This propulsion system, whilst unknown to us, is similar to that described by other witnesses.) When asked where they came from, the man pointed to the sky without any further detail; shortly afterwards he firmly invited HM to leave.

French researcher Leo Noury has discussed the controversial Ummo case. In Madrid, a young dactylographer advertised for work during the 1960s. Two 'Danish' doctors asked him to type some scientific articles. Both were tall and blond, no different to any other human being. One day they asked him to type a paper on their 'home world', the planet Ummo, 14 light years away.

He thought they were pulling his leg until one pulled a small transparent ball from his pocket. It started to levitate, and in it was a recording of all the scenes from the dactylographer's home the night before. They advised this was just a sample of their technology. This entire episode was debunked as a hoax by some researchers. (Oddly enough, French physicist Jean Pierre Petit claims that part of his work on Magnetohydrodynamics (MHD) propulsion systems was made possible through the Ummo letters.)

A family holiday?

Some cases leave us wondering and undecided. US investigator John Schroeder interviewed five independent witnesses to an unusual case in St. Louis USA in May 1970. At about 10.30p.m., a family of four people arrived at the front desk of a high-rise motel. They appeared to be a husband and wife, no taller than 4 feet with two children, only a little shorter. At first the night clerk thought they may be dwarfs, but their features and bodily proportions were that of almost perfect human specimens, and they looked very similar: "they could have been cast from the same mould." He then wondered if they could be indigenous Mexicans or South Americans, some of whom are very short.

The man, and his son had shiny black hair, and youthful unlined faces, and his wife and daughter had long bright blond hair. The father and son both wore dark, tailored expensive suits, and the mother and daughter twin dresses in pastel peach. With pale skin, their eyes were large, dark and slightly slanted 'like those of Orientals', and their lips and noses smaller than average. The staff said they could have been wearing wigs, they weren't sure. When they spoke, their voices were strange: "somewhat like that of a ventriloquist".

The man's voice was slightly falsetto when he asked for "a room to stay", and seemed confused when given details, eventually placing a large roll of currency on the desk. The wife said nothing. When asked his name for the register he said, "A. Bell". When asked where they were from the man pointed his arm skyward and said: "We come from up there...up there." His wife pulled his arm down and said in an unusual voice: "from Hammond, Indiana." The staff did a quick identity check. Although their names and addresses were false, with no identifiable car parked outside, the transaction was allowed. They had, after all, paid in cash.

The bell hop took their bags to the room. The dining room waitress said their behaviour and eating habits were strange. She had confirmed for them that 'milk was from a cow' and the vegetables were grown on a farm. They required their food be cut into small pieces, which they sucked rather than chewed.

They did not seem to know how the elevator worked, and when the bell hop tried to turn on the television the man got angry saying it would hurt the children's eyes. The staff were so perplexed they decided to follow this strange family when they checked out to see where they went. All the entrances had security alarms, and the only exit was past the desk via the front door.

At 7.30 a.m., when they had not come down, the bell hop went to the room, and found it empty, the television unplugged and the keys on the desk. No other exit had been opened and the door alarms were still operative. Who were these strangers, and where had they really come from? Was it just a family holiday to planet Earth?

Travis Walton

Sometimes we don't know if interactions are planned or accidental, such as the 1979 case of Travis Walton, who was hit by a beam of light from a UFO. Obviously injured, he was taken onboard the craft and attended by a group of small aliens, who were about five feet tall, bald, with chalky white skin and large brown eyes. He was then taken to a second group of 'humans', one of them about six feet tall, muscular, with brownish/blond hair, clean-shaven, dark complexion, hazel-gold eyes and wearing a blue uniform with bubble-shaped helmet. Two other men and a woman there were identically dressed, but did not wear helmets.

In his book *Ultimate Encounter*, Bill Barry quotes Walton as saying: "He was a man, just like a human being ... he was human enough, so if I was walking down the street in a crowd, he'd be an unusual-looking person in passing ... I thought he could be an American just as far as I could tell."

After five days, Travis was placed back in Arizona, some distance from the forest where he had been removed.

Travis wrote of his experiences in his book *Fire in the Sky*. Of just as much interest in this case, is the way it was depicted by the media and film makers, who distorted the entire event, presenting the entities as 'classic' Greys, and portraying horrendous images onboard the craft. Was this just Hollywood trying to make a buck, or did national security have a hand in trying to scare the living daylights out of the public?

Humanoids in London

An astounding account was revealed in Sir Peter Horsley's autobiography; *Sounds from Another Room*. Sir Peter was once the Deputy Commander-in-Chief, of British Strike Command. He was also Equerry to Prince Philip for seven years, and they often discussed UFOs as the Prince had an open mind and was interested in the subject. Sir Peter was fascinated by UFOs, after receiving many reports from pilots and servicemen.

During the 1950s Prince Philip received an interesting report from Squadron Leader Peter Caddy, when his duties took him on board the Royal Yacht. Caddy, some other officers, and other interested people, had formed a group and claimed they were in telepathic contact with 'Space Brothers.' They claimed the Visitors were concerned about the growing nuclear threat and other environmental issues facing Earth in the aftermath of World War Two.

Caddy said they told him to produce a paper titled; *An Introduction to the Nature and Purpose of Unidentified Flying Objects* and make 26 copies to be given to specific high ranking officials and dignitaries, including Prince Philip.

Another 'buff' was Air Chief Marshall Sir Arthur Barrett, who introduced Sir Peter to his friend General Martin.

In 1954, Sir Peter Horsley received a telephone call from General Martin, inviting him to a meeting that night in the Chelsea flat of a Mrs Markham. When he arrived, the General was not there. However, Sir Peter was introduced to a Mr Janus, a slim, middle-aged man with greying hair and a soft voice., who wanted to know what Sir Peter knew about UFOs. After a while Sir Peter stopped and asked Janus why was he interested, to which he replied that he wanted to meet Prince Philip.

They had a long discussion, and Sir Peter was a little unsettled that Janus seemed to be able to read his thoughts. Janus basically felt that the Prince was a man of 'great vision' who understood the importance of the relationship between man and nature, something necessary for future galactic harmony. He also reiterated the message of other Visitors that humanity was not ready to venture out into the galaxy until it had learned to respect the preservation of life everywhere.

Janus had an excellent knowledge of space technology, confirming that extraterrestrials were here observing Earth, and stressed that interference was not allowed. The Visitors can adapt to our environment and move around freely, relying on their advanced extra-sensory, thought-reading, hypnosis, inter-dimensional and other mental powers.

Sir Peter contacted another senior officer on the Prince's staff, but when he rang Mrs Markham there was no answer. General Martin became evasive, and he found Mrs Markham had 'moved out in a hurry.' He never heard from her or Janus again. It is obvious Sir Peter thought Janus was a Visitor, and was wondering whether his telepathic abilities had alerted him that Sir Peter was 'of two minds' about informing the security authorities.

After his autobiography was published in the 1990s, one senior official commented it was unfortunate that "the public will learn that the man who had his finger on the button at Strike Command was seeing little green men."

This wasn't the only unusual case to be reported out of London. British researcher Jenny Randles wrote of an incident in 1976 when she and Peter Warrington were contacted by a man claiming to be an alien, living as a human here on Earth. He wished to prove himself by meeting a certain scientist. The 'alien', who looked like a normal middle-aged man, was insistent, and Randles was surprised when the scientist, Professor Eric Laithwaite, actually invited them all to meet him in his Imperial College University laboratory in London.

The alien proffered suggestions as to how Laithwaite could further his work in the development of magnetic-field based propulsion systems. The UFO researchers did not understand the science, but the professor took copious notes and taped the entire interview. Jenny noted later that it was around the time Laithwaite announced the solution of a fundamental problem he had been struggling with. When the researchers apologised for taking up his time, Laithwaite smiled and said: "This is not the first alien I have met!" He added that some ideas for his magnetic levitation propulsion system had been offered some years earlier, in another meeting with a man claiming to be an alien.

There are other cases reported where we cannot be sure whether someone was just a normal human being, or an integrated Visitor.

Cyril Jones, a photographer with his own private pilot's license, reported on a strange incident which happened Thanksgiving morning in 1954. He was only sixteen, and the youngest employee at a service station in north-western USA. The weather was dreadful, and at about 10 a.m. a very unkempt man came in.

He was about five feet eight tall, medium build, with clear grey eyes, and salt-and-pepper hair. He had obviously been travelling for some time, as he had a two-day growth of stubble, his scuffed brown shoes looked old, and his tan trench coat soiled and tattered. He was seeking directions to the town of Columbia, in California's 'Mother Lode Country'. Cyril knew the town was mostly deserted, and queried how and why he wanted to go there.

The stranger pointed to his intended destination on the map, saying that a person living there, who didn't know he was coming, had cancer, and he could save him. Time was of the essence, and he had already travelled all the way down the Al-Can Highway from Alaska. The transmission on his old car had just failed after his arduous trip through Canada, and he asked if he could use their lube room and rack to repair it.

Cyril's two workmates went out into the driveway, and he followed, leaving the stranger in the office, behind the closed door. As his workmates left in their vehicle, they were full of criticism, saying the customer was 'whacko' and 'full of shit'. When Cyril returned inside, the stranger repeated every word of that conversation. There was no way he could have lip-read or overheard what was being said. Before Cyril could say anything, the stranger advised he could read their thoughts, as well as knowing what they said. Cyril wondered if this guy was for real, and where he had come from. The stranger looked him straight in the eye and said: "Young man, I am very real."

They pushed his broken-down car into the workshop. Cyril was fascinated and astounded with both the array of instruments that covered the dashboard, and unfamiliar items in the trunk. The stranger worked with precision and expertise when repairing his vehicle, and Cyril realised he seemed a well-educated and intelligent man. Except for his mind reading trick, he seemed like anyone else; yet there was something about him that was not ordinary at all.

As he worked he spoke to Cyril in a quiet articulate manner. Cyril had thought he was in his fifties, but the man told him he was very old, had outlived several wives, and had many children, grand-children and great grand-children. He spoke of living in various parts of the world, and his many adventures.

He then turned the conversation to the Andes and the Himalayas, where there were ruins of mysterious cities. He spoke of beings from elsewhere in the Universe, who landed their space craft there and other places on Earth which had special powers for those who know how to tap into them.

He went on to say there were beings who exist just beyond our ability to see, in a different dimension. They were here to help and protect us in our hour of need, but we had to believe, and sincerely seek them out. Primitive people made contact all the time, but we had lost this ability once we became civilised.

Cyril asked him about the pyramids, and was told the Great Pyramid was built by an ancient race of people who had since vanished from Earth. It was not a tomb, but a mathematical statement about this planet, and its relationship with the Sun, Solar System and Universe.

He went on to explain auras, the invisible force field around all living things, and psychic and telepathic abilities. We are all born with these gifts, but our culture teaches us, from a very early age, not to trust our psychic powers and to ignore intuition.

The stranger continued talking and explaining the entire time he was repairing his car. Although Cyril did not understand everything he talked about, he got the occasional opportunity to ask a question out loud. For the most part, the stranger seemed to anticipate what he was going to ask. As Cyril watched, the man repaired his car in record time, with incredible speed and precision.

After about an hour, he closed the bonnet, pressed the starter button, and the engine sprang back into life. Before donning his old trench coat, he shook Cyril's hand and thanked him, saying; "There is not enough time to tell you much today. Look into these matters on your own and keep an open mind. You'll be a better person for it."

He backed off the lube rack, and with a wink and a grin, drove off into the remainder of the day. Cyril still asks himself; was the stranger in the storm from here or from out there?

Chapter Two

Humanoid Visitors

Many Visitors appear human, so much so as to be indistinguishable from the average person in society. Rosemary Decker discusses these humanoid extraterrestrials in numerous articles and her book *35 minutes to Mars*. She alludes to probable Visitors in many religious texts, saying: "Visitors, either extraterrestrial or ultraterrestrial (from a parallel universe), have been reported and recorded in writings countless times from ancient days up to the present. They can be from midget size to very tall, from stocky to very slim, with skin tones from blonde to golden tan or brown, even slightly blue, or greenish. Eye colour varies from blue and green, to golden, brown, and very dark, with shapes varying from Aryan to Oriental and wrap-around.

"Old texts, from China across India, from Persia into the Near and Middle East, describe others looking so much like us that when dressed like us, they often pass in our streets unnoticed. These could be genetically our close kin, and if so, what of their mental, emotional and spiritual endowments?

"From countless reports, both ancient and modern, one characteristic that stands out is mental telepathy, which bypasses the emotional complex and goes directly mind-to-mind. It is not an attempt to control the recipient, but simply to communicate clearly."

Dan Fry

Dr. Dan Fry, an engineering executive, with over thirty years' experience in Aeronautics and Rocketry Science, claimed an unusual and enlightening experience on 4 July 1949, while stationed at the White Sands Missile Proving Ground in New Mexico.

He inexplicably went for a walk one hot night, and was startled when a 30 feet wide object landed near him. It was about 16 feet high, spherical, flat top and bottom, and the colour of silver polished metal. As Dan inched closer he noticed it had no visible seams, doors, or windows.

A voice came from the craft, telling him this was a remotely controlled sampling craft, and the 'man' was speaking to him through a communications system from a mother ship, some 900 miles above. He apologised and advised that they had superimposed their will on him to lead him to the landing site, something they rarely did unless warranted.

The voice, who said his earthly name was 'Alan', over time imparted the following information: A research ship from a Galactic Federation had been monitoring Earth more closely once we invented aeroplanes and flight, so they could chart our progress to the next step – Space.

Alan told Dan that other civilizations in the galaxy find us of great interest. Firstly, they believe we were genetically engineered much earlier by another advanced intelligent race, which used the Earth as a testing ground for a diversity of life forms. Secondly, our humanoid race is in so many different stages of development at the same time, from stone-age cultures through to modern nuclear-powered communities.

The problem on earth is that we lack spiritual basis, and cannot control our increasing inventions and technological growth. In fact, they control us. (This was articulated in 1949. Our development of 'doomsday' weapons and recent dependence on digital technology confirms this early prediction.)

Some of their people have been sent here to help and advise us, as we need assistance to achieve lasting peace. Without this we cannot attain the understanding needed for our advancement and continued existence. Alan said he was part of this continuing mission, but he needed Dan's help for his forthcoming assignment. He and his people had advanced technology, which let them live on self-supporting space ships. He was neither American nor from Earth, and his current assignment required him to infiltrate our society as both.

While his people, who had been coming here for centuries, were biologically and physically similar to us, it would take him 4-5 years to become accustomed to our different atmosphere and stronger gravity, and learn to speak our language fluently. Also, the sampling craft was checking our atmosphere for micro-organisms to identify any immunity he might require.

After Dan agreed to help, he was allowed to enter the craft for a 30 minute 'joy flight', during which time he noticed that the ship rotated, and reached an altitude of about 35 miles. As he travelled, Alan explained the physics, gravity and propulsion of the vessel. He also advised that we all possess mental telepathy, an ability we rarely use, and they had recorded Dan's 'frequency pattern' for future use.

Alan also described how tens of thousands of years ago their ancestors had lived on planet Earth, on Lemuria or Mu. They were scientifically advanced with comparable weapons, and eventually became involved in a devastating war with the people of Atlantis. Some survived in the Himalayas and others escaped to Mars, which at that time had water, vegetation and a better atmosphere and temperature. (I have pondered on this. We have many myths about Lemuria, Atlantis, and the Anunnaki who, if Alan's information is correct, may pre-date his people. Are these ideas contradictory or complementary? If accurate, they suggest human history may be many thousands of years older than we realise. Further, current thinking suggests that Mars has been uninhabitable for a much longer time.)

This encounter had a radical effect on Dan's personality and thinking. A few months later a small glowing ball appeared, giving him instructions to leave textbooks and newspapers etc. for Alan to study. These were collected by a sampling device and then returned. Fry then helped Alan and his colleague, Vera, with birth certificates, passports, bank accounts and professions.

George Adamski described how easy it was in the 1950s to arrange false ID materials for aliens to 'set themselves up', if required. While Dan, and others were possibly involved in espionage activities, I don't think anyone was ever charged. Perhaps the government and military didn't need the publicity!

Dan Fry had other meetings with Alan and in 1954 was told to write his experiences and pass the message to others, because our social and spiritual values do not equal our material science, a fatal flaw in previous civilisations which were annihilated. Efforts to change must come from humans themselves. Dan felt it would be futile, the media would distort the message, and he would be ridiculed. Alan agreed but encouraged him saying: "Ridicule is the barrier which the ignorant erect between themselves and any truth which frightens or disturbs them."

Dan kept in covert contact with Alan who told him that there were other alien races here, with different agendas (and of great interest to the author, if there have been breeding programs involving particular bloodlines.) Another meaningful disclosure was that They can tune into our individual frequencies, and if necessary probe our minds or superimpose their will on us. This certainly explains some of the experiences reported by contactees and abductees.

Was Dan being misled? Other White Sands employees certainly saw UFOs, and believed in them. On 20 August 1949, six weeks after Dan Fry's first encounter, astronomer Clyde Tombaugh (who discovered the planet Pluto in 1930), and his wife, were "petrified with astonishment", when they saw two rows of parallel yellow-green lights travelling silently across the sky. The same year, missile expert Colonel MacLaughlin commented: "Many times I have seen flying discs following and overtaking missiles in flight at the experimental base at White Sands Proving Ground."

Details of advanced physics, which Alan told Fry, were proven in later years. Dan also commented that some information had been exceedingly useful to him in his own work. There was no way it could have all originated in his own mind.

In 1989, realising he was aging, Dan wrote a letter titled *The Sad Time of Parting*, to his friends. He mentioned two books he was writing, and hoped to finish. The most important, *When in Cairo*, would "deal with the problems and concerns of Alan in his struggle to keep the world at peace. It is about 70% true and 30% fiction, which is necessary to avoid disclosure of the true names of some of the characters, who still need security. Those of you who have read *To Men of Earth* will find little difficulty determining who the characters actually are." (The author had US colleagues, personal friends, who were Dan Fry's contemporaries. They knew him well and believed him.) Astronaut Gordon Cooper knew Dan when he was in charge of instruments for missile control and guidance at White Sands. He said "I have seen my share of wide-eyed UFO fanatics and lunatics – Fry was not in that category. I found him totally credible."

An interesting anecdote in Gordon Cooper's memoirs was his reference to Valerie Ransome, who also claimed contact with extraterrestrials. She said her contact had warned of a technical problem with the space shuttle. Cooper trusted her apparent telepathic powers, and risked his own credibility by advising NASA, who found the information was correct, and rectified the problem.

Telepathic 'Technology'

In his memoir *Selected by Extraterrestrials*, William Tompkins tells how he was subjected to ridicule after claiming that several pretty little 'blond Nordic alien' secretaries telepathically gave them technical information while he was working on secret military projects with large corporations.

I wondered how this telepathic interaction and information was imparted, and stumbled on a case reported in the 1999 *Australian UFO Bulletin*. The witness was a scientist employed by the Northern Territory University in Darwin; while he did not recall any experience involving a UFO or aliens, he had been suffering an intense headache. He was in bed, and felt what seemed to be an 'energy force' penetrating his head and entire body. The pain was so bad he couldn't sleep, but it suddenly eased off and he saw a picture of a large screen in his mind. There was writing, numbers and brackets, like very long formulae, projected on the screen.

He said out loud: "What the hell is that?" A disembodied male voice replied that it was the formulae for a very special material used for certain parts and components in the building of spacecraft and advanced technology. He asked what the material might look like, and the large screen in his mind displayed a large grey object that was oval, and like metal moulded together. It had a smooth, glossy surface finish, with no visible signs of welding, bolts, or screws.

The scientist said: "The picture of that component remained in my mind a long time after the screen disappeared. I continued to lie in bed, in the dark, after the image and voice had gone, refreshing my memory of the experience. I lay awake all night, certain it wasn't a dream – it was real. What I was shown was not from beings of this planet!

My friend and colleague Margaret Fry recounted the case of the Tite family, her personal friends for some years in mid-Wales, which gave further insights into the *mind's* ability to see a projection, as distinct from the actual vision of our eyes:

John Tite was totally blind, had been for 14 years, and relied on his wife – 'his devoted eyes'. She had gone out one evening, leaving him in their home, a houseboat on the tow-path of the canal. Their young daughter was asleep, when John realised that their houseboat was filling with smoke – it was on fire! He groped about for his little girl, and with her in his arms, made his way onto the deck. But where to from there?

He felt himself being gently lifted, and deposited with his daughter, outside the venue where his wife was. He claimed that during this experience he "saw a UFO." Margaret suggested that it was "in his mind's eye."

"No," he insisted, "I actually saw it, I saw the craft that rescued us. I did not know about UFOs. I am totally blind, but I saw it, and since then, when they are in the vicinity they show me symbols in the sky. I would like to know what these symbols mean."

Of course, given the difficulties of his blindness, there was no-one in rural Wales who could help.

South America

Other researchers have heard from witnesses repeating the same cautions that Alan had expressed to Dan Fry. Gordon Creighton of *Flying Saucer Review* translated a 1957 newspaper article from Argentina; an Air Force guard had an encounter with a flying saucer. A disembodied voice spoke to the guard from the craft, saying they were here to help, as our misguided use of atomic energy threatened to destroy us.

The same year a similar message came from Dr Guimaraes of Brazil. This Catholic professor reported a contact with humanoids who advised not only of the danger of nuclear weapons, but also of scientific experiments being conducted with flagrant disregard for the possible consequences, including damage to our atmosphere. He encountered the 'beings' one evening, while relaxing on a beach in Sao Paulo. Two men alighted from a landed craft and communicated both telepathically and verbally with him. They were both some 1.8 metres tall, with normal youthful faces, fair complexions and long fair hair.

He accepted their invitation to go for a ride in their 'ship', and noted another two or three similar men inside. When they returned him to Earth they made an appointment to meet him again shortly after. However, the Brazilian Air Force heard about this, and planned to send some jet fighters. The professor decided not to go.

More 'integrated' Visitors

Dan Fry is not the only person who claims he had directly helped our 'guests' to integrate into society. While some dispute his authenticity, Howard Menger, stated that he had helped and interacted with several such 'people', male and female, since 1932. They looked human and their masquerade was so detailed and believable they mingled with and presented themselves as normal members of the community. The complex and detailed account of Howard Menger's claims and experiences are contained in the book *The High Bridge Incident*, written by his second wife, Connie.

In 1960 Menger recounted his claims, but told people this was only to stop the unwarranted attention and harassment from the press. During his 'retirement' he worked on little-publicised inventions designed to harness free energy and allow mankind to build their own flying saucers. Along with his contemporary George

Adamski, Menger made so many extraordinary statements, the entire episode was held up to ridicule and dismissed at the time.

Another contactee brought into disrepute was Dino Kraspedon who wrote the book *My Contact with Flying Saucers*.

Kraspedon and a friend were driving in mountains near San Paulo, Brazil, when they saw five flying saucers, and at a later date went on board one. The human-looking commander later visited Dino at home, dressed as a priest and they had a long conversation about science, physics, society and religion.

Several years later Kraspedon started accurately predicting disasters and events around the world. He was finally arrested and jailed, accused of planning to assassinate government officials, to take over the government. He said his extraterrestrial friends would come to his rescue, but they didn't! One wonders if they 'put him up to' the political agenda?

It was then revealed his real name was Alidino Felix, and he was accused of being a hoaxer. Some researchers still consider his reports, psychic abilities and advance knowledge were such that his claims cannot be easily dismissed.

The Space People's motives were in some way those of necessity rather than kindness. It had been suggested the Earth is 'in quarantine' until we either destroy ourselves or our self-cleansing is complete. Their problem is that if we achieve independent and unlimited space travel first, we would pose a threat to other species in the galaxy.

Other communications have been less benign. Timothy Good reported that Orlandi Ferrandi of Brazil encountered humanoid beings and their craft in 1956. Their communication included the warning that if our experiments or warfare endangered stellar harmony – *They* will regrettably have to destroy us. I have also interviewed a witness who related an identical message.

Not all contactees warned about our own dangerous use of new technology and weapons. Many spoke instead of impending natural cataclysms.

George Adamski

The best-known flying saucer contactee of the 1950s, George Adamski, still attracts enormous ridicule. However, Adamski's accounts of 'Orthon', a young 5'6" sun-tanned alien, with shoulder length sandy-coloured hair, and his message and demeanour, are entirely consistent with most reports of the time. While many 'orthodox' UFO researchers still cringe at any mention of his name, many well-educated people who knew Adamski personally, believe his initial encounters with aliens were valid. Many messages which George relayed make more sense today than they did 60 years ago! Researchers sympathetic to Adamski consider he was deliberately given wrong information later on. This misinformation, combined with George's more ludicrous claims and increasing eccentricity, tended to discredit the entire episode.

Basically, Adamski first contacted a blond-haired humanoid being in late 1952, after a saucer-type craft landed in the desert near Palomar Gardens in California. George had taken six friends into the desert with him, and they watched him from a distance as he met one of the craft's occupants, Orthon. (Adamski's contact looked quite human, and later, when he cut his hand on the space ship, Orthon bled red blood like any other human.)

Interestingly, from comments made to these witnesses, Adamski already knew the spacecraft would to land at that place and time. Any allusion to a supposed message from a Ouija board or psychic, was merely a cover story for the prearranged event, which required witnesses for confirmation. While Adamski claimed UFO sightings from 1946, it seems he had been in contact with these entities long before, but never wrote about this or spoke of it publicly.

Adamski's childhood remains a bit of a mystery. When he was a small child, his family migrated from Poland to the US. His father died when he was very young, and a mysterious family friend financed and arranged for him to travel to Tibet to study with Buddhist 'Masters'. (Perhaps it is co-incidental that Tibet is said to have a long association with aliens; some close to Adamski suggest he was being prepared for his 'mission'.) Fred Steckling, one of George's colleagues, told his son that Adamski's mother also had 'experiences'.

After spending time studying with mystical practitioners, Adamski returned to the US, publishing his book *Wisdom of the Masters of the Far East* in 1936, and lecturing on Eastern philosophy. An enthusiastic amateur astronomer, George also lectured on 'space ships' and authored a little-known book, *Pioneer of Space*.

Orthon didn't want his photograph taken as he had been in Los Angeles several times, and didn't want to be recognised! Was he associated with Alan and also infiltrating our society? Adamski certainly claimed 'They' were living among us, naming further contacts – *Ramu*, *Firkon* and *Kalna*. He detailed meetings with them in public places in the city. George occasionally mentioned the various 'on-world' money-making ventures his friends used to fund their undercover operations. These activities included diamond-trading, involvement in the shipping industry, and a cafe where fellow space people could meet.

There are many reports, that while on overseas trips in several countries, George was seen meeting 'mysterious, young, blond-haired men' in restaurants or in his hotel room. These men also seemed to be present in the background at lectures or meetings. Apparently, George insisted on staying at large hotels where these meetings would be more difficult to observe. While they intended to be undetected, and only two Visitors at a time appeared, Adamski was less than discreet when indicating their presence to his human companions.

Usually Adamski's communications with humanoids were telepathic (he 'taught' telepathy himself for many years). At other times, they were spoken. (Orthon's spoken language was described as 'musical', sounding like a mixture of Chinese and some ancient tongue.)

Adamski's Space People claimed they had been living amongst us for some time, and part of their message makes a lot of sense to me. They stated that cults which believed vast changes to the Earth would occur and Space People would rescue a 'chosen few' were wrong. Natural disasters affect all planets, and the resulting death, injury and devastation are not punishment from God, but merely come from being in the wrong place at the wrong time.

George warned that Space People were not gods, and should not be worshipped as such. However, they have progressed further than humans, spiritually, and have great understanding and compassion for people on Earth. We are here to learn lessons in loving each other and nature, and to appreciate the laws of The Creator. Most importantly, individuals must learn to think for themselves, and not necessarily accept official or popular opinions, or religion as fact.

Adamski wrote three more books; *Flying Saucers Have Landed* (co-authored with Desmond Leslie), *Inside the Spaceships* and *Flying Saucer Farewell*. He reported trips into space and visiting a mother ship. (While large, this was apparently small compared to their craft several miles in length in outer space.) However, there was a growing problem with his lectures and writing. George breached strict limitations he had been given on what he could divulge, such as details of alien technology he had seen, and some of the Visitors' *modus operandi*. As time went by, George increasingly embellished the information provided by his contacts with his own opinions and exaggerations. This undermined his credibility, although some descriptions he gave of outer space etc. were proven fairly accurate soon afterwards.

There are conflicting reports that Adamski met with several world leaders to pass on various messages. Maybe he did meet some – maybe he didn't meet others. Some witnesses claim he met Pope John XXIII on 31 May 1963, and gave the Pope a small package he had received from a Visitor two weeks before in Copenhagen. At the time, the Pope was confined to his room, very ill, and died two days later. (Vatican officials deny this meeting ever happened and there are conflicting reports.)

Nexus magazine April-May 2007, published an article *The Omega Secret* by Cristoforo Barbato, which claims a Jesuit priest in the Vatican confirmed Adamski's meeting with the Pope. Barbato states the Jesuit described how the Nordic aliens, even though technologically and spiritually evolved, were very much flesh and blood. They had 'discovered' the Catholic Church, espoused Christ's messages, and convinced Pope Pius XII that they could help the Church in its beneficial missions with social and political world situations.

The Jesuit said Pope John XXIII inherited the agreement and beneficial support from the Visitors, but kept it secret. The Pope had reservations about trusting these newly converted alien beings. Just before his death Pope John had decided to cease any direct contact with them. He determined the Church must operate separately to the Nordics. Pope John Paul II continued his work by spreading their message of how we must care for the Earth and each other.

No-one seems to have asked exactly what messages Adamski gave to various individuals or known what they were about. Did they differ from what Adamski was saying publicly? Personally, I suspect these private messages were so disturbing that although George did pass them on, nobody, Visitors or humans alike, could risk him publicly divulging the ultimate truth. (It has been suggested that they concerned Planet X/Nibiru.) Whatever information Adamski imparted, all parties ensured he would be discredited a short time later.

While Adamski was very political, despising governments and capitalism, he did raise mankind's awareness as to the error of its ways and who, and what, may be out there in the vast cosmos. Perhaps his hectic schedule contributed to his death from heart failure in 1965.

Many of the humanoid contactees around the world ignore the very real possibility of deception. They believe their alien Visitors are benevolent, and come with a higher purpose to help mankind survive the troubled times to come. Many have been subjected to an organised campaign of ridicule. At the height of the Cold War, peace, love and ban-the-bomb campaigns were the last thing the Military, Government, and arms manufacturers wanted to hear. All western governments had major challenges at that time. Most important was to keep ahead of the arms race, and to develop new technologies secure from foreign interests. The implication that technologically superior entities and their craft could enter our airspace with apparent impunity, greatly alarmed authorities.

Adamski and his contemporaries worried the authorities and FBI, who suggested such contactees were subversive, and could in fact be Russian agents – their messages designed to hinder US progress. In some ways, their concern was understandable; Adamski did postulate in some of his talks that communism was the only way to go, and that one day Russia would lead the world.

Interestingly, during the late 1950s, Adamski alluded to an invasion from space by aliens <u>less friendly</u> than those he liaised with. He proposed a Space Exploration Program, to replace the existing Military-Industrial complex and the US economy's dependence upon warfare. Adamski believed such a project would unite the Earth peoples, and the production of space craft would help defend the world against unwanted incursions from space.

Many contactees receive messages and visions of future calamities which will affect our Earth. These warning messages typically predict world-wide destruction, and massive death tolls.

The actual time frame of the forecast cataclysms usually varied greatly, creating scepticism as to their validity. Predictions included a wide range of man-made disasters such as war, pollution, global warming, and more-exotic cosmic phenomena, such as asteroids or the passing of the mythical planet Nibiru. Others predicted a sudden tilting of the Earth's rotational axis, and terrestrial polar movements, which have occurred in the past. There was also mention of the eight super-volcanoes around the world. (The eruption of just one, and its subsequent ash cloud, would cause catastrophic damage to the environment, and the death of an enormous number of humans.)

Given the complexities of the entire scenario, we can't be really sure if these entities are benevolent or not. Are aliens working as one, or are there various species with competing interests in different countries? Given our own propensity for duplicity, do we play one alien species off against another? Or, is the human race being manipulated? The vast amount of misinformation, disinformation, half-truths and downright lies promulgated by all parties, means we just don't know the truth at this stage.

There does seem to be a different approach and contact instigated by the human-looking Visitors, to that of the 'Grey' and 'Reptilian' species:

1. Most humanoid cases *invite* contact rather than force abductions.
2. Humanoids do not usually 'appear' in bedrooms, or manifest through walls. They require the contact to be outside a building.
3. Witnesses frequently recall humanoid contact, while other extra-terrestrials block memories in the witness's mind.
4. Humanoids stress and respect free will in humans. Other species insist they have a right to violate our bodies and basic rights.
5. While humanoids impart information, they rarely dominate the minds of contactees.
6. Although they can communicate telepathically, humanoids speak fluently in many languages.

We can understand why Visitors quietly integrate into our society, not making their presence known. If detected, they would be apprehended by the authorities and interrogated, or worse. Today, billions of religious adherents will not accept the possibility of extraterrestrial life, preferring to settle for angels or demons.

A different physiology

Jean Sider, a veteran French UFO investigator, detailed a case from Amiens in 1932, when an unconscious female car accident victim, was taken to a local hospital. The attending doctor, Victor Pauchet, was considering a blood transfusion when he discovered her blood was not a recognisable human type, and had a bluish colour. Officially, 'she' had been admitted as an Englishwoman called 'Smith'. The hospital's reaction was to place her in a guarded locked room with barred windows.

When the police arrived later the woman had disappeared from the locked room; the crashed vehicle had also vanished.

Warren Aston discussed another incident, over 40 years later: (Dr Leopoldo Diaz reported this incident during a 1978 interview on Radio WOAI in San Antonio, Texas.) In 1976, when Diaz was head of surgery in a major hospital in Guadalajara, Mexico, a man came in and requested an examination because he had been travelling extensively. The doctor soon realised he was not 'human', and the man advised he had come because he wanted someone respected and influential to pass on a message.

He said how many people from his planet were living undetected among us, trying to help us avert catastrophe. He and the doctor had a long discussion about the Earth's future, religion, and other matters. After he left, the doctor was so impressed, and concerned about our future, he flew to New York in an unsuccessful attempt to have a United Nations delegation initiate an investigation.

Why the Cover-Up?

Secret governments are expert at both the concealment and the psychological, subconscious manipulation of information. In well over 30 years a lot of the truth has been embedded in movies, especially the most popular, widely watched sci-fi television series. This has a dual purpose. It is a devious method of getting the general masses to accept the possibility of other intelligent beings, at least in our own galaxy. It also introduces, and hopefully fosters an acceptance of the incredible covert technology that we have secretly developed, most probably with alien assistance. However, if anyone dares to proffer any evidence to verify that it is in fact really happening, they can be accused of sheer fantasy, based on watching too many of these fictional productions.

I have noticed that while various government authorities in western countries have been a little nonchalant about reports of Grey, reptilian and other various aliens they try to discredit the reports and witnesses of humanoid aliens. Gene Roddenberry, the genius who brought decades of *Star Trek* into our lounge rooms, concentrated on all kinds of wild and wonderful adventures in outer space in centuries to come.

Roddenberry was extremely well informed as to future technology, much of which I suspect had alien origins. Why then did he create the excellent series *Earth; Final Conflict*, with instructions that it should be made after his death? Why was it not shown on so many media outlets as his previous productions? I suggest because it concentrated upon aliens present on Earth, who if they wished, could resemble us. The initial humanoids in this series, who were reasonably friendly, but scheming, gave us some advanced technology. There were hints of genetic manipulation programs. Roddenberry detailed other, less pleasant beings arriving soon after. Was it much too close to the truth for him to reveal during his lifetime?

Another interesting television series *The Event* was pulled after nine of its first 21-episode season. This was a fictional tale of human-looking aliens – some in 'detention' and some living secretly in society after their spacecraft crashed.

There were some thought-provoking aspects to this series before it was brought to a sudden halt. The aliens, although they aged more slowly, were genetically compatible with us, and had married and produced children with our normal population. Although some wanted to get the chance to return to their own planet, others had been sufficiently integrated to want to remain here.

While the accusation of a great conspiracy or cover-up could be made, it must be remembered that a few in our society are a little deranged. It may be unwise for them to know that some Visitors are very much like us, for fear they may become delusional. I have received several disturbing phone calls from very unstable people claiming their innocent neighbours and fellow citizens are 'evil aliens'.

There are even more pressing reasons for authorities to suppress all the messages imparted by the Visitors. Understandably, the military cannot relinquish their weapons programs unless all the other countries also agree. Large corporations are not willing to abandon new innovative technologies or power and profits just because they may be misused by our population, and who is to determine which are beneficial or not?

Further, these ethical celestial humans, if their message was widely spread, could cause their earthly brothers to adopt them as de-facto leaders, thereby defecting from their own political and religious spheres.

It is not so simple as some believe. In relation to the long predicted natural disasters and cataclysms, the fear or anticipation of such occurrences can cause massive social upheavals worse than the event itself.

Alien Co-Operation in the Twentieth Century

Another, more disturbing possibility has crossed my mind. Some researchers suggest that these particular aliens were present in the first half of the 20th Century. Several also maintain that at least one species of aliens helped the German Third Reich, promising Hitler control of the world. This could explain their rapid technological advancement, but not necessarily the Fuhrer's preoccupation with eugenics and racial perfection.

(It must also be considered that in the early 1950s, the craft photographed by Adamski and other witnesses closely resembled those allegedly found in captured Nazi blueprints. Was there a connection, or were Visitors merely imitating the technology of the day?)

By 1942, with disastrous losses on the Russian front, it was obvious Nazi Germany was on the back foot. Hitler himself was starting to lose touch with reality, thanks in part to Britain's secret weapon – the vast number of occult practitioners who combined to direct a telepathic 'cone of power and whispers' in the Fuhrer's direction. It seemed to succeed then, as it had done against the Spanish Armada.

Some claim that these particular aliens did not approve the Nazi behaviour and mass exterminations, but many of the Allies had official, racist segregation policies, some not even recognising their indigenous populations as full citizens. Regardless, it seems that in about 1941 there was also interaction with the US-UK alliance.

Other researchers consider it was a different, competing species who had assisted Hitler's opponents. Had the military fathers of some of the contactees come in contact with these particular aliens in the latter half of the War? We will never know. Nobody is talking, and those that do seem to come to a sticky end.

For those who subscribe to an alien presence and motives, there are so many varying and contradictory theories. Some of their contacts give a clue, but we can never know for sure. Certainly, many experiencers have reported messages that we are developing dangerous weapons and new discoveries. We could endanger other parts of the Galaxy, and certainly destroy ourselves and planet Earth. They reiterate the same pleas for peace, love and harmony.

No advanced alien intelligence would give us the equivalent of its own technology, but may provide sufficient knowledge to help us progress and mitigate the damage we are creating to the environment. I have considered the possibility that they have imparted enough knowledge to enable us to discontinue our reliance on fossil fuels, and nuclear power. Other forms of less detrimental and free easily-accessible sources and technology would assist our recovery if disaster struck.

Despite any good intentions of the aliens, whoever 'They' are, UFO technologies are dangerous in the wrong hands. One witness reported that: "They don't like the clandestine operations that only benefit a handful of people trying to commandeer the knowledge for their own selfish purposes."

Even 'Simple Simon' knows that 'brotherly love' over the globe is not going to happen! Vicious conflicts are occurring ad infinitum, and we see the rise of radical religious societies, intent on dominating the globe. Innovations such as the League of Nations have failed, the United Nations and mutual co-operation among various countries remain fragile – the USSR collapsed and the EU is not so united anymore.

Many academics postulate that a society must first live in peace in order to successfully develop the technology to venture into outer space and other planetary systems. Otherwise they will have destroyed themselves with that very same technology. If a society had one only government, albeit a harsh, dictatorial authority, this would also curtail the possibility of self-annihilation. Is this a solution attempted by the Visitors?

One could argue this hypothesis with regards to the rumours, and indeed some evidence, where the Third Reich and Hitler were concerned. Is there any truth at all in the allegations that since World War 2, more than one species of alien has covertly penetrated deep into the politics of various First World countries via their large, powerful corporations? Of course, if all humans were conveniently micro-chipped, out Visitors would not only know who was their 'property', it could also produce a compliant population.

Chapter Three

Rosemary and Millen

The two most influential UFO researchers/investigators in my life have been Rosemary Decker and Millen Le Poer Trench. I was privileged to call them close friends. Both were highly intelligent, but never sought the limelight and often worked quietly behind the scenes, contributing to many studies, and supporting others who had experienced troubling contact or abductions. They promoted the idea that aliens were present on this planet in ancient times, and that mankind is partly a result of alien genetic engineering and modification.

They also had a more secretive side, some of which I have only discovered in recent years. Both were in contact with humanoid Visitors on Earth during the mid-twentieth century, and I suspect facilitated their activities here – spreading the message of mankind's need to improve its ways, and adopt safer technology, before we destroy ourselves and this planet.

I was exceptionally fortunate, Rosemary stayed with me when visiting Australia, and we corresponded for nearly 30 years. She imparted so much information in the hundreds of letters I received.

Rosemary Decker

Rosemary was born in New York, into an old birthright Quaker family, on 9 June 1916. She was raised in Chicago, later moving to Oregon for a short time, and then to California for the rest of her life.

She was well educated and a gifted author and artist. Despite gaining a PhD she never used the title 'Doctor.' Rosemary devoted most of her life to being an educator, specialising in, and writing a book about, teaching children with learning disabilities. She also had strong spiritual values, and quietly performed much charity and social work.

Rosemary's family was technically minded, although they varied in their support of her UFO work. Some were fully on-board; others more sceptical, possibly due to the politics of their workplace and employers. One was an electrical engineer within a large corporation; another in the Navy in the District of Columbia, yet another a physicist and university professor.

She rarely divulged her own experiences, and once commented: "I learned quite early in childhood to keep 'mum' about it, though I suspect my father had some experiences himself, and was equally quiet. He did recognise it, and in a kindly way warned me, when in my teens, against ever permitting myself to be exploited by the unscrupulous ... Glad I heeded his counsel!"

She married, had two children and later becoming a divorced, solo parent. In her later life, some of her 'kin by marriage' confided they'd had close encounters of their own.

Throughout her life, Rosemary embraced the study of space and maintained a strong interest in UFO research. She was, for many years, a historian for the Mutual UFO Research Network (MUFON) and mentor and research assistant to many investigators, including myself. Her massive contribution to research on both Mars and ufology was quiet, and without the recognition she never sought, but richly deserved. She passed away in January 2009, being laid to rest in the Masonic Cemetery in Fallbrook California. (If Rosemary did have any connection to the Masons, she never mentioned it to me. While many have bias against Freemasons and subscribe to multiple conspiracy theories, it must be noted that their roots date back many centuries. They advocate principles of tolerance – social justice, democracy, and the worth of the individual, regardless of social or economic rank.)

As well as lecturing at many venues, Rosemary contributed articles for a multitude of publications. She spoke at many international conferences on a variety of subjects including *The Early UFO Era/Contactee Phase* – Rosemary told me she 'already had a good beginning for that!'

In 1956 President Eisenhower established a Citizen Ambassador Program to promote international goodwill and exchange of knowledge across a broad spectrum of disciplines; Non-political, non-religious and inter-racial. In March 1995, the Program sent out its first UFO Delegation. This entailed Crop Circle Studies, Parapsychology, ESP, and included telepathy and other areas of research related to UFO phenomena. Rosemary was one of the Delegation of eighteen experts who visited Britain and Ireland under the directorship of Dr. Leo Sprinkle.

Rosemary and George Adamski

Rosemary's research interests started early in life. She enjoyed amateur astronomy, meeting like-minded enthusiasts and was a friend of George Adamski long before his famous meeting with Orthon in the desert in 1952. She took advantage of Adamski's access to larger-than-average telescopes to view the wonders of the night sky. Rosemary also pointed out, that in order to diminish Adamski, *TIME* magazine erroneously reported George as working at a 'hamburger stall'. This was not true; Adamski and his wife were tenants who rented accommodation behind cafe premises owned and operated by Alice Wells at Palomar Gardens.

The Visitor

When Adamski began making more and more outlandish claims, some of his acquaintances in the local community were having their own contacts, and wisely decided not to speak out. Maybe this was a good thing, because I have no doubt at least one government 'spook' would have infiltrated the gatherings, at a very early stage. Many experiencers were carefully surveying the situation first, then quietly confiding in only a few people they felt they could trust.

Rosemary Decker related one such case, concerning Mary, who had a close encounter many years before. Not wanting any publicity, she had said nothing and only confided in Rosemary:

"In April 1958, while Mary and I were talking on the phone late one night, a very remarkable thing happened. While talking she suddenly interrupted her train of thought, asking 'Do you hear that sound overhead?' (We only lived about six miles apart.) I heard nothing, but offered to go outside and listen. I heard something like a jet ... *but it remained stationary* ... Back on the phone I reported hearing it ... observing that since she heard it from the telephone in her kitchen, it was probably closer to her than me. We agreed I'd hang up while she went outside with binoculars and a Polaroid camera ... she said she'd phone me back in 20 minutes or so.

"However, the time passed, and it was nearly an hour later when my phone rang. I was startled to hear her say my name, and then simply to burst into tears ... 'No, nothing to be alarmed about ... 'Yes, there was a large, long ship and some small craft ... but they're *all gone*. 'All I have is a snapshot of the little one that came close ... 'I'll never sleep tonight; may I come over?'

"I put on the coffee pot, and in about 20 minutes she arrived, with the photo, white-faced but a little more composed. She'd been standing by her car, searching the sky with her binoculars, when she heard footsteps behind her. A tall man approached – he was the same visitant who had come many years earlier. Her knees went wobbly, and the man partly supported her as he led her into the house by the kitchen door.

"For half an hour or so they conversed, and he offered to come several times in the near future. He gave her a few suggestions regarding our research, and departed, suggesting she call the friend she'd been on the phone with. (She'd forgotten all about me – naturally enough – but somehow, he must have been aware!) Mary's small Polaroid snapshot proved nothing, though I knew it to be real. Photographic analysis was not so technologically advanced in those days, and Mary didn't want any publicity."

While Rosemary trusted me enough to confide some details to me, she always kept everything close to her chest. I never discovered what Mary and her Visitor had discussed.

What was of particular interest to me was that Rosemary was already acquainted with all witnesses to the first Adamski-Orthon meeting. She once let it slip that she and her friend Millen were at Mt. Palomar that day, when the group all returned in a state of great excitement. Over the next few weeks Rosemary spoke to each witness, individually and in private; they all confirmed the event and circumstances.

"Living within an hour's drive of Adamski all those years ago, he was the first contacted person I investigated. Yes, he was contacted, although his ego was inflated beyond a safe point, and he subsequently suffered the consequences. I have spent days, over several years of my life in the early to late 50s, in/at his open house weekends, where he had several good telescopes, donated by friends and admirers. Due to his hospitality, I met fascinating people from many States and countries, where we learned from each other and Adamski, each sharing their own experiences. It is a background I am grateful for."

Eventually, along with other friends and supporters, Rosemary felt compelled to withdraw her support for Adamski, despite their long association: "He developed a great fear of undercover security agencies, and ignored the warnings and advice given by the Visitors. We were all concerned about his well-being, and grew very worried about his later ego trips and false claims, but he was not reachable by reason."

This personality problem, which also discredited other early contactees, troubled Rosemary, who said, "I asked Dan Fry (who maintained a stable course) if he understood the situation. He replied with one of the finest bit of counsel ever given me: 'You simply cannot know the intensity of the pressures, exerted from many sources, on the lives of contactees, unless you have walked in their shoes – as I have. Without condoning their blunders, be compassionate and be patient. We are in no position to judge them. Always keep in mind *their* Basic Purpose; to assist and enlighten – *and support them in that.*"

Rosemary did say one thing in Adamski's defence: "My Uncle Bill owned a property near some acreage that Adamski and his colleagues had. He told me he had seen various original negatives of Adamski's spacecraft at the same time they had been photographed. He assured me that he considered them to be genuine, and that he had seen three craft himself, in silent triangular formation in the night sky while engineering in Saudi Arabia in 1949-50."

(Attempting to discredit Adamski, the *London Evening News* of 19 September 1975, claimed that his most-famous flying saucer photograph was that of a bottle cooler made by a Wigan, Lancashire firm. The next day a refrigeration engineer named Nicholson came forward on radio to state he had designed the cooler in 1959, six years after Adamski's photographs were first published. When challenged, Nicholson produced his patents, and noted that he had copied the design for the bottle cooler shade from the photograph in Adamski's book.)

Networking

Rosemary maintained her friendships with the original witnesses to the Adamski-Orthon meeting, and often mentioned the Baileys, and George Hunt Williamson.

She was well acquainted with Canadian engineer Wilbur Smith, Dan Fry, Leo Sprinkle, George Andrews, Brinsley le Poer Trench, Zechariah Sitchin, Gordon Creighton, Whitley Strieber, George Wingfield, Wendell Stevens, Richard Hoagland, Hans Petersen, Ida Kannenberg, and other UFO groups and authors-investigators active today. She quietly worked with many researchers around the world, introducing and putting them in contact with each other. She liaised extensively with leading astronomers and scientists studying the Solar System, especially the Moon and Mars.

Rosemary was very careful in keeping confidences, especially when helping scientists with their own ground-breaking research. She was always meticulous in her research, and felt some investigators were too accepting of data without sufficient critical analysis. In private, she was outspoken about some well-known hypnotherapists, claiming that during some abduction regressions they asked leading questions that would conform with their own theories and beliefs.

Encounters

Rosemary was good friends with Leonard Cramp, a UK engineer, and was very impressed with his fourth and final book *The A.T. Factor*. He confided in her that he had enjoyed a number of contacts with friendly human-looking extraterrestrials, who had visited his farm. He commented; "We must take into consideration the fact of thousands of years of earthly reports of the Visitors' human-like appearance, and the genetic kinship with homo sapiens (some are in the *Bible*, some worldwide.)" They apparently offered suggestions for his research into gravity.

In 1991, another expert, whose name I must withhold, also confided his personal meetings with Visitors to Rosemary; "They had occurred several years before, and were definitely friendly. He felt that most intelligences who are observing Earth's crisis are benign, and concerned not only for all our life-forms, (including Man), but also for our neighbouring planets."

Some of Rosemary's associates told of high-ranking military officers who liaised with the Visitors on many occasions. They had learned, for their own safety and security, that people like Adamski were not the best of contacts. A couple of retired officers, mentioned that while the Visitors could communicate telepathically, they spoke perfect English and were indistinguishable from humans.

While admitting her own long-term contact with the Visitors, Rosemary only confided a small portion to me: "If the audience ever ask, I only ever mention my close encounters of the first and second kind, which my daughter and I experienced together, some years ago. One happened in 1963-64 when we were driving one night, and our 'friends from above' saved us from falling over a cliff in the snow and ice. You wouldn't believe it, we had a second encounter the next morning in bright sunlight.

"Millen and I were neighbours in the US, and along with several other friends in California, watched saucers go overhead many times. Occasionally they stopped to hover, reverse, and do aerobatics. Once, after attending a lecture by George Hunt Williamson (one of the Adamski's 'desert witnesses'), at the Recreation Centre in Vista, California on 11 January 1958, we both saw, along with many other witnesses, what I can only describe as a gigantic mother ship hovering for over an hour. Man-made satellites were just making their first ventures above the Earth. And no, flying geese and the planet Venus do not have domes and portholes, but some of the craft we observed did!"

Rosemary noted that George Williamson had done some excellent work on his trips to South America, but after he went public with his contactee experiences, he had a hard time adjusting to being treated as a charlatan, and eventually withdrew and became reclusive.

"Another time, when Millen and I were together, one afternoon in Ireland, we saw a classic flying saucer. It was glinting silvery in the sun, poised and hovering silently just off the peak of Errigal Mountain, and was widely reported in the local press the next day. I suddenly realised that the vicinity was heavily laden with quartz, as was our area back home, and wondered if there was an affinity between spacecraft and quartz."

Contacts

I asked about earlier years, but Rosemary was more reticent. She said that her first contact with a 'friend from a faraway place' was on 14 January 1953, but involved telepathic communication. She also commented; "I am so grateful that my experiences did not include seeing any of those little robot-type extraterrestrials. They seem to be manufactured rather than actual people. No wonder folks get frightened."

Another time she mentioned a Visitor who left for 'Home' in 1960 – his last words to her and a friend were: "And do take care of your body." In 1995, in another correspondence to a colleague she wrote, "Don't recall if I told you that the friend and mentor from 'Upstairs' suggested to me (on the phone, shortly before he left) that I might want to write a book on the Mars-Earth connection someday. He even offered a title for the book! (That was over 30 years ago! Plainly my time scale and his were a bit different. No wonder he said: 'Try to cultivate patience,' to Millen and me, just as he was about to leave.)"

Comments such as this confirmed my suspicions that Rosemary and Millen were liaising with the Visitors. She once wrote: "My contacts were such fine ETs, and our close cousins genetically." As Rosemary was a friend and colleague of Dan Fry (who admitted providing false identity documents for Visitors), I wonder about Rosemary and Millen's involvement with helping Visitors access human society.

Rosemary made some interesting observations about the Visitors; "There is an order in their authority structure. Many of us who experience both human-like types and the small, large-headed humanoids, consider that the human-like people, although seen less often, seem to be in charge of the operations. In describing the human-like types, one has to keep in mind that they are more advanced than Earth-humans. Telepathy and ESP abilities in general are fully natural to them, and there are some physiological differences. Obviously, there is some genetic connection with *homo sapiens*, which is apparently a hybrid race, as our Bible and other early sacred books inform us."

Ancient Aliens

During her extensive research into ancient history, Rosemary liaised with Zechariah Sitchin on several occasions. Rosemary admired Sitchin's extensive research into the historical, archaeological and linguistic evidence for his thesis that today's human is a hybrid race, developed by a technologically and genetically advanced human race from beyond this planet. She supported his contention that they had crossbred with early, primitive humans, citing the Biblical 'Nefilim', Sumerian 'Anunnaki' and Egyptian 'Gods'.

Rosemary qualified her opinion in that: "being human, Sitchin does make mistakes. His vision is short in one area. He does not see that visitors can be coming from systems beyond our own solar family of planets.

"The Nephilim, ('those who came down') saw that the daughters of men were fair, and took wives, parenting men of great renown. I believe that was a secondary cross-breeding, much later than the one that produced the Adam of the second section of the Book of Genesis. No wonder Earth-humans have such a broad range of types."

Rosemary certainly toyed with the legends of Atlantis, and that when it 'sank beneath the sea', some of the survivors settled to the east in Ireland. She was very interested in the ruins at Newgrange, in the Boyne Valley, where the vertical side walls are dwarfed by an immense high dome rising from them. Archeologists have discovered that the original builders had surfaced the top completely with glistening white quartz.

Rosemary wrote: "The important purpose of this 5,000 to 6,000-year-old building has been known for a fairly long time. The opening, which leads to a long, narrow corridor, was engineered to bring a thin beam of the rising sun, at winter solstice, to fall on an object at the end of the corridor. After all the intervening millennia, the function of this 'calendar' still continues.

"Many engravings, inside and out of the building, apparently relate to astronomical knowledge, much of which has not yet been de-coded. A lot of scientific research has been undertaken by the experts. Its actual design as an ancient structural calendar and astronomical centre is unique.

"As with Stonehenge and other age-old monuments, the engineering skills are mind-boggling. The architects could not have been 'primitive barbarians'. They had very extensive, sophisticated mathematical and engineering abilities, although obliged to use very simple materials. An example of their ingenuity is the way in which they crafted the dome to be absolutely water-proof. To this day, the structure remains dry inside, although the quartz coating wore away many centuries ago."

Holograms

Rosemary, in addition to historical research, devoted many years to the study of holograms, crop circles and Mars – her specialities.

She did not consider all sightings were actual craft, and when reviewing one local US case, claimed: "They were 'holograms' – I believe somebody 'upstairs' was surely producing them!"

She also considered the possibility that some religious apparitions of the 'Lady' may have been holograms. She had researched the Lady of Guadalupe,(1539), up through into the 20th century- Lourdes, Beauraing, Cairo, Fatima, Garabandal and Medjugorje.

"The 'Lady' had varying aspects of physical appearance, changed facial expression, and had direct person-to-person communication, usually apparently by voice, sometimes telepathically. In at least three of these occasions it was well attested that that space-craft were associated with these apparitions.

"It was demonstrated in the case of the well-witnessed and responsibly documented case in Knock, (Ireland), in 1879, where three 'figures' were standing next to the church. They did not move much, but seemed to 'slide' back when curious witnesses got too close. One young lad jumped over the wall, and peeked over at a book one was holding. There was writing on the page, but he was disappointed as 'he couldn't read it'!

"One devotee, Bridget Trench, 'clumb' over the low rock wall, approached the Lady, and knelt to clasp her hands around the feet and kiss them. To Bridget's amazement, her hands went right through the Lady's feet, although they still appeared in natural 3-dimensional form."

Rosemary explained. "Based on accumulated evidence from all possible sources, I have formed the opinion that the apparitions are, in general, produced with an advanced technology, and are what we term 'holograms'. That is 3-D projections, by concentrated light beams, passed through prisms from a source located elsewhere. Among *homo sapiens*, it is a science in its infancy, but undoubtedly long known, and highly developed, elsewhere in the Cosmos.

"You may be wondering why I didn't express an interpretation of the 'Virgin' apparitions and communications? My impression is that, whoever 'she' is, the motive is constructive. The method is suitable to reach those millions of people who have a strong affinity with, and devotion towards 'Mother Mary'. It appeals to their higher emotions, and through them the possible awakening of the heart centre, altruistic love, and the peaceful resolution of problems.

"It makes sense for an accepted authority figure to focus and augment the tremendous potential energy of the faithful, to be expressed in beneficent living, tolerance towards others' religions and nations, and peaceful relationships."

Rosemary combined her research into holograms with investigations into the ever-increasing cases of crop circles, not only in British fields, but around the world. She was convinced they were actually 3-dimensional, with cryptic mathematical equations and instructions.

The Moon and Mars

For about 500 years there have been lights and transient lunar phenomena reported. Rosemary liaised with a lot of astronomers, engineers and geologists, (many ex-NASA scientists), regarding the anomalies on the Moon and Mars, and the possibility they were intelligently constructed. Many started by working on their own projects, and later became a 'Team of Independent Mars Researchers'. In 1994 Rosemary helped organise a small local conference-networking weekend for some of them. She reported that, "most of the experts agreed that we needed to gain 'real space flight' – not the clumsy, expensive and excessively dangerous rocketry currently employed. Instead of fighting gravity, hopefully it can be harnessed, as electro-magnetism has begun to be."

Her research into the Mars connection spanned over 40 years, and she wrote to me that one crop glyph was a real mind-blower. "Someone at the 'Mars Mission Group' has found correlations with world-wide crop patterns and Martian monuments in the famous Cydonia region; mathematical, angular and geometric. Perhaps forces from 'another side' are affecting our chemical/physical side and trying to show us possible ways to use unfamiliar universal and/or Earth energies. Probably an interaction of both."

In 2004 she published her book *35 Minutes to Mars*. Her research had taken decades, and liaison with many astronomers and other respected experts. In the foreward she acknowledged the assistance of Manly Hall (*The Lost Keys of Freemasonary*), Lowell Observatory, Dr E. Slipher, Richard Hoagland and many other respected authorities. She also spoke of the lunar anomalies detailed by Patrick Moore and Percy Wilkin, and discussed man's connection to the Cosmos and Galactic Man.

It is worth mentioning the known facts about the geography of and anomalies on Mars and our Moon. While certain aspects of Mars and its history are still controversial, we do know that its two moons orbit in opposite directions.

The Moon has many oddities. Experts are still trying to determine its age; one rock was reputed to be 5.2 billion years old – a billion years older than those on Earth, although there may be a prosaic explanation as to its origin. It is the only known moon in the Solar System a stationary, near perfect circular orbit. Its size and distance from the Earth ensure it exactly covers the Sun during an eclipse, something Isaac Asimov commented on, saying: "There is no astronomical reason ... it is the sheerest of coincidences." (The moon's diameter is 400 times smaller than the Sun, and 400 times closer.)

Unlike many terrestrial bodies, our Moon is believed to have a tiny solid metal core, and impacts of various kinds upon its surface, cause it to reverberate and 'ring like a bell'. Some scientists believe that the Moon may be partially hollow. (Carl Sagan proposed that Phobos, Mars' Moon, may also be the same, because it also appears to be hollow with a rigid exterior shell.) At the moment, with our still limited knowledge of the cosmos, some are suggesting that both the Moon and Phobos could be artificial satellites.

While it is said that the moon has no magnetic field of its own, moon rocks were analysed as being magnetised. Mankind has known for thousands of years that the Moon affects Earth's tides and many of life's biological cycles. Many have observed 'moon madness', and the effect of our companion in space on the psychology and behaviour of some people.

Working with Contactees

Rosemary claimed the Visitors had given her the following advice in the early 1950s: "Be an observer". As a result, she worked quietly behind the scenes, often counselling people who had been traumatised by their experiences. She actually assisted me in my work with both Jane and Elizabeth, and also shared some of the cases she had been involved with, especially where more than one generation of the same family was involved. She did not permit me to publish them at the time, but many years have now passed. Due to their positions in society, the strict confidentiality regarding some witnesses still has to be maintained.

In this account, she said the details came from the witness's memory and not through hypnosis, so there were some 'gaps'. In 1988, a US university professor and his son were travelling along a highway at dusk. They were forced off the road by an 'unseen force' and encountered about nine small humanoid figures nearby – some were examining their vehicle. They were just over 4 feet tall, with thin bodies and limbs, but comparatively large heads and slanted eyes. There was also a taller 'normal' humanoid who took them through to a spacecraft in a secluded clearing in the nearby woods.

"They were all communicating with us telepathically," the professor said, "but my next memory was of being in a brightly lit room, where an implant was placed in my right nostril and beyond. There was also an injection near my thyroid area, and another near my thymus gland. The taller friendly man guided us back to our vehicle where we drove back to the highway and resumed our journey home."

While his son suffered no after-effects, the professor has noted that sometimes marks come and go at the sites of the two injections. Health-wise his immune system has improved, and many signs of 'male aging' seem to have been reversed. He also has developed some psychic abilities.

In 1989 Rosemary visited an 81-year-old woman, living on an isolated property in the US; "Thirteen years earlier, in the mid-1970s, when she was 68, she and her husband were abducted. She clearly remembered the unpleasant medical exam, but the 'nightmare' came later from fellow humans. Her husband has since died but some detail had been leaked to the media, causing unwelcome contempt. An embarrassed relative tried to put her in a mental facility, and she was subjected to harassment, including life threats and her dogs being killed."

What Rosemary then told me was quite amazing. Some may explain this as being a spiritual experience, but it was consistent with those contactees who actually hear a voice. "About 2.15 one morning, while praying for help, and pacing the floor in an agitated state, she heard a voice say one word; 'CUP'. She looked around, nobody visible, then the next word; 'COFFEE' followed. She made the coffee, and the anonymous voice said; 'SIT!' By this time, she just meekly obeyed, later hearing the words; 'WRITE NEWSPAPER', which she thought would only worsen matters. The message was repeated three times, so she wrote and 'poured out everything as it came to her'. Within 24 hours or so rescue arrived in many forms."

Rosemary noted her friend Ida Kannenberg was one of the fewer older contacted people (past 50) when her experiences first began rather late in life. "She wrote her book, *How to Come to Terms with Your UFO/Alien Encounter* to provide comfort and common sense to close-encountered individuals who have met with insult or worse when they attempt to get help from fellow humans such as psychologists, investigators etc. following-up lost time and/or an abduction. I am glad she has included some humour into it all!"

We were once discussing some personality clashes in one of the research groups, where some had wanted to debunk all the witnesses as being delusional. Rosemary was always exceptionally secretive about her own contacts, but at that time made the following observations: "I have no doubt that most of the larger organisations are, to some degree, infiltrated by official agencies, incognito. There is certainly a fear that the facts could become known. For this reason, I do not share either my own or others' greater knowledge with any of them. On the few occasions when recording specific instances, I withhold names and sometimes reverse sexes as well. I have urged several lecturers to be much more cautious than they tend to be. I am very glad you have learned caution.

"Some people lack discretion, and quite a large number are merely toying with the UFO field, enjoying the mystery, and would be disappointed or even paranoid if they perceived clearly. It is a pity that they have to be so petty – but par for humanoids on planet Earth. Doubly sad, because the main reason for all these recent visitations is the world crisis the Earth-human has been creating, endangering air, water, earth and a myriad of life-forms, not to mention human beings themselves. Co-operation and tolerance are crucially important, as you have observed and experienced all too often."

In 1991 I asked Rosemary her opinion about the humanoid-aliens presence among us? She considered for a moment: – "The 'Big Picture' of this visitation era? The questions and the answers are so many; so of course, no-one has THE answer. There is still so much even the most assiduous of us haven't learned, no matter how many years we've applied to the field. One factor does predominate and seems to be plain beyond all doubt. There is a tremendous, over-all effort on the part of beings from other places/other grades of substance to **shake Earth humanity awake** at this time of world crisis unprecedented in known history."

She also alluded to the television live *Cover-up* program, which was completely stage managed – telling the witnesses exactly what they had to say: "It gave an unbalanced picture of the facts, by not only leaving a vast amount of data unsaid, but also widely publicising the unethical abduction/genetic tampering by other alien races. In my opinion most people, who were, and still are contacted by friendly visitors, never make their experiences public. I believe some of officialdom's aims were realised; but not that of flushing out close-encountered persons into the open."

Rosemary often glossed over, or didn't discuss, the implications of reversed alien technology being used for the wrong purposes. In 1989, she shared the following thoughts with me: "Taking this 'reality' seriously implies the requirement to accept responsibility and therefore DO something to improve conditions. You and I and many others have widened horizons, and used our individual skills as best we know how. My work with learning-disabled children for the past 27 years is the main thrust of my contribution. Others are engaged in ecological reform, animal protection, holistic healing, anthropology, education and many other fields."

I often wondered if Rosemary was really 'of this Earth'. She certainly had a regular human family like the rest of us, but she was small, just like the other women. Her energy levels and intelligence were so exceptional, was there some genetic enhancement in her heritage? She had connected with, assisted and changed so many people from all walks of life. Rosemary also had a beautiful soul, so pure and loving. I could never bring myself to tell her that 'love and peace' would not always solve our problems. The global situation has only worsened in the years since; sometimes we have to fight the evil before it takes over the world.

I have been enriched in so many ways by knowing Rosemary; her life was more influential both locally and internationally, than we will ever know. She once wrote an analysis of her 'overview': "The UFO scenario unfolds in an orderly, phase-to-phase progression. Undoubtedly this unfolding will continue as long as there is hope Earth's humanity will get a glimmer of its cosmic heritage, and take the necessary steps upward on the long ladder to its Liberation – <u>while there is still time</u>."

Millen Le Poer Trench

Rosemary's friend and colleague, Millen, was an important and integral part of Rosemary's life and research. After Millen's death in 1995, Rosemary said, "Now I can include her contributions to the field, including the fact that she was also a contactee. I always respected her request for anonymity – contact-wise, and her very quiet way of working largely behind the scenes. I can be more open now she has 'moved on'. I nearly always leave out my own personal contacts – I always have. I must stress though, despite our close contact and involvement with the Visitors, neither Millen nor I have ever been abducted or abdoctored."

Millen's grandmother was Italian and her grandfather a French-Afghani, who migrated to the US. She lived with them until the age of 12, when she returned to her parents' home. Her other grandfather was also Italian, and between the two of them Millen had a good education in ancient civilisations and literature. Rosemary once let it slip that Millen's godfather was a Visitor, hence her enhanced abilities.

As early as 1930, when she alluded to her first contact, Millen studied the folklore, and historic and religious records of peoples as diverse as the Sumerians, Egyptians, Tibetans and Amerindians. This brought her to the conclusion that Earth had been visited for millennia by advanced peoples from elsewhere, extraterrestrials, and from other realms – 'other dimensionals'. She possessed much esoteric knowledge, and besides her UFO writings had worked with Kahil Gibrau, a relative of the Dalai Lama, and many others. She was highly intelligent, and in her youth, had also 'flown planes'.

Millen often commented that visitations had begun to recur on a much-accelerated scale within her lifetime, as Earth humanity approached a learning crisis that may entail a survival crisis as well. Millen and Rosemary had family connections, and as neighbours, were 'the dearest of pals' for over 50 years. It is apparent from Rosemary's comments that Millen also had contact or an association with a Visitor, whom they both referred to as 'D' in their correspondence.

It became obvious that 'D' was integrated into our society. He was also connected to both families, but not actually in the traditional way. 'D' had met and interacted with a couple of young university students, who become influential world leaders later on. (In 1991 Rosemary forwarded some reports to me, indicating that another man in Alabama may also be an integrated Visitor.)

Millen always wrote in a cryptic way. One comment to me was: "In my book, life as we understand it, is molecular, and DNA is by no means the First Chapter." In 1959, she wrote to Rosemary regarding their mutual contact, and the first piece of advice 'D' ever gave her: "Take the face value of any statement. If other values bubble up out of your accumulated data, claim them as your own creation. Puzzling over 'hidden meanings' in this universe has caused a lot of people to miss the bus."

Millen and Rosemary were part of a team researching Brinsley le Poer Trench's (later to become the Earl of Clancarty, a member of the House of Lords) 1960 classic, *The Sky People* which introduced our ancient civilisations/legends and the

Mars-Earth connection to UFO literature. Millen, who later married Brinsley, was reluctant to fully reveal her life history, especially her UFO connections. She always avoided the limelight, preferring to quietly assist and counsel others. In fact, she was highly intelligent author, who usually used a pen-name.

Brinsley Le Poer Trench and Gordon Creighton

After their marriage, Millen spent much of her time with Brinsley in London. He wrote several books about man's ancient ET heritage, but stopped once he and Millen parted. He never properly acknowledged Millen's research contribution.

Brinsley had also been an executive for respected aviation magazines. In 1956, he edited and combined the two publications *Flying Saucer News* and *Flying Saucer Review*, and helped form the British UFO Research Association (BUFORA) in 1959. In 1967, he founded UFO research group *Contact International*, which collected data from around the world. Members used their information to suggest theories on propulsion, origins, and behaviour.

Brinsley's colleague, researcher Gordon Creighton, was raised on a farm in Hertfordshire, and became editor of *Flying Saucer Review* after Brinsley. Creighton was a Freemason, and an exceptionally intelligent multi-linguist. He translated foreign material, had connections to the British Government, and his own UFO sightings whilst in China as a diplomat. He also served as an Intelligence Officer in Whitehall for several years. Gordon's research, into both psychic phenomena and extraterrestrials, led him to express concern about extraterrestrials, living in a parallel dimension, who remained imperceptible to human senses, unless they chose to manifest.

Gordon, very much a scholar and diplomat in his own right, expressed deep concern about Brinsley "espousing a number of wild and absurd ideas such as 'Holes at the Poles', 'Hollow Earth' and the exploits of the ridiculous bogus 'Tibetan Lama' Lobsang Rampa, which certainly did us no good!"

While Gordon could be critical of his ideas, Brinsley's books are excellent for their historical research. Brinsley may have offended some with fundamental religious beliefs, but he often referred to the Bible. He reiterated comparable messages being given by the Visitors, and talked of them 'walking among us'. He also made an observation which had occurred to me – the similarity in construction of the universe down to the simple atom.

In 1998 Brinsley raised the matter of UFOs in the British House of Lords, and briefly headed an all-party study group. (It is interesting that while Lord Hill-Norton advised over 1,000 objects, unidentifiable to the witness, had been reported in 1996-7, UK airspace had not been compromised by unauthorised *foreign* military activity. He declined to provide any identifications.)

In a 1982 newspaper article Brinsley was quoted as making the following claims; "There has been a cover-up by governments of the USA, Russia and Britain. A UFO actually landed at Earl Mountbatten's home in Hampshire. It crashed and the remains are being kept for research purposes, but the public is being kept in the dark. There is a race to be the first to discover their free electro-

> magnetic power, the secret of which will give ascendancy over all other countries."
>
> Brinsley went on to say, "President Eisenhower is supposed to have met aliens, by arrangement, at Edwards Air Force Base in 1953, and he decided that they are so advanced the world is not ready for open contact. This information came directly to me from an Air Force pilot, who was present at the confrontation as an advisor. The aliens suggested an education program to prepare the way, and I believe the films *ET* and *Close Encounters*, are part of that program."
>
> A few years after Millen's marriage to Brinsley le Poer Trench, they parted, and not on the best of terms. Millen migrated to Australia incognito. I once asked how much of Brinsley's books was her work. She was silent on the matter, but expressed regret that he 'changed what she said'.

It is only since their deaths I have realised how exceptionally knowledgeable Rosemary and Millen were, not only about benign human-type Visitors, but the more insidious Greys, other extraterrestrials, and their motives and agendas.

They had both obviously worked quietly with some very influential people regarding covert and undesirable activities of other entities, but never discussed that aspect with me. It was as if they interacted with each person on an individual 'need to know' basis.

Recently I have been asking myself just *how connected* both these friends of mine were to the Visitors? I have been able to gather they had both had personal contacts before 1952. They also knew in advance of Adamski's meeting in the desert with Orthn, but chose to stay back at Mt.Palomar – why? Was Adamski the 'chosen one' to pass on messages?

I often wonder about what they knew, as both had extensive collections of early UFO material. After her death, Millen's material was passed on to Rosemary for safekeeping and further research. A few years later, Rosemary's home burned down in California's forest fires, and everything was lost!

Chapter Four

Close Encounters

During the many years I have been involved with the UFO scenario, I have noticed that most contactees report a much-improved and heightened psychic ability. It seems that telepathic communication plays an important part in many contacts, and it could possibly be a combination of the Visitors having a greater mastery over psychic abilities, plus some form of technical assistance. Many gifted humans believe we all have these powers, but are not fully aware, and don't know how to use them. Is there some inhibiting factor within our subconscious?

In my younger days I was friends with a young priest, and we got talking about the paranormal, ESP and other psychic phenomena. I was surprised when he freely admitted to the existence of all these latent abilities in fellow beings. I asked why he denied these things from the pulpit, and realised the wisdom of his answer:

"These abilities are essentially neutral. They can be used for good or evil. To let my congregation become aware of or develop these senses would be like opening Pandora's Box. They may behave responsibly for a short period, but the day would come when somebody would anger them, and the temptation to retaliate with their newly developed powers, would be too strong a temptation."

In some paranormal events, where the practitioner can physically affect actual objects, it has been suggested that this is an interaction, not of mind to mind, but of mind upon matter or reality. This concept goes to the theories relating to a universal consciousness, and effecting an outcome by will/mental force combined with an actual result, which is compatible with some of the initial results in ongoing physics research, and quantum mechanics.

Rosemary Decker had great understanding of the problems UFO contactees experienced in their lives. She gave me this article to publish in my *INUFOR Digest* or a book at a later date, and I am including a condensed version here, as her wisdom and compassion needs to be shared with all. Further, most of her observations apply equally to experiencers I had been working with.

The long-term effects of Close Encounters
By Rosemary Decker

"A chick, once hatched, can never return to the shell" - Old Proverb.

In order to get a clear view of the long-term effects of close encounters on the 'encountered', we need at least a brief review of typical short-term effects; those of the first few weeks, months or years following the event. That the initial effects on the person's life and personality is disturbing, often extremely so, should not be amazing when we consider that their entire personal universe has, in a matter of moments or hours, blown wide open.

As the initial, emotionally protective shock wears off, the contacted person becomes aware that not only must their pre-concepts of what is scientifically possible be modified; *their entire concept of earth human's place in Creation must be reconstructed.* All this takes time to sort out, naturally, and the witness, contactee or abductee has an intense need to communicate with someone who will listen empathetically and without judgment.

It is just at this crucial point that additional difficulties often arise, which will affect his personal life for years to come. Out of a sense of duty, he may take his story to the police or military. There, he may be shrugged off as either addled, hoaxing or lying. He may be interrogated so exhaustingly or so frighteningly, that he spends the rest of his life regretting his actions.

He may confide instead to a trusted family member who fears he has gone 'round the bend', and he consequentially suffers rejection in his home community. He may already be a UFO researcher, who feels that the logical and safe place to take his confidence to is his local organisation. Unfortunately, this can be quite traumatic – the entire group may exhibit suspicion and turn their backs. In order to save his position and status in the community, he then stays silent, and years later hesitate to trust anyone, however much he would like to retrieve his 'lost time.'

In short, the most distressing emotional scars experienced by encountered people are not always resultant from the initial alien contact, but from the insensitivity, distrust and abuse at the hands of their own fellow man. *These may have to be lived with indefinitely.* Nevertheless, over many years of investigations, starting with incidents in the early 1950s, I have found the long-term effects on the lives of the majority of involved persons to be remarkably positive.

The subject has, over the years, become more acceptable, and many experiencers don't feel so isolated at the event. Government agencies and the media in general usually kept reported incidents to a minimum, and when ignoring and suppression were impossible, often resorted to debunking. Unlike the early days of 'open' encounters, abductees don't have to carry the burden of proof alone. Since they often beat a path to the door of a therapist or hypnotist in the hopes of 'finding out what happened', their position has become more credible, and sympathy usually replaces censure.

The exception to this generally improved situation is the close-encountered who is *himself* a researcher. In the words of one of them, "At first I tried to explain what happened to my colleagues in scientific and ufology circles. I soon realised this was very unwise. The few spoken to gave me decidedly strange looks, and I knew if I mentioned the subject again I'd destroy any credibility I had as a reputable researcher. I have remained silent regarding the experience for the last nine years."

Of the 24 'encountered' I have worked with, nine were researchers when the contacts occurred, and most had also learned to keep silent. Of the 24 (which I have all met personally, and followed through on) run a wide cross-section of occupations. Half were/are in professions ranging from aerospace through anthropology, astronomy, engineering, social sciences and the ministry. Several were scientists or engineers, had careers or were officers in the armed services, others homemakers, two were teachers, one a secretary, plus a musician and another a small business owner. All have managed very well, in the long term, most of them still living and active in their chosen work – some just getting into their stride.

Of the two in aerospace engineering and research, one writes excellently (though rarely) on extraterrestrial technology. The other scientist, soon after his encounter, attempted to communicate some of what he's learned to a limited number within the scientific community. He has since sought to keep a lower profile in this regard, and recently co-authored an outstanding book on astronomy.

One, a noted science fiction author, kept the 'connection' from friends, family and church, but through writing the books managed to get across some advanced ideas and concern for the dangers our present Earth race is imposing on itself and on the planet that sustains us.

The minister and priest, happy with their broadened horizons, and more concerned than ever with the need for understanding and co-operation between peoples – both within and beyond their own religious doctrines – have come under the censure of their respective churches. The priest has been forbidden to use church time to communicate the source of his widened horizons, but during his holidays makes use of every possible hour.

The social service officer and the newspaper journalist, both already UFO researchers when the contacts occurred, were given a rough time within their immediate groups, and have pursued their subsequent research on their own.

Looking at all 24 of these people as a group, across the span of over 30 years, certain elements are seen to occur throughout. At least 11 persons' contacts involved some telepathy. A few remembered a childhood encounter – usually following the adult incident, or series of incidents. Different races of humans/humanoids were involved. Some looked enough like us to go unnoticed in our streets (with appropriate dress and hair style!)

In several instances, children of the involved contacted person, or a neighbour's children, were peripherally involved. This usually showed up as an immediate and intense interest in the stars and in the question of Life in Outer Space. Those whose bodies had been temporarily paralysed and/or examined felt that the physical restraint was the most upsetting. For those with 'time loss' the need for at least one empathetic listener was especially crucial.

Almost all of those in the group felt the long-term benefits have far outweighed the cost of the temporary loss of 'balance', so often accompanied by broken human relationships. Among the recognised gains that occurred most often; an increased sense of creativity and constructive purpose, coupled with augmented alertness; An awareness of telepathic communication as a potential in human development; A developing sense of fellowship between themselves and others 'in the same boat', whether personally acquainted or not, and an interest in the 'Ancient Astronaut' aspect, and the visitation alluded to in legendary and scriptural writings worldwide.

They also developed a growing interest in the human mind, brain and personality, an increased awareness of the wonders and magnitude of the Cosmos, and most importantly a greater concern for the well-being of our ailing planet.

Of course, there have been gains specific to the individual as well as more general ones I have not observed. But if there is one close up being shared by all, is that which 'topped the cream' in Dr. Leo Sprinkle's work with 225 self-reporting witnesses/contactees over a period of years;

"Emerging evidence supports the speculation that contactees view themselves as changing from 'planetary persons' to 'Cosmic citizens' ..."

Chapter Five

The European Wars

Evidence of many extraterrestrial craft and visitations may well have been lost in the chaos of warfare, but witnesses, researchers and historians managed to uncover several tantalising glimpses.

World War 1
In his later years, former German Air Force Ace, Peter Waitzrik made a fascinating report. He recounted an event in the spring of 1917, when flying over Belgium. He was piloting a Fokker triplane on an early morning mission, when he saw a glittering silver disc, with undulating orange lights, in the clear blue sky ahead. It was about 40 meters in diameter, and at the time, having never heard of flying saucers, he was terrified. He had never seen anything like it before, and thought it must be some kind of American reconnaissance plane.

Baron Manfred von Richtofen, the 'Red Baron', was flying alongside Waitzrik, and immediately opened fire. The strange craft 'went down like a rock', shearing off tree limbs as it crashed into the woods. Peter was then astounded to see two 'little bald-headed guys, probably bruised and battered,' climb out and scamper into the woods.

Peter and the Baron both reported the incident and were told not to mention it again.

Spanish Civil War
In 1936, at the height of the Spanish Civil War, villagers of the town of Pollenca on the island of Mojorca watched three glowing objects in the sky. Described as 'plates, giving off luminosity', the witnesses first thought they were some new form of weapon Hitler had promised Franco. The craft flew over the island at an altitude of about 10,000ft, and did not engage in the hostilities below.

In February 1938 forces fighting at Penon de la Mata, north of Granada, reported being buzzed by a cartwheel-shaped object, which had spokes coming from a round centre. Described as looking 'like a Mexican Hat', it was a dull aluminium colour and there were curved black portholes around the side. As it flew southward into the distance, it appeared to be rotating counter-clockwise.

Researcher Manuel Carballal reported that in July 1938 two military officers near Granada saw a disc-shaped craft hovering about 60 metres away. It was about 36 feet in diameter, and gradually lowered a column, containing two humanoid figures, from underneath. When it reached the ground, it projected a circle of blue light, which increased in circumference over the ground until it reached several witnesses. The light dimmed and the column retracted fully. The top and bottom halves of the object began rotating in opposite directions. It gave off a powerful white light before disappearing into the sky at great speed.

Researchers Mariano Melgar and Juan Benitez document another 1938 case: One hot summer morning a young lad was minding the cows on his family's farm in Munico near Avila, in central Spain. He saw a silver disc-type object, about 18 feet in diameter, descend from the sky and land nearby. It was surrounded by constantly flashing lights, and made a buzzing or humming noise which stopped after a door opened, and three figures emerged.

The boy could see all forms of devices through the open door. One figure stayed inside on guard, while the other two seemed to be collecting soil or vegetation samples. Twice when the youngster tried to approach the craft, he was repelled by some form of ray gun. After about 15 minutes the other two re-entered the craft, and the sentry actually waved to the boy before the object took off and flew away at a low altitude, spinning on its axis.

A variety of Soviet, Western and German aircraft took part in the Spanish Civil War, but none are known which resembled a domed, light-ringed disc.

Mussolini's Italy

In June 1933 a circular disc made of a grey metal, some fifty feet across and only seven feet thick, is reported to have crashed near Maderno, Lombardy, in northern Italy. It had been seen travelling silently, but faster than any known aircraft, and local Italians thought it was a secret prototype of the enemy.

Mussolini immediately ordered the wreckage be recovered, and it was taken to a hangar at the Sesto Canende airfield in Ticino. Italian ufologists suggest it was an unmanned, remote control craft, as no 'bodies' were ever mentioned.

Over the next three years, Italian scientists concluded the disc was not made on Earth, but came from a more advanced civilisation elsewhere. More sightings of superior craft were reported during that decade, and the Italians permitted scientists from Nazi Germany to access and inspect the object.

The Italians kept the matter top secret, but Mussolini made a very unusual comment during a speech on 22 February 1941: *"The United States is far more likely to be invaded, not by Axis soldiers, but by the less-well-known, though rather warlike inhabitants of the planet Mars – who will descend from outer space in their unimaginable flying fortresses."*

Hitler's Germany

Much controversy surrounds reports of early European and Nazi German contacts with extraterrestrials, and the possible development of flying discs and similar craft. Russian researcher Vladimir Terziski maintains that an 'alien tutor race' co-operated with German scientists in secret, from the 1920s, and enabled massive technological progress with antigravity and other advanced scientific concepts. (It would be interesting to know if this 'co-operation' was due to the physical presence of 'alien tutors' or to telepathic suggestions and information, as described by contemporaries in other countries.) Between 1920 and 1945, thousands of patents were applied for in Germany (but not always granted).

Terziski claimed the Germans produced their first hybrid antigravity circular craft, the RFZ1, between 1920 and 1930, and Fritz von Opel devised the first rocket powered automobile the *Opel-Rak* 1 in 1928.

Two innovators 'taken' to Britain after World War 2 were Dr F Moderson, and Hans Coler, a Naval Captain who researched new sources of power during the 1920s. Coler suggested that electrical energy could be derived without a chemical or mechanical source. In 1925, he invented the *Stromzeuger* (Current Generator), then the *Magnetstromapparat* (Magnet-Current Apparatus).

When Adolf Hitler seized power in 1933, the Nazi party took control of all rocket and aircraft development. In later years John Lear, the son of aviation pioneer William Lear, claimed that a UFO crashed in Germany shortly before the War. The Nazis had been reverse-engineering UFO technology in secret underground bases, for their rocketry and other programs.

(I once asked a European acquaintance what her father did during the War; she said he was in the Air Force, seconded by the Nazis to help reverse-engineer a flying saucer. Umberto Visani's article in the *Ufologist, Vol 17*, mentions the June 1933 UFO crash and retrieval in Italy. He concluded that the reverse engineering was completed later in Germany.)

Humans sometimes erroneously equate an unusual object with something they are already aware of and recognise. In *UFOs for the 21st Century Mind*, Richard Dolan details a report from Canada's North West Territories in 1936: The witness was performing a pre-flight inspection on his plane when he saw an ellipse-shaped object in the clear blue sky. Describing it as a magnificent airship of a light aluminium colour, he said it had no portholes or windows. The craft did not emulate an airship. It was stationary for a moment, then rotated to the east and departed out of sight at a fantastic speed. Was this one of Germany's experimental prototypes?

Certainly, unusual objects were reported in skies near the Arctic Circle. From 1930 'aeroplanes' were seen, sometimes on a daily basis, in all kinds of weather unsuitable for conventional craft, over the North Pole, Lapland, Sweden and Norway.

In 1933 in Saskatchewan Canada, three witnesses saw a landed disc in local marshland. It had a ladder coming from it, and several small men standing nearby seemed to be making repairs of some kind. They were dressed in silver, one-piece suits, and the whole area seemed to be deathly silent. The witnesses were unable to drive any closer that night, and when they returned a couple of days later the craft and occupants had gone. There were marks and footprints on the ground.

In the mid-thirties the Russians moved part of their air force to the Kola Peninsula because of the 'ghost-fliers' coming from the north. On different occasions, several witnesses described the occupants as being human-looking 'Orientals'. While some suggested they may be Japanese, the description is reminiscent of 'men in black', and some contactees report the Visitors as being 'Oriental' in appearance.

As well as seeing strange craft in the skies, the Russians are said to have been developing new technologies during the 1930s, and in 1935, tested a craft made from transparent material. In his book *The Soviet UFO Files*, Paul Stonehill discusses Robert Bartini, who designed more than ten experimental planes for the USSR. Bartini was originally an Italian communist and sympathiser who moved to Russia in 1923, after the 1917 revolution.

He specialised in super-magnetic fields, and discovered aspects of the space-time continuum which could allow an object, such as an airplane at a fixed point, to become invisible to outside observers.

The Russians have an enduring interest in the paranormal. Another Russian immigrant, Konstantin Tsiolkovskiy, originally from Poland, was a famed pioneering rocket scientist. As early as 1920 he wrote: "Intelligent beings are found in endless number ... the spread of life from one solar system to another, even from the Milky Way to other galaxies is entirely possible ... Certainly, advanced extraterrestrials possess the means of interplanetary travel ... If life does not spread, but remains tied to its home planet, it will remain incomplete and fated to a sad end. In the Cosmos undoubtedly exist more-developed beings ... a huge number of planets and other inhabitable bodies are already colonised so that the Cosmos is rich with higher life forms."

Tsiolkovskiy wrote extensively about alien visitation and interaction with Earth, and what he considered their motivation and behaviour would be. His theories were so accurate, appearing decades before reports and messages received later in the century.

Nazi Germany had many top-secret research facilities. For example, the Hermann Goering Aeronautical Research Institute at Volkenrode provided many scientists who later became instrumental to the United States' space program.

Professor Hermann Oberth (1894-1989)

Born in Transylvania in 1894, Hermann Oberth was fascinated by Jules Verne's lunar fictions, and the possibility of travelling into space. By the age of seven he had a little 'Notebook of Inventions'. He developed an early aptitude for mathematics, and in 1909 designed his first rocket ship. By 1912, he formulated a multi-stage space rocket using liquid hydrogen and oxygen as propellant.

Due to ridicule by his peers, it wasn't until 1923 that Oberth's book *Die Rackete zu den Planetenraumen*, (The Rocket into Interplanetary Space) was published. In his biographical article on Prof Oberth, Dr Ernst Stuhlinger notes that this book includes a detailed discussion of the modern high-performance precision rocket: "Propulsion, combustion, pump and pressure feed systems, tank design, thermal protection, air and jet vanes, gyro control, inertial guidance, flight mechanics, thermal and aerodynamics, zero-gravity effects, life support systems, re-entry, and the dangers of radiation and meteors in space."

Oberth envisioned the use of rockets and satellites for "mail services, meteorology, earth observations. astronomy, radio relays, astronautical research, solar and planetary studies, and space sciences in general." In 1929, he released his second book *Ways and Means of Space Travel* and described a combustion chamber and nozzle for liquid oxygen and propellants.

He served in the Medical Corp. in World War 1, and during the 1920s maintained contact with fellow pioneers, the American Robert Goddard, (1882-1945), and Russian Konstantin Tsiolkovsky, (1857-1935). A pioneer of the Space Age, and way ahead of his time, Oberth nurtured Wernher von Braun, who worked on the Peenemunde rocket team for the German Army, and was later instrumental to the US Space Program. When in charge of V2 rocket development at Peenemunde, von Braun brought Oberth to the facility in 1943.

Viktor Schauberger (1885-1958)

A life-long inventor with many theories regarding natural power, energy and turbines. His inventions include round, bulbous objects, but were they actually flying discs? Controversy still rages, because at the end of World War 2, all technical experiments, data and their associated scientists were 'repatriated' by Russia and the Western Allies. Various UFO researchers insist the Third Reich was indeed developing flying saucers, while others de-bunk this. Shortly before his death, Schauberger claimed he was involved in a secret US disc program.

Rudolph Schriever

A Luftwaffe aeronautical engineer, he was assigned to Heinkel in 1940, where he designed disc-shaped Vertical Take Off and Landing (VTOL) craft, and produced the V1 rocket. In 1943 Schriever piloted a V3, 30 feet in diameter, with a fixed central cabin, around which a ring with adjustable vanes rotated to provide thrust on both vertical and horizontal planes.

In 1944 his program was moved to Czechoslovakia, where he was joined by Viktor Schauberger, Klaus Habermohl, Giuseppe Belluzzo and Richard Miethe, who had previously worked with Werner von Braun at Peenemunde. Together they produced a superior disc craft – with plans for even more advanced prototypes.

Just before he died in the 1950s, Flugkapitan Rudolph Shriever claimed that the prototype for a 'flying top' which he had designed, was tested in 1942. He also claimed that in 1944 he created a larger version, but its initial test in 1945 was cancelled, and the machine destroyed, due to the advance of the Allies. He was adamant that the discs sighted over Europe in the following years were evidence that his papers were discovered, and his work stolen and completed.

The German rocket program only ended in 1945 with the V7 and the development of the *Kupelblitz*, a round symmetrical airplane, which in many ways resembled a flying saucer. It is believed there was a prototype as early as 1943, a 35-feet diameter spinning saucer.

Hermann Oberth once said the V7 may have been responsible for some UFO reports towards the end of the War. It is probable V7 research was more advanced than has ever been disclosed, but it was probably not responsible for all sightings. There would have been only a few prototypes, and the Third Reich's ability to produce aircraft, equipment and weapons was severely hindered by then. In the last two years of the war, Germany's manufacturing capabilities were severely disabled by constant Allied bombing raids.

Certainly, all major powers were developing aircraft capable of vertical take-off and landing well before World War 2, to eliminate the need for long runways on vulnerable aerodromes. German research may have started as early as 1932.

In the early 1930s the United States had proposals for a 'low-aspect-ratio craft', incorporating circular wing platforms. The US Navy's prototype for a propeller-driven 'Flying Pancake' (designed by Charles Zimmerman) appeared in 1942. Shortly afterwards Chance Vought designed his more sophisticated XFSU-1, and jet-powered versions were developed later.

World War 2 – the *Foo-fighters*

Towards the latter stages of World War 2 many Allied and Axis pilots reported 'foo-fighters' – small, strange glowing objects which followed their planes for miles before accelerating away. Both sides thought they were a secret weapon from the enemy, and were concerned by their incredible agility and high speed.

Aircrews flying missions over Europe were alarmed when aerial objects, mostly red or green lights, but also described as glowing globes, small amber discs, flat round silver objects, round speedy balls of fire, or as clusters of discs, would follow their every move at unbelievable speed. (Today we would probably classify these smaller objects as 'drones'.)

It soon became apparent that while foo-fighters could pose a threat to aircraft, they usually seemed to be just observing. They did not actually attack or show hostility to Allied or Axis planes. They did, however, have the potential to disrupt missions, and could interfere with internal combustion engines, even from a distance. Some planes would become highly electrified, and experts later concluded this may have been due to the objects having an exotic propulsion system which ionised the surrounding atmosphere.

Foo-fighters were reported by both Allied and Axis airmen, and despite many open and covert investigations, it has never been determined exactly what the objects were or where they came from.

Some authorities concluded they were neither American nor German, and a few researchers insist they were an advanced Nazi technology, so secret that even German airmen weren't told about them. (In an excellent series of articles, *Heart of Darkness,* British researcher David Sivier concludes that the Nazis were not responsible for the foo-fighters.)

However, suggestions some foo-fighters were actually advanced Nazi prototypes, still persist. Renato Vesco, an Italian aircraft engineer, published a book in 1971, about his work for the Germans at a huge underground facility in Lake Garda, Northern Italy.

Vesco had access to technical papers captured after the war, and mentions a remotely-controlled *Feuerball.* Its specifications and capabilities certainly describe some of the foo-fighters features reported, but doubts persist as to whether any of these craft got beyond the blueprint stage.

Vesco gives a detailed account of the Nazi's technological progress, including secret bases and factories where the *Kugelblitz* and other advanced craft were developed. He names scientists who continued developing technology 'requisitioned' after Germany's defeat, especially in Britain and Canada. After the war, Renato worked for the Italian Air Ministry and Ministry of Defense.

Today, most UFO investigators conclude the foo-fighters were mostly extraterrestrial remotely-controlled drones, on observation missions. However, did these foo-fighters have 'other', subtler effects on airmen?

In 1944 Jaques Drabier was a fighter pilot in the Free French Air Force, when three foo-fighters intercepted his plane. They projected a green beam of energy which completely enveloped him. This seemed to activate a vision of a commanding starship. He claims that such visions, and psychic abilities, continued for the rest of his life.

Researcher John Ringer writes that foo-fighters were also reported by pilots in the Pacific war. One report was made to HQ V11 Bomber Command (Pacific Theatre) on 2 May 1944. When aircrews did report the foo-fighters, they were given strict instructions, under the *Official Secrets Act,* never to talk about it, and often not to record it in their log books.

It is considered unlikely that the Germans would have shared any such technology with their Japanese allies.

British researcher Andy Roberts thoroughly investigated the foo-fighters and wrote an excellent article in the July 1988 *BUFORA Bulletin,* Number 29. Roberts disagrees with the German secret weapon hypothesis promoted by Renato Vesco, as they were seen often throughout the war years, from 1940 onwards. Furthermore, they were witnessed all over the major theatres of war in Europe, Scandinavia, Africa, the Middle East and Asia.

On 5 April 1943, Gerry Casey, a respected aviation writer and former US CAA/FAA inspector, was training pilots at the Air Corps Ferry Command base, Long Beach, California. While on a flight instrument practice trip on a BT-13, a craft came in at a moderate dive towards them at a perfect intercept angle. Gerry prepared to take evasive action, but the object made a wobbly turn, and aligned itself off his left wing, in perfect formation. Its adjustment to their altitude and course was perfect and instantaneous.

At was a radiant orange and appeared to shimmer in the bright sunlight. After a short while its aft-end made a slight alteration and it shot away, turning white as it disappeared in a climbing turn toward the ocean. The airmen estimated its speed as being about 7,200 miles per hour.

They reported the craft was round to elliptical in shape, with a round-hump topside, a smaller duplicate bump underside, and no visible openings or glass indicting a cockpit. It did not have a propeller, or any other type of propulsion that they could determine. They could not accurately gauge the size of the craft as they were not sure how far off their wingtip it was, but estimated it was anything from 35 to 75 feet in diameter.

Gerry did not take a photograph, because he had heard that Lockheed were producing a new experimental craft. He later realised that Lockheed only had the P-38 pursuit, and didn't fly the first P-80 jet until January 1944.

Encounters with much larger craft also occurred, and it was only in their twilight years that some brave souls felt able to speak out. Several British researchers commented on a case from 11 August 1944, when retired radio/radar operator Ronald Claridge broke his silence at age 80.

Ronald was in a Lancaster bomber, returning from a night raid on oil refineries in Southern France, when his screen suddenly went blank. As he advised the pilot, they both noticed a string of lights, about a thousand yards away from their starboard side. Ronald went up into the astrodome to have a look. He saw an enormous disc, with very bright circular yellow-changing to intense white, lights around it; "something like portholes in a ship." The Lancaster planes were some of the largest flying during World War 2, but this craft was huge – many times larger.

After about three minutes the object suddenly shot ahead and was gone. There was no engine noise or vapour trail. Ronald recalled that while they were all stunned, they also felt a strange sense of calm. He said that although they had not heard of

UFOs or flying saucers, they knew this was 'not of this world.' When they returned to base they were forbidden to record the event in their log books, and told not to ever speak of the experience, not even with each other.

One could argue the foo-fighters were the product of clandestine assistance from alien visitors, but the huge disc was definitely not the product of any combatants. William Tompkins, claims in his book *Selected by Extraterrestrials*, that secret agents, imbedded in high positions in Nazi establishments, advised that less-than-pleasant 'out-of-this-world aliens' gave Hitler advanced technology. Authors Louis Pauwels and Jaques Bergier are both convinced the Nazis were in contact with an extraterrestrial race, before, during and after World War 2, who helped construct small 'Adamski'-type saucers. This will always be a contentious subject, and since much documentary evidence was embargoed in 1945, there is still no definite proof either way.

On 27 May 1943 when Allied planes were attacking Essen, the crew of one British plane watched a cylindrical, silvery-gold object hovering over their 400-strong group. It was much larger than their Halifax 1A bomber, and seemed to have portholes evenly spaced along its length. After a very short time it moved away, then ascended out of sight at incredible speed.

In October, 1943 the 348 Bomber Group encountered scores of small silvery discs over Schweinfurt, Germany. Many researchers suggest that many of the smaller objects sighted by airmen must have come from a much larger mother ship somewhere in space, well away from detection.

In 1940, the British first implemented the use of radar, under Lord Dowding. Their screens routinely picked up blips of objects which flew too fast, too high, and manoeuvred in such a way they couldn't be conventional aircraft.

Pilots and aircrew photographed these 'craft' whenever possible. Military security took possession of all negatives and the reports were themselves heavily censored. Dowding was obsessed by these radar 'anomalies'. In 1942, at the age of 60, he retired from the RAF. However, he still had access to subsequent classified information, and maintained a serious and outspoken interest in UFOs the rest of his life, despite attempts by authorities to discredit him. He lectured on the subject, verifying the enormous body of evidence on their existence, and Government attempts to 'cover it up'. In 1954, he said: "Naturally flying saucers exist and they do come from other planets. The cumulative evidence for this is overwhelming, but it is not permitted to be made public."

By 1944 the official British military UFO files and investigations were assigned to General William Massey and Sir Victor Goddard, who continued a lifetime study into the phenomena. During a public lecture in London in 1969, Goddard disclosed much of what the RAF knew of these unidentified craft and their effect on humans.

Enormous numbers of reports came from the continent, and unusual objects were reported all over the world. In 1941, the crew of a converted British troop carrier, in the Indian Ocean, saw a 'globe' hovering overhead. It was about half the size of the full moon, glowing with greenish light. In 1942, a Dutch sailor reported a large illuminated disc, which circled over the Timor Sea for several hours before disappearing at high speed. In 1943, Allied bombers were followed by a UFO after a raid on Japan, and in May 1945 a large cigar-shaped object, accompanied by three smaller discs was sighted off the coast of Okinawa.

An elderly Australian gentleman told me how he was a 'gunner' on an Air Force plane during World War 2. They were flying from New Guinea to Darwin: "We were over the Torres Strait when this huge round disc, as big as us, came overhead. We were really freaked out, and then it moved and flew alongside of us for a short while, before it shot off at a hell of a speed."

Even the Russians encountered strange craft during World War 2. *UFO Encounters* 277 reported on a 1944 Soviet mission to bomb oil refineries in Romania. When Boris Surikov and his commander Major Bajenov were flying over south-west Ukraine, they saw a large ellipse-shaped object flying towards them. It was larger than the (much later) Buran space shuttle, and about twice as long.

They were at an altitude of about five kilometres, and as the object passed their entire plane started vibrating, turned a fluorescent colour and seemed to become electrified. Worried that the plane would catch fire, they jettisoned their bombs early, and said nothing during their debriefing.

Surikov said: "We'd read in the newspapers about new German weapons, but we'd seen nothing like this!"

Alien Artefacts

While a few researchers insist that all UFOs seen during World War 2 were advanced German technology, the United States was already aware that some were of extraterrestrial origin.

William Jones and Dr Irena Scott detail a very credible report from the daughters of Reverend Turner Holt, who held a Doctorate in Theology, and was a community leader and minister at his local Christian Church in Ohio.

Reverend Holt's cousin was Cordell Hull, Franklin Roosevelt's Secretary of State, and a Nobel Peace Prize winner.

One day in Washington D.C., Cordell swore Turner to secrecy and took him to a sub-basement in the Capitol Building. There Turner saw wreckage of some kind of round craft – 'metallic material' that had a silvery colour never seen before. It seemed to be a vehicle which had been completely dismantled.

There were also four large glass jars of formaldehyde, each containing an unknown creature about 4 feet tall. Reverend Holt never referred to them as extraterrestrials. or whether he knew where they came from. He said Cordell told him they were afraid it could start a panic if the public ever found out. This was a family secret, which Reverend Holt wanted revealed once he and Cordell died. Holt's daughters indicated they wanted publication delayed until they had also died.

It was only later that I joined the dots. A little-known report from April 1941 tells of a craft that crashed in Missouri which was retrieved and stored underneath 'the largest, most important building in Washington.' This happened during the Presidency of Franklin Roosevelt who knew of the incident and the retrieved artefacts. This incident was later reported by UFO researchers Raymond Fowler, Len Stringfield and Ryan Wood. After a very thorough investigation, they concluded the event most probably occurred as stated.

The witness was the widow of Reverend William Huffman, a Baptist Minister called out by local police to what they thought was a plane crash outside town. What they found was debris and the remains of a shiny metallic 'saucer'.

There were three bodies, not human, each about 4 feet tall, with very long hands and fingers. Their bodies were hairless and limp, with oval slanted eyes, slit mouths and two small holes for a nose. Huffman provided the requested blessings for the three dead occupants, and then walked up to the wreckage. He looked inside a broken portion of the 'command module' and could see a small metal chair and gauges and dials he could not recognise. He also noticed there was some kind of hieroglyphic inscriptions and writing inside. When the authorities arrived, he was instructed 'not to talk about this.' However, he told his wife and family when he returned home.

Were these the same retrieved artefacts seen later by Reverend Holt?

During 1941, senior US authorities must have known about such incursions from outer space. On 7 December 1941, the Japanese bombed Pearl Harbour. Bob Baumgartner was 22 at the time, and a military policeman on guard during the attack.

People magazine, 6 March 1990, features an article about how Bob, then 71, had spent years collecting reports supporting his claim that during the raid he and many servicemen, saw two giant silver discs, at least 300 foot in diameter, hovering in the sky. They lingered after the Japanese bombers left, as if surveying the damage, then disappeared into the upper atmosphere at high speed.

Baumgartner unearthed official US army documents which substantiated his claim, and quoted one report as stating: "They were on a surveillance mission for an unknown, and possibly extraterrestrial, power."

He was surprised to find the Japanese had also noticed the discs: "In fact, Japanese war files reveal that one of the planners of the attack, General Takashi Komazura, had ordered a retreat when he saw the mammoth flying saucers, but was overruled by General Tomoyusku Yamashita."

Los Angeles 1942

In the weeks following Pearl Harbour, the West Coast of the United States experienced several blackouts due to reports of unidentified planes invading Californian airspace. On 23 February 1942, a large Japanese submarine surfaced and shelled an oil refinery in Santa Barbara.

Two days later, one of the most witnessed UFO encounters occurred over Los Angeles. In the early hours of Wednesday morning, 25 February 1942, witnesses saw a large round craft, some 7,000 feet up. It was likened to the hub of a bicycle wheel, surrounded by gleaming spokes. It appeared to hover over Culver City and Santa Monica for some time.

The area was blacked-out, air-raid sirens and massive searchlights were deployed, and over a thousand rounds of ammunition fired. All anti-aircraft shells exploded on the bottom of the intruder without causing damage. Five other craft came into view and passed the first, before it slowly departed.

The objects were tracked on radar, and witnessed by thousands of people. Many claimed they saw groups of planes approach the object, shoot at it, then turn away. The US Army later denied having any of its fighter planes in the air.

Attempts were made to play down the incident, and suggest a conventional explanation. Despite numerous reports, newspapers did not print a single description of the objects, and government sources claimed it was a 'false alarm'. Most residents quietly disagreed, but noted that no bombs were dropped, and any damage and injuries had been caused by their own forces' massive shelling.

US authorities wondered if they were of Japanese or possible Russian origin. (It later transpired that Soviet agents also tried to unravel the Los Angeles event, thinking it was some new American craft.) Some US authorities were quietly concerned at the possibility of alien intervention.

Uncensored magazine, of March-June 2015, published a top-secret memo written by George Marshall to the President: "Regarding the air raid over Los Angeles, it was learned by Army G2 that Rear Admiral Anderson ... recovered an unidentified airplane off the coast of California ... with no bearing on conventional explanation ... This Headquarters has come to the determination that the mystery airplanes are in fact not earthly and according to secret intelligence sources they are in all probability of interplanetary origin ... As a consequence, I have issued orders to Army G2 that a special intelligence unit be created to further investigate the phenomenon and report any significant connection between recent incidents and those collected by the director of the Office of Co-ordinator of Information."

This and other reports, may indicate there were five smaller craft in the sky, as reported by witnesses, and that one of these may have been intercepted.

In 2010 researcher Robert Wood published documents obtained by former Marine, Timothy Cooper, on 6 September 2000 under the Freedom of Information Act. In these letters from 1942, President Roosevelt discusses the Los Angeles incident, and mentions an existing 'Interplanetary Phenomenon Unit'. Later correspondence from 1944 is addressed to a 'Special Committee on Non-Terrestrial Science and Technology,' indicating US authorities knew full well what they were dealing with. These documents also refer to the crash recovery reported from Missouri in 1941.

Stephen Spighesi makes an amazing revelation in his book *The UFO Book of Lists*. He published the following notation added to a 1947 memo by FBI Director J Edgar Hoover: "I would (aid the Army Air Force in its investigation) but before agreeing to it, we must insist upon full access to the discs recovered. For instance, in the Los Angeles case the Army grabbed it and would not let us have it for cursory examination."

In addition to the Los Angeles event, General MacArthur was being plagued with reports of unidentified craft in the Pacific Theatre. Analysis of possible threats was further complicated because MacArthur's ships, planes and radar often reported essentially different objects. Gigantic cigar-shaped craft would emerge from the ocean and fly off at speed.

Like his British counterpart, Lord Dowding, MacArthur developed an intense interest in UFOs. In his final address to students at West Point (12 May 1962) MacArthur stated that 'one day mankind would be confronted with evil beings from outer space'.

These encounters raise the question as to who They were – extraterrestrials, or Nazi or Allied personnel with a craft and technology far more advanced than has ever been admitted?

Chapter Six

After World War 2

I am also interested in less-publicised incidents, especially in Europe and Scandinavia, which relate to flying saucers and humanoid aliens; their possible presence then and over the following years.

The Swedish 'Ghost Rockets' of 1946

Technically, Sweden remained neutral during World War 2; but was this really so? Sweden had attracted the interest of western security agencies for some years, and during the 1950s the British Directorate of Scientific Intelligence (DSI) compiled a report; *Examination of German Secret Weapons in Sweden*.

Swedish researcher Anders Liljegren investigates UFO phenomena in Scandinavia, and has collected interesting data from many Swedish archives.

Liljegren found that sightings of unidentified aerial phenomena were far more numerous immediately after World War 2 than has ever been acknowledged by Western governments.

(These events differed from wartime cases, when numerous wreckages were located. In 1946 Scandinavia alone reported over 100 instances where rocket-shaped or luminous objects appeared to crash into the sea or into lakes, but no debris or evidence was ever found after extensive searching. Sightings often occurred in widely-separated spots within several hours of each other – some researchers claim this is a common pattern in UFO phenomena.)

These post-war UFOs were frequently described as being metallic with spool-shaped bodies, often with small fins. They were relatively slow moving, about airplane speed, which did not correspond with the lightning speed of V2s. (What was never reported at the time, was that three days before the first substantial sighting, a man in south Sweden witnessed a disc-shaped object and its occupants land in a glade near Vegeholm.)

The Swedish military conducted comprehensive investigations. It was feared, initially, that the unidentified objects were rockets or remotely controlled weapons test initiated by the Russians, who had repatriated Nazi technology and rocket scientists at the end of World War 2. (It was another year before the Russians launched their first V2-type rocket, which had none of the capabilities of the craft seen over Sweden.)

The Swedish military committee reviewed incidents going back to the 1930s, but their attempts to source the 1946 'ghost rockets' proved futile. (An interesting anecdote is that Swedish Air Director Henry Kjellson investigated a crashed V2 rocket in 1944 and participated in the 1946 review. Later in life he wrote about the possible use of advanced technologies by ancient civilisations.)

Swedish Intelligence Agencies considered that the strange objects possessed a technical capacity not attributable to any country on earth. Other scientific peers also made thought provoking comments. Dr. Menzel, in the US, was sceptical, but said: "We are dealing with beings from another solar system entirely."

In his book *Flying Saucers From Outer Space*, Donald Keyhoe documented a report from Norway in June 1952; A disc, glowing with a bluish-coloured light, was seen to descend over an electric power plant. A few weeks later, six Norwegian jets flying over the Hinlopen Straits, reported their radios were jamming. On further investigation, they found a blue metal disc, 125 feet in diameter, wrecked on the snow below. Later, Norwegian authorities denied any such occurrence.

South Australian man, Rolf Lunnisted, tells of a perplexing experience he had as a young eleven-year-old in his native Norway in 1954: On Saturday nights, he was allowed to visit a friend who lived ten minutes away through the forest. They would listen to the radio together, and at 10 p.m., once their favourite program finished, Rolf had to return home immediately.

One night he left 'on the dot', but suddenly found himself lost in the forest he knew so well. He was a bit disconcerted, but knew all he had to do was walk down the hill to the open fields below. However, there was no hillside – it was a different forest to the one he knew! Now scared, he started running through the bushes, and after quite a few minutes stumbled, exhausted, into a clearing.

In the middle of the clearing was a large 'rock' which changed colours from red to purple, green and yellow. He went towards it and 'snuggled up' in his exhaustion, feeling a strange sense of peace. The next thing he knew, he was inside 'something full of lights', with a man standing nearby.

The man spoke to Rolf telepathically saying his name was *Keon* and they were there in peace. They had been coming here for thousands of years of *our* time. He said they were keeping an eye on our progress, but had a code of conduct not to interfere with humankind. If things became too bad they would 'have to stop it'. Keon added they were not the only ones watching over Earth.

Keon also told Rolf that they did not use our primitive methods of thrust, power and speed to travel. Instead they had anti-matter, other dimensions and technology we had never heard of. He then said: "Rolf, I have picked you to hear this because you believe in matter, space and the universe itself as a living body." He wanted Rolf to get home safely, and said he might meet him again.

Suddenly, Rolf found himself only 50 metres from his own front door. The biggest surprise was to come. He realised he was early. Somehow, he had travelled back in time by at least 30 minutes or more. It was now 9.55 p.m. and the same radio show which had finished before he left his friend's home was still playing. He was hearing it for the second time that night!

He confirmed meeting Keon since then, but would not go into any detail.

In 1947 the Greek army called in a team of engineers to investigate what it thought was Russian missiles flying over their territory. They were definitely not missiles. However, the investigation closed abruptly, and foreign scientists arrived for a private conference. Like many experts, Paul Santorini, who was involved in the Greek investigation and believed in an ET presence, waited until his senior years before further disclosure. In 1967, he made the following statement: "There is a world-wide blanket of secrecy about UFO activities, because the authorities did not want to admit the existence of forces against which Earth has no possibility of defence."

The French were also aware of the UFO phenomenon; Pierre Clostermann, a French Air Force 'ace' commented: "Flying saucers have an extraterrestrial origin. Neither the Americans nor Russians can construct machines of this sort. The characteristics of the discs are clearly superior to the present possibilities of science." His thoughts were confirmed by fellow countryman Louis Breguet, an aircraft manufacturer, who said: "The discs use a means of propulsion different to ours. There is no other possible explanation. Flying saucers come from another world." Gabriel Voison, an aviation pioneer joined the debate: "Those extraterrestrial explorers are separated from us by a gigantic barrier higher than the Himalayas – our retarded technical knowledge and our haughty ignorance."

Admiral Lord Hill-Norton, former Head of the British Ministry of Defence, has stated that: "There is a serious possibility we are being visited, have been for many years, by people from outer space, other civilizations. It behoves us to find out who they are, where they come from and what they want."

One insider has stated that US Admiral Conway reported to Secretary of Defence James Forrestal that: "Several different alien craft have, and continue to fly in restricted air-space, and possess unknown ray weapons." In 1947, the *Majestic 12* committee was convened on James Forrestal's recommendation, to investigate further.

During a press conference on 4 April 1950, President Truman stated: "I can assure you that flying saucers, given that they exist, are not constructed by any power on Earth." To a certain extent his claims were validated just over two years later. In July 1952 UFOs cruised, at low altitude, over the White House, only to evade, at incredible speed, any pursuit by Air Force jets.

Our governments have long stressed a need to sustain varying power structures on Earth, and maintain technical superiority over rival nations. There is still fierce competition to retrieve and back-engineer any alien craft to learn their propulsion energies and other secrets. It has been suggested, on several occasions, that government agencies promote the belief in UFOs to mask their own experiments, and avoid costly compensation claims if anyone is injured when tests go wrong.

The major powers are certainly aware that unidentified craft of extraterrestrial origin exist, and their concerns classify such events way above Top Secret. What intrigues me is the insistence, by some of the upper echelon, that it is imperative to mount a mission to Mars in the foreseeable future – why? It was not of strategic importance at that time, given our limited military technology and its vast distance from Earth.

An interesting draft document has recently come to light, purportedly written by Dr Robert Oppenheimer and Albert Einstein in June 1947, a month *before* the Roswell crash event, and less than a week after a similar incident was reported at Socorro on 31 May 1947. Titled *Relationships with Inhabitants of Celestial Bodies*, it confirms the existence of UFOs and outlines possible future friendly or hostile interactions with aliens. They envisage mining on the moon, and creating an artificial atmosphere there. The danger of nuclear war, and the necessity of reaching an agreement with other countries regarding nuclear weapons, is also stressed.

The Scottish Conference report (see box opposite) may be questionable, but *Flying Saucer Review* published an account, based on a conversation overheard between a physicist and a member of Naval Intelligence: They discussed the incredible technology of saucers seen in World War 2, and how they first thought these were a new secret enemy weapon. It was discovered they had just been small craft sent out from a mother-ship orbiting out of sight.

About the beginning of March 1955, five UFOs landed in England. Some were unmanned, but others had occupants who looked just like us. Friendly contact was established with these Visitors, who were scientists. It was suggested that some remained and mingled with the general population

In his book *Alien Liaison*, Timothy Good describes a meeting in the US in 1957, where an alien of Caucasian appearance, met with international scientists. He addressed them telepathically, and let them inspect his saucer-shaped craft. He described the concepts behind the technology, but most of the audience had trouble grasping the new physics. He also told them that "beings like himself had infiltrated amongst us". The supposed initiator of this report later tried to deny it, but given other leaked information, one can but wonder.

In 1956 the United States set up *Project Horizon* to put a US army base on the moon. In 1958, the more sophisticated National Aeronautics and Space Administration was established. NASA and the US Military began contracting out a wide range of aerospace projects to big business corporations.

Secret Meetings

Arms races and space races are now entrenched in our society, but sometimes opponents will collaborate in the face of a common threat. Author Paul Stonehill details research by Yuri Stroganov, who reports that the USSR's Ministry of Defence formed a UFO Research Committee in 1955. Stroganov claims that Russian intelligence chiefs met with counterparts from France, Britain and the USA to discuss the problem in 1956. They agreed upon the necessity to keep the issue top secret and maintain a unified approach in handling witnesses, the media and UFO research groups.

Official agreements to keep the UFO-alien issue top secret take on new meaning when considered along with a little-known report dating back to the early 1950s. A New Zealand investigator received a letter from a respected US researcher who used to work in a cafe. One of the regular patrons was a young American pilot. Chatting over lunch one day, the pilot mentioned that he had just been sent on a mission to Australia, where he landed at a vast airport.

A gigantic spacecraft was already there, and he was introduced to a group of friendly, intelligent, good-looking men. He was told they were scientists from other planets, and he was to fly them to Scotland for a meeting. He liked these visitors and was impressed with them and their conduct.

The pilot had flown them to Scotland, and remained with his plane while they attended the conference. He said that scientists from many of the world's nations were also present.

When the conference ended, he flew them back to Australia and their spaceship before returning to the United States himself. There was some talk at the time of a little-known conference in Geneva, but little has been said about the Scotland meeting. There were still secret facilities in Britain's remote north, which had been used for covert training and operations during World War 2.

The pilot was told the spacecraft was too large to land at any British airport, and of course it would have been too obvious! It stands to reason that the relatively uninhabited far north of Australia would have been more secure, well away from prying eyes. What better facility than **Carson's Field** in the Northern Territory (later to become RAAF Base Tindal)?

The American 43rd Engineer Regiment began constructing a large runway at Carsons Field, in 1942 to service Consolidated B-24 Liberator heavy bombers. Completion took several years. It was never actually used for its original purpose and remained a 'bare base' until refurbished in the late 1960s. It opened as a permanently manned RAAF Base in 1989.

(Other less-likely possibilities are: **MacDonald Airfield**, built by the Australian military in 1942 – the runway there was 6,000 feet long and only 100 feet wide; or **Fenton Airfield** which catered for B-24 Liberators.)

Further covert projects began to build large, underground military facilities to house these developments. Most secret technology and prototypes created for military and space projects were produced by these powerful corporations, who employed ex-Nazi scientists and engineers who worked either by choice or coercion.

Britain, Canada and Australia were also involved in assimilating German technical personnel, and in 1946-7 all had teams actively recruiting staff for their own government's hi-tech projects. It was essential to develop these new technologies and keep them from the Russians. (Later on, some of the eminent scientists involved publicly supported the alien hypothesis, and several became 'whistle-blowers', claimed an alien presence and assistance in research laboratories and underground bases.)

Whose technology?

In 1952 Canada began *Project Omega*. British-owned Avro-Canada developed its own program to build a flying disc. This was discontinued in 1954 with rumours that the experimental craft failed. Many commentators considered this was just a smoke screen to conceal further developments, such as the highly-advanced *Project Y2* in 1955. The United States began *Project Silver Bug* in 1955, to develop versions of flying saucers and discs.

While some UFO sightings and crashes may be due to our own experiments, others were probably not. One Skunk Works engineer was quoted as saying: "Some UFOs are ours, and some are theirs." It is also worth considering that some flying saucers seen in the 1950s were more 'terrestrial' and of a fairly basic design, very similar to Nazi plans discovered at the end of World War 2. Other sightings in that decade were of much larger, more sophisticated machines. These were unlikely to be our advanced technology, which manifested itself in later years.

The US, UK and their allies' shared anxiety over a possible alien threat increased in the years following. There are several alleged crashes and entity retrievals in 1947. In 1951, 5,000 crew of a convey of seven US Navy ships, witnessed a large cylindrical craft hovering 400 feet above the largest aircraft carrier in their fleet. It was 8,000 feet long and 500 feet in diameter, and one analyst suggested that we were dealing with a superior Galactic force.

On 30 July 1952 a RAF fighter pilot, on a training mission over West Germany, was intercepted by a gleaming silver metallic disc which flew alongside his plane before speeding off. It had a diameter of about 100 feet and ground radar tracked it at speeds in excess of any known aircraft.

British UFO investigator Nick Redfern reported the UK had another scare in September 1952, involving his own father, a RAF radar mechanic. (This account was verified by independent sources.) Over the course of two days UFOs raced over the UK, Bay of Biscay, and English Channel at speeds of up to 2,000 miles per

More retrieved craft

Do we really know how many crashed discs our scientists have retrieved and back-engineered? While many news-stand UFO magazines have a preference for spectacular but unsubstantiated journalism, in 1978 *Official UFO* published a comprehensive report regarding one such retrieval:

Pacesetter II, a Shell Oil Company rig was drilling 90 miles off the coast of New Jersey, when it struck metal 600 feet down. A lowered sonar device recorded a metal object, about 50 foot in diameter. When the object was brought to the surface, all that was visible was a central area on top with small rectangular openings all around. The remainder was covered with barnacles. Once cleaned up, it showed a disc shape, complete with original shine.

A high-ranking US Federal representative (the informant), three Shell officials and a physicist arrived by helicopter. The physicist entered the object from an opening at the bottom, and returned dumbfounded. He said he didn't know what it was made of; it wasn't steel. Furthermore, he could not figure out the propulsion mechanism or the equipment inside. He then enlisted the help of other workers on the rig to dismantle the mysterious object.

The physicist carbon-dated it at 600 years old, and determined it was not radioactive. He and a rig mechanic re-entered the craft, and after about 20 minutes a whirring sound was heard. A large cylinder emerged from underneath the belly of the craft. A sliding door opened and the two men came out. The physicist was holding a solid, silvery object, about the size of a basketball, which he had found in the exact centre of the craft.

He let go of the ball but it didn't fall, and explained that its composition had so far defied analysis. He thought it was an 'anti-gravity' machine. Its purpose? ... to make the craft simulate a planet with its own gravitational pull, thereby preventing the occupants floating around during flight.

Another helicopter arrived with five CIA agents, who said they were taking possession of the object, and put it on their ship which would arrive soon. While they argued with the Shell executives as to legal ownership of the salvaged craft, the physicist continued dismantling more panel boards from the control room. He commented he'd not seen equipment like it before.

He and the mechanic, much like 'boys with toys', brought a few smaller items up on deck. He pointed a cylindrical tube towards the water, and pressed a red button on the end. A thin white ray shot out with a blinding flash, and travelled about a mile before petering out. Next, they got a small 'control box', pointed it at the craft and pressed the button. A conning tower panel slid open, a 3-foot metal rod emerged, and when manipulated skywards, they pressed a second button. An electrical bolt, like lightning, shot skywards and punched a hole in the clouds 10,000 feet above.

By the time they had collected more small 'gadgets', and thought better of testing them out, the CIA ship had arrived. Everything was confiscated.

hour. They were tracked on radar and were much too fast for the Meteor fighters sent in pursuit.

Another ex-RAF officer confirmed that during that two-day period they located an enormous object, "the equivalent mass of a battleship," hovering for at least 18 minutes, in the stratosphere high above the English Channel. It then split into three parts which zoomed off at an incredible speed. One headed north, one over to France, and the third disappeared in the eastern Baltic region. The personnel involved did not talk about the incidents until they were elderly, and no longer in the armed services.

Australia

Australia also received reports of unidentified objects with advanced technology. In *Contact Down Under*, I detailed the well-known case of Naval pilot James (Shamus) O'Farrell in 1954. One night while on a routine flight over countryside to the west of the Nowra Base, O'Farrell unexpectedly encountered two strange craft which 'paced' him for some time, before departing at incredible speed. They were tracked by radar, and reported by witnesses on the ground. To this day, they remain unidentified.

In 1956, another report came from just outside Goulburn, west of Naval Base HMAS *Albatross* at Nowra: Late one winter's night, a motorist stopped his car to watch a very bright light hovering about 100 feet above the ground.

Getting out of his car, he walked to the fence at the side of the road and noticed farm animals running around in a distressed state. The light was so bright he could not make out any shape. It remained for another five minutes before suddenly shooting off at high speed, into the night sky.

In 1958, in the same sparsely-populated area, the wife of a Goulburn sheep shearer had risen at daybreak to see her husband off to work. As she looked out her kitchen window she saw a "clear shaped object" hovering about 500 feet above a nearby paddock. Five or six smaller disc-shaped craft flew up and entered it. The larger object then took off at great speed and disappeared.

In 1967, four planes, each holding two pilots and flying at 25,000 feet near Jervis Bay, Nowra, sighted an unknown craft in their airspace. One of them was diverted to intercept and identify the intruder. When they got within five miles it headed southwards at an inconceivable speed. Other reports were also filed, but all were fobbed off with an unacceptable excuse.

By the 1970s there were several secret craft and technology of our own in the skies. Among its less-publicised roles, HMAS *Albatross* south of Sydney, had the task of monitoring UFO activity. On several occasions fighters and bombers were scrambled to pursue evasive objects in the nearby sky. We can assume the Naval Air Arm would not be chasing known or friendly craft.

> ## 'Motherships'
>
> A review of many reports indicates the humanoid aliens withdrew from open contact around 1960, leaving only their people who had quietly integrated or assimilated into society. At times, they even invited contactees to go with them.
>
> We can only speculate the reasons for their departure, but several possibilities come to mind: In 1957 the Soviets placed the first *sputnik* satellite in Earth orbit, heralding our increasing surveillance of space and sky. We were also starting to develop technology, similar to theirs. Another possibility was the arrival of another, less-benign alien race, which I do not discuss in this book, but which other investigators mention at some length.
>
> There are a couple of early reports of huge craft, which are highly unlikely to have come from this planet. (They may have been larger 'mothership' vehicles for housing smaller 'scout' craft, more suitable for landing on Earth.)
>
> One was reported by a former RAF member, and documented in the *Flying Saucer Review*. In August 1949 the British held *Operation Bulldog* – military exercises designed to test air defences. Just after midnight one day, an enormous object travelled from west to east parallel to the South Coast of England. Its size was estimated to be that of a freighter or passenger ship, about 15,000 to 20,000 tons, travelling at about 3,000 miles per hour, at an altitude of 50,000 feet. It suddenly increased speed, shot upwards and disappeared out of range at about 100,000 feet. The next day, all log books and records disappeared, replaced with new Duty Watch Books.
>
> Major Donald Keyhoe discussed a 1956 encounter by a Navy transport plane flying westwards across the Atlantic to Newfoundland: A giant metallic, disc-shaped craft – at least 30 feet thick and nearly 400 feet across, with an uneven glow around its rim, raced up from below, and tilted as it passed them. It then swung around and paced them at a distance of about 100 yards.
>
> Gradually the craft pulled ahead, tilted upwards and accelerated out of sight at an incredible speed. The Navy crew were met and debriefed by US Air Force intelligence officers, and later by the Navy. After several days a government scientist arrived, and showed photographs, one of which looked like the strange disc. After identification, the scientist would not answer any questions. Our own air-power was no match at the time.

One person at HMAS *Albatross* advised me that this prompted years of talk in the base about UFOs. Apparently, military counterparts described an incident with the British Navy during the Cold War: When on a routine flight over the Atlantic, a large, submerged, disc-shaped object, approximately half a mile in diameter was spotted. It was described as 'yellowish', but this could have been caused by the water's colour. Instead of following usual procedure and buzzing the object until it left the area, they were told to 'blow it up' and not ask any questions.

The following years

Since the 1970s there has been an explosion of publicity about UFOs and aliens. At times, it has become so overblown by lies and disinformation it is hard to know what is the truth.

We only went to the moon a few times, but while lunar exploration has now been put on hold, we quickly went further out into space, launching *Voyager 1* and *Voyager 2* in 1977. These have been followed by more data-gathering missions in the decades since. As these missions continue, we are learning a great deal about space and our Solar System, much of which does not correspond at all with our initial expectations from twentieth-century astronomy and physics. Scientists now freely debate major theories in public, including those of Velikovsky and Einstein.

United States President, Jimmy Carter, was quite open about his personal sighting of a UFO in 1969. While never disclosing any information, he had been privy to while in the White House, he could not make good on his promise to publicise all UFO data held by US officials. His 1977 address, is embossed on Voyager, before it was sent into space. If you read the words carefully, they are very revealing in themselves. Most people are not aware that part of it is a quote from African contactee Elizabeth Klarer:

This Voyager spacecraft was constructed by the United States of America. We are a community of 240 million human beings among the more than 4 billion who inhabit the planet Earth. We human beings are still divided into nation states, but these states are rapidly becoming a single global civilisation.

We cast this message into the cosmos. It is likely to survive a billion years into our future, when our civilisation is profoundly altered and the surface of the Earth may be vastly changed.

Of the 30 billion stars in the Milky Way galaxy, some – perhaps many – may have inhabited planets and spacefaring civilisations. If one such civilisation intercepts Voyager and can understand these recorded contents, here is our message.

"This is a present from a small distant world, a token of our sounds, our science, our images, our music, our thoughts and our feelings. We are attempting to survive our times so we may live into yours.

We hope someday, having solved the problems we face, to join a community of galactic civilisations. This record represents our hope and determination, and our good will in a vast and awesome universe."

The governments of the world have always been very tight-lipped about UFOs and extraterrestrials, usually explaining them away as natural phenomena or misidentifications. Even when UFOs appeared over US nuclear weapons facilities, interfering with or shutting down missiles, the ensuing security clampdown prevented any disclosure of the facts. Any investigator brave enough to publish details was promptly discredited and ridiculed.

Alien Co-operation

I often wonder about what really goes on in Australia where experimental technology and alien collaboration are concerned. Occasionally I receive a communication from 'insiders', but cannot tell if these are genuine or disinformation.

Sometimes public servants, bound by the *Official Secrets Act*, did not hold it in such high regard as their military counterparts. A friend who worked in the UK with the RAF, told me that UFO reports from both military and civilian pilots, came across her desk on a daily basis. An Australian Ministerial secretary saw monthly reports of UFOs in three categories; *identified, unidentified for now*, and *unidentified, to be concerned about*.

Perhaps the security agencies biggest problem is employees who confide in partners or family. At the end of 1996 I received a call from Canberra. 'Martin' actually wanted the telephone number of UFO Research Queensland. He nervously told me how he and his girlfriend 'Rebecca' worked for the Department of Defence, as did his friend 'Robert', an ex-pilot.

"Rebecca's boss has asked for certain files. However, the second in charge of an Air Force base has told her not to give them to him – her own supervisor! She was told to either destroy them or return them to him at the base.

"Rebecca was scared, and spoke to me of small experimental craft – two car lengths long with wings, on the ground. The wings fold out. The pilots were small, and the base either counselled people who had sightings or ridiculed them." At this stage, Martin mentioned a well-publicised incident where Rebecca had felt sorry for the witnesses, and guilty about keeping quiet.

"She claimed some sightings were staged; that it was replicated technology. This was not supposed to become public but it is out of their control as "the nature of the craft is such that it can become invisible if it wants." Rebecca said that she had seen it, and that space travel is much further advanced than we realise.

"She then mentioned the Visitors and said they were not dangerous. The new ones are timid, the old ones were not. She went on to tell me there were retrievals where they used 'good flash trucks,' but no-one would ever know. She was reluctant to give any more details, but mentioned something about a 'Global Particle Beam' Defence System – did I know what she meant?"

I did know, and while Martin had my full attention, I was not about to volunteer any information, and just let him continue confiding his fears.

"I was at a loss as to what I could do to help with Rebecca's predicament," Martin said. "I spoke to my brother, an ex-paratrooper stationed at a military base. He believed Rebecca, and said four US military officers were drunk one night and bragged they had 'anti-gravity and tech-links to aliens.' My older brother John has links to the Joint Intelligence Organisation. He has photos, the public did not know about the Army being in 'smaller' areas. He told me that it's

> the old cliché 'If you know too much they will kill you', and went on to say some witnesses to retrievals did disappear."
>
> It was hard for me to decide what to do with this report, and I have sat on it for twenty years. UFO researchers are often fed false information deliberately, but this account certainly corresponds with other leaks around the world. 'Sensitive' programs are always compartmentalised. In 2010, the *Washington Post* reported that the US military chain of command is routinely undermined as personnel are ordered not to reveal to their commanding officers about top secret programs, especially those concerning UFO technology and extraterrestrial life, to which they had been recruited.
>
> There was little I could do to help Martin and Rebecca with their predicament, except to suggest that sometimes 'discretion is the better part of valour'. Whether they spoke to other research groups is something I don't know. I have refrained from detailing any codes or file or base names. It is up to the reader to decide. However, it does add further to the speculation that not all sightings are extraterrestrial; some may be our own experimental craft or reverse-engineered alien technology.

I can well understand the necessity, on many levels, for strict secrecy. Perhaps Sir Winston Churchill said it all in his famous quote: "The truth is so precious that it must be protected by a bodyguard of lies."

We often hear comments about the 'invisibility' of some craft. One of the primary goals of any military is to make their own aircraft, especially those on spying missions, invisible to the eye and undetectable by enemy radar. We have succeeded, but only to a limited degree, with Stealth technology and other more innovative programs. Simultaneously, the major powers are employing countermeasures and enhancing their technology to better detect such craft.

I have received sufficient reports to convince me that *some* craft, whether they be worldly or alien, have mastered the art of invisibility. One difference I have gleaned from the reports – only my own theory – is that some 'cloaking' technology is used.

Our own stealth innovations displace the atmosphere as they fly. However, alien craft tend to create a rippling effect, especially as they come into view.

This leads to the logical question as to why any alien objects are deliberately making themselves so obvious? What are their motives and agenda? Then we must also consider the craft we are not able to detect. These are questions to which the answers could be hypothesised forever.

Limiting weapons of mass destruction

In the decades following World War 2, some major powers agreed upon several arms control treaties. It is not known whether the alien message had any influence on this, or if our leaders finally developed some common sense.

Physicists have told me that there was always a worry about the very first atomic and hydrogen bomb test detonations. There was a slight possibility these might trigger an unbounded chain reaction that would immediately consume the entire planet. Wilbur Smith once divulged that he had seen a photograph of a very large hydro-nuclear explosion on Bikini Atoll: "It showed a large fireball ... well over 100 miles in diameter ... projecting out from it were solar prominences, great tongues of activity ... about 25-50 miles in size ... chain reactions taking place in the Earth's atmosphere ... very significant and worrisome."

We realised there was a need for some control over our dangerous experiments. Beginning with the *United Test Ban Treaty* (1963) we progressed to military actions in outer space (1967); *Non-Proliferation of Nuclear Weapons* (1970), and the *Seabed Arms Control Treaty* (1972). In recent times, there have been limited agreements regarding biological and chemical weapons. Some experts correctly state that these measures are technically 'tokenistic', as the world's most powerful countries already have sufficient weaponry to destroy all life on Earth several times over, and other rogue nations are not prepared to toe the line.

While limiting nuclear and other planet-destroying technologies, we continue many devastating 'conventional' conflicts, usually in third world countries. On the other hand, we have continued with our exploration into space and the Solar System, even participating in some limited joint projects.

New technologies

Scientists have long recognised our planet is at risk from asteroids whose orbits intersect Earth's orbit. Anything more than 100 meters across is a potential threat, yet difficult to anticipate. In the US, federal funding is made available for better equipment and a *Near Earth Asteroid Tracking* program (NEAT) is managed by the Air Force and scientific groups. NASA and the European Space Agency are developing better technologies to detect these rogue bodies.

Some Visitors warn their contactees of a coming natural disaster. Perhaps they are concerned about our possible detrimental response to an asteroid threat. The current consensus is that it is safer to intercept and 'nudge' a rogue asteroid into a safer trajectory rather than 'nuking' it – this could produce a bombardment of smaller, damaging rocks and radiation.

Space surveillance for incoming asteroids and aliens, is not the only project our governments have in mind. A few decades ago we launched our first satellites with sophisticated telescopic cameras to observe minute details on Earth, of not only 'enemy' installations, but also public events and people on the street going about their everyday lives. These provide continuous scrutiny of any target and relay it back to base, with absolute secrecy and concealment.

We now have remotely-controlled drones, operated by artificial intelligence. Besides their military value, satellites and drones are being widely adapted for commercial use, which increases misidentifications by UFO enthusiasts. The downside of this technology is its enormous potential for undetected nefarious use, and one of our primary concerns has to be nuclear or biological terrorism.

The many satellites which now orbit the Earth, provide a primitive 'defence shield' around the globe, and 'eyes' into outer space. They also form an important part of our digital technologies and communications. These can monitor and manipulate many things in our everyday lives – all types of electronic instruments, appliances and devices.

To reach the nearest stars would require impossible amount of our current fuel propellants. We need technology which will generate vast amounts of thrust for a very small amount of input energy. In 1998, NASA initiated its *Breakthrough Propulsion Physics* program. Scientists are constantly devising radical systems, although some are too costly or difficult to actually conduct experiments. We have yet to master time travel, or journey across the galaxy with ease, but many other visionary projects and research have, or are likely to become a reality. They include nanotechnology, sub-atomic technology and photons, lasers, scalar, particle and psychotronic technology, bio-machines, electromagnetic weapons and energy beams, phase-conjugation, exotic propulsion systems, gravitational waves, neutrinos, Higgs Boson, cold fusion, microwaves, pulsed strobes, holographic technology, magnetic fields and super-conductors.

An enormous amount of experimentation has been devoted to anti-gravity. A pioneer in the field was Thomas Townsend Brown who in the 1920s developed a complex theory into gravitational fields (the *Biefeld-Brown Effect*) with professor Paul Biefeld. After the war, in 1953, he planned for a disc-shaped anti-gravity combat craft, called *Project Winterhaven*. While he suffered considerable disappointment at the hands of some of the large corporations, he continued with his electrogravitic research. It is interesting that a scientist of his calibre went on to found a UFO research organisation in October 1956!

Other researchers still study the Earth's vibrations, harmonics, energy grids and ley-lines, long known and utilised by indigenous and other paranormally inclined cultures. Canadian scientist John Hutchinson pioneered discoveries into magnetic fields in nature and modern society, and several researchers are positive we can derive all the energy we need from nature, the cosmos, and the power of the Earth's rotation, gravity and/or its magnetic field. Another area of on-going interest is the use and effect of sound vibrations and frequencies.

Some experiments, such as the Hadron Collider, and the search for dark-matter are controversial, as is the HAARP project which interferes with the Earth's ionospheric pressures. While many worry about the 'flow-on' effects of these technologies, we are constantly assured the effects are minimal. The list of innovative research and discoveries goes on and on as we advance our technology and automation potential.

Over the last century, many scientists have contributed to our great technological leap forward. Given the observations by some, that they made their discoveries with 'assistance', we can only wonder if some of our geniuses had inspiration from the Visitors. Newton, Boscovich, Poincare, Lorentz, Faraday, Teller, Maxwell, Beardon, Riemann, Planck, Schauberger, Searle, Tesla and Einstein are some of the better-known mathematicians and physicists who contributed to today's theories and discoveries, some of which do not always complement each other. There are many other unrecognised scientists and engineers who have, and still are, assisting our future progress.

There is new ongoing research into quantum physics, and entangled particles. Basically, two once-correlated subatomic quantum particles can remain correlated, and instantly influence or mirror each other, even when separated by great distance – interfering with one has a spontaneous effect on the other. These 'wave functions' or 'packets' have been likened to 'warping of space and time' and have scientists disputing and debating whether or not Einstein's Theory of Relativity and the Speed of Light Constant still apply, and if it is possible to combine Quantum Mechanics with General Relativity to create a Unified Theory of Quantum Gravity. Already some of the research has led to new innovations, including the possible founding of an 'alternative quantum Internet', which would be difficult to covertly tap into.

When finally resolved I think this aspect of science will give us a better understanding of both the UFO/alien and some psychic phenomena. (One theory under consideration is that the speed of thought may exceed the speed of light.) IBM scientist Charles Bennett improved on 'streaming theories', and physicists Bose, Home, and Zeilinger developed quantum superposition.

Certainly many contactees report the same 'beam of blue light' which carries them into a space craft, and this information may be of interest to our scientists. Some experts theorise this research, still in its infancy, may lead to teleportation, making *Star Trek's* – 'Beam me up, Scotty' not so far-fetched after all!

At the start of the 20th Century, the Wright brothers finally managed to get their flimsy little plane airborne, and people scoffed at the idea of other habitable planets and 'life' out there in the universe. Just over half a century since we have landed on the moon, and now we have discovered the existence of many 'exoplanets', including seven in one solar system only 40 light years away.

Now we have interplanetary rocket ships, permanent space stations and pilotless aircraft and drones. Our technological progress in the last century has been mind-boggling. Did we really accomplish all that on our own merits? I don't think so! But if, perchance, our primitive civilisation could make this great leap forward without assistance – what superior technology could an advanced alien species have developed?

Chapter Seven

Those in the Know

Much has been debated about the 'saucer crashes' at various locations in the late 1940s following World War 2. German scientists had been seconded to Russia, the US, and other countries to work on space and defense projects. If anybody was aware of the presence of UFOs, aliens, or reverse-engineered alien technology it would be them, as well as the pilots, military and some political leaders of the day. Many of these people were quietly confirming these things do exist, while the public was being told the opposite.

In his book *Alien Liaison*, Timothy Good mentions information he received from Hans Petersen, who served in the Danish Air Force for 27 years. Hans had a letter from a now-deceased US Army Brigadier-General, who was contacted by aliens he called 'the boys upstairs'. They looked totally human and could communicate both telepathically and in perfect English. They asked him to become their 'physical earth-man contact' with various national and religious leaders. It had to remain strictly secret, as if revealed, he would become worthless to both them and the tasks he was performing.

Paul Hellyer, an aeronautical engineer and politician with a private pilot's license, was elected to the Canadian Parliament in 1949, and served for 40 years. As Defence Minister in the Pearson Administration during the Cold War, he was privy to much confidential information. He received all UFO sighting reports, of which 80% were misidentifications, and about 15% were genuine unidentified flying objects.

Hellyer was always very outspoken on UFOs, and confirmed a sighting by himself and his wife outside Toronto. He made numerous speeches on the subject, including to the Russian media. He believes that aliens live among us, and said it was likely that at least two species, the 'tall whites' and 'nordic blondes', worked with the US government.

Whenever challenged, he always denies using any information or knowledge obtained while holding his government portfolios. Witnesses approach him personally, and every week he receives three to five emails.

In August 2014, he reportedly stated on Russian television: "Some guests from outer space actually live here on planet Earth." Interviewers claimed he also said: "Some of them look just like us, and they could walk down the street and you wouldn't know if you walked past one. You'd probably say: "Oh, I wonder if she is from Denmark or somewhere." Aliens could share more tech with us, if we warmonger less." Hellyer claimed the Visitors are concerned because we are not good stewards of the planet's environment, wildlife, or our fellow man. They also worry about our use of nuclear weapons, because it does not just affect us - the Cosmos is a unity.

Hellyer also claimed the subject is so top secret that one government bought the rights to a book, to prevent it being published. He has long advocated full disclosure: "We really have to know, and have a right to know." *The Huffingtom Post Canada* reported that at the Citizen Hearing on Disclosure in Washington, DC Hellyer claimed at least four species of extraterrestrials, some with different agendas, have been visiting Earth for thousands of years.

Wilbur (Wilbert) Smith, an electrical engineer, was head of Canada's *Project Magnet* from 1950-54. One of his ambitions was to harness the energy of the Earth's magnetic field, and he initiated *Project Magnet* in 1950. The aim of this study was to learn as much as possible about UFOs and use this data to duplicate their performance.

He had already learned, from a meeting of Canadian scientists and engineers with an American physicist in Washington, that flying saucers certainly existed. In 1961 Wilbur commented: "I showed Admiral Knowles (US Navy, Ret.) the small piece of a flying saucer which the USAF kindly loaned me for examination. That was July of 1952." While Smith was unable to ascertain that they operated on 'magnetic principles', he did get confirmation that scientists had not been able to duplicate their performance, and they did not originate on Earth.

Until his early death in 1962, when Wilbur was working on an anti-gravity device, he struggled to define the nature and technology of UFOs. My friend, Rosemary Decker, was also friends with Wilbur Smith. Rosemary helped by providing contact with witnesses and contactees, who provided many valuable observations, insights and information. While Wilbur did not admit any direct contact with the Visitors, Rosemary suggested some had occurred. He confirmed his involvement with others in mind-to-mind telepathic communication, and spread a similar message to that given Adamski by Orthon.

Various US presidents have cautiously commented. Dwight Eisenhower said: "I believe that it is not correct to say that flying saucers are only from one planet." President John Kennedy stated: "I am convinced that indeed spaceships exist and that they come from another world." President Ronald Reagan is said to have told film producer Steven Spielberg, during a screening of *ET*: "There are probably only six people in this room who know how true this is!" He also publicly referred to the hypothetical situation of the world uniting if ever facing an alien threat from space.

Further confirmation came from other US sources: NASA Press Chief, Albert Chop, is quoted as saying: "I have long been convinced that flying saucers are of interplanetary origin." Jeff Peckman of Colorado, claimed that before Ben Rich (CEO of Skunk Works) died, he said: "some UFOs are ours – and some Theirs. We have learned from crash retrievals and some hand-me-downs."

Japanese authorities have also commented on the matter. In 1967, Air Self-Defense Force Chief, General Kanshi Ishiwaka stated: "UFOs are real and they may come from outer space ... UFO photographs and various materials show scientifically that there are more advanced people piloting the saucers and motherships."

The Russians have been less outspoken. British newspaper *The Guardian*, (23 November 2002), quoted a *Pravda* claim that Stalin was a UFO-obsessive, and didn't believe the crash at Roswell was a weather balloon. He ordered his senior scientists to investigate this and similar events. In May 1990, former President Mikhail Gorbachev stated that: "The phenomenon of UFOs does exist, and it must be treated seriously."

By the 1990s the Russians had several research institutes and military departments secretly studying UFOs. The most surprising revelation has been the suggestion that alien rocket remains had provided vital technological knowledge for the Soviet space program, and that there was a Russian report of a crashed UFO and occupants. Russian UFO investigator Anton Anaflow mentions crashes and recovered extraterrestrial biological entities.

It would be naive to assume that Visitors have only infiltrated and integrated with a few countries. While some societies discuss this, it is never mentioned in Russia. I have friends from Siberia who talk in hushed tones, and was surprised at a very public UFO report made by Kirsan Ilyumzhinov in 2010.

Ilyumzhinov, is the leader of Russia's southern region of Kalymkia, a small Buddhist area on the shores of the Caspian Sea. He stated in a television interview, that on 18 September 1997, he heard someone calling him from his Moscow apartment balcony. He went out and saw a 'half-transparent, half tube spaceship'. Kirsan went inside, and met human-like beings in yellow spacesuits, who gave him a tour of their craft. Apparently, all communication was telepathic, and they advised him they had come to Earth to take samples.

Although Ilyumzhinov claimed he had witnesses, fellow politician Lebedev, suggested President Dmitry Medvedev investigate him. Lebedev noted that this was not just "a bad joke", and Illyumzhinov may have "divulged state secrets".

The most credible witnesses of all could be our astronauts, who usually maintain total silence when asked in public about who or what might be 'out there'. During US Moon missions, audio transmissions from astronauts used a delayed tape technique, which gave Mission Control up to three minutes to edit any 'inappropriate' messages. Ham radio operators in Australia often claimed they had tuned into these frequencies and heard pre-censored dialogue which indicated sightings of unexplained objects.

On 6 March 2001, astronaut (and later Senator) John Glenn stated on the US television Show *Frasier*: "Back in those glory days, I was very uncomfortable when they asked us to say things we didn't want to say, and deny other things. Some people asked, you know, were you alone out there? We never gave the real answer, and yet we see things out there, strange things. We know what we saw out there, and we couldn't really say anything.

"The bosses were really afraid of this. They were afraid of the War of the Worlds-type stuff, and about panic in the streets. So, we had to keep quiet, and now we only see these things in our nightmares, or maybe in the movies. Some of them are pretty close to being the truth."

Alien influences on scientists and technology

It is significant to me that Hermann Oberth, and contemporaries Lord Dowding, Winston Churchill and General MacArthur all developed life-long interests in UFOs, alien life and intelligence. I can only speculate as to why these western leaders, privy to highly-classified information and secrets, should consider extraterrestrial beings, their advanced intelligence and craft worthy of a lifetime interest.

After World War 2, Hermann Oberth was instrumental in the US Moon program, and devoted much time and effort to philosophical pursuit of advocating peace and harmony with our fellow men and the environment. While Oberth never said where or how he gained his advanced knowledge and theories, he strongly subscribed to an extraterrestrial hypothesis and advocated exactly the same message contactees had received from the Visitors.

In 1954, Oberth published an article in the *American Weekly*, titled *Flying Saucers Come from Distant Worlds*. He began with the statement: "It is my thesis that flying saucers are real and that they are space ships from another solar system. I think that they are possibly manned by intelligent 'observers', who are members of a race that may have been investigating our earth for centuries."

In 1955, he was commissioned by the West German government to conduct a three-year study into the UFO mystery, and in 1960 he addressed the UFO Congress at Wiesbaden. Oberth was also contracted to head the US Jupiter Space Program, and on completing his contract in late 1959, suggested the US took UFOs much more seriously than it admitted publicly. He indicated that scientists were trying to duplicate UFOs propulsion systems, and predicted that within five years we would be able to travel to the moon in a craft propelled by electromagnetic means.

In 1962 Oberth published a more detailed paper about these flying machines and occupants, theorising on their possible origin and technologies, such as artificial gravity fields. His vast knowledge of the subject is thought-provoking, way ahead of mainstream thinking at the time. He once commented that we had been "helped by people of other worlds". Hermann Oberth's comments led many to think he was confirming two widely-held beliefs: firstly, that German scientists had worked with alien technology long before World War 2, and secondly, that the US Air Force was reverse-engineering a crashed saucer.

Oberth wrote a book in German detailing channelled messages from alleged extraterrestrial sources, most of which encouraged mankind to change its warlike ways and care for the planet. When conveying the alien's message about our capability to make this earth uninhabitable for humans, he quoted them as saying: "It would be a shame to lose and waste the efforts which your God expended on you and his creation."

(It is interesting that this message alludes to mankind being created by an individual 'God' rather than a universal, all-encompassing deity. I don't intend to court controversy here by analysing this further.)

Wernher von Braun spoke out in 1959, telling *Neues Europa*: "We find ourselves faced by powers which are far stronger than we had hitherto assumed, and whose base of operations is at present unknown to us. More I cannot say at present. We are now engaged in entering into closer contact with these powers, and in six or nine months' time, it may be possible to speak with more precision on the matter." Of course, he did not speak of the matter again, but in later interviews admitted he believed there could be life in other Solar Systems. He was reticent and non-committal on whether UFOs were extraterrestrial.

Nikola Tesla

Have some of our eminent scientists been given limited knowledge to aid our progress? One of our most notable, Nikola Tesla, actually mentioned 'an interplanetary communication system', and was well aware of telepathy and psychic phenomena. Tesla claimed that he spoke to aliens, and that some of his discoveries arose from sudden inspiration. Did he receive communications from Mars or extraterrestrials? This remains controversial.

In 1893 Tesla developed a system of energy transmission and telegraphy without the use of wires – "dependent instead upon 'drawing electricity from the earth', and driving it back into the same at an enormous rate, causing a ripple or disturbance which could be carefully attuned to receiving circuits." He wanted to expand his theories to incorporate inter-space communication using light.

Tesla was a visionary, way ahead of his time, who envisioned life on other planets. He made the following comment: "Reasoning beings ... would adapt themselves to their constantly changing environment. I think it is quite possible that in a frozen planet, such as our Moon is supposed to be, intelligent beings *may dwell in its interior*, if not on its surface."

In one interview Tesla stated: "Psychical telepathy does not exist as a reality; but the transmission of thought from mind directly to mind is a wonderful phenomenon, worthy of scientific study." This revelation brought some ridicule, and perhaps made other scientists more cautious in disclosing similar experiences they may have had.

Tesla made astounding discoveries and theories. Mostly known for his work with alternating currents, he discovered electromagnetic energy propagation effects, which he proposed using to make electricity freely available for the masses (by transmitting, and magnifying through the ground rather than the air). He also toyed with 'radiant energy', 'scalar vectoring', early research into photons and, one of his favourite subjects – the 'ether', as being an important part of the universe.

His patents include direct and polyphase current devices, the Tesla Magnifying Transmitter, many wireless and telegraphy systems, fluorescent lighting, turbines, pumps, airplanes, mechanical oscillators, and thermo-magnetic motors. He devised applications for high-frequency and high-potential currents including apparatus for generating controls, circuits, systems and insulation.

UFO researchers today are interested in his 'death-ray', which gained much publicity when the headlines *Tesla at 78 Bares New 'Death-Beam'* appeared in the *New York Times* on 11 July 1934. Many ridiculed him as a mad scientist – but wait a minute! Tesla only wanted his ray used for defensive purposes; it only had the ability to stop the operation of 'all cars, planes and ships' within a four-mile radius! (This is consistent with many close encounter reports where a vehicle is disabled by a UFO. We may need to re-evaluate such incidents, and consider the possibility that earthly agencies use Tesla's discoveries.)

Albert Einstein, Tesla's contemporary and a fellow genius, never claimed contact with extraterrestrials, but did not deny their existence. Einstein was very aware what that statement had cost Tesla. Also, he and Tesla strongly disagreed on the Theory of Relativity. All of their views on relativity, gravity, energy, and atomic particles are under reconsideration at present. (Tesla also incorporated concepts of time and the curvature of space in his theories, but considered that the speed of light could be exceeded.)

There is much more to Nikola Tesla – his genius, abilities and comprehension of physics and the universe. Much of his research may have 'never seen the light of day' – his secretary advised all his notes and files were taken soon after his death (aged 86), in 1943. Tesla once said: "If you wish to understand the universe, think in terms of energy, frequency and vibration." (These are concepts the Visitors often allude to.)

While people scoffed at Tesla's claim of extraterrestrial contact, an interesting anecdote came to light after his death. A Mr. Matthews and his son Arthur had worked with Tesla in the past. They stated his claims were true, and that 'sky people' had landed several times on their Canadian property to see how they were getting along with Tesla's 'Anti-War Machine'.

The 1954 Moon film

Australian researcher Mike Farrell brought this case to my attention: the SBS television series, *Eat Carpet* featured a French item on Tibor Nagy, a Hungarian migrant to the US who settled in Massachusetts in 1941, and spoke little English

At 10.15 a.m., on 15 April 1954, Tibor was driving along a deserted, rural highway with his wife in the front seat, and twelve-year-old daughter in the back. Nagy said; "We were all alone on the road, when a huge shadow stopped right above us and brought our car to a standstill ... nothing would work ... My wife screamed! My daughter started crying, and I told them not to be afraid. It seemed like 'the night fell around us'.

"I don't remember how much time later ... I opened my eyes and we were still in the car, but it was 'vibrating gently' and in a large white room. I got out and right in front of me, I saw the Moon coming at me. So, I took out my camera, which I always took with me when we go out to visit, and I filmed. I was shaking with fear. Good God, I was frightened!

"At the same moment I was filming, my daughter woke up, and I had to explain to her that I believed we had been picked up by a flying craft. Then a man stepped into the room. He seemed like us, but he was wearing a helmet on his head, and I couldn't see his face.

"He didn't say anything – but we 'understood' that we need not be afraid. I could film whatever I saw, but not the inside of the ship. I remember perfectly saying ... 'Yes sir' ... and my daughter yelling, 'We're higher than the Moon.' I watched and filmed until I ran out of film. Then I felt like we were 'falling'.

"When I opened my eyes, my wife and daughter were now both in the back seat of the car. We were a few meters away from a road we didn't know, which turned out to be some miles away from where we were taken. I turned to my wife and daughter, saying that God wants to test us – be brave!"

Three weeks later, on 6 May 1954, Tibor was called before Senator Lawley's Committee of Inquiry, but he could only testify in Hungarian, and wasn't believed. The results of a second hearing held a few weeks later, remain secret.

Tibor didn't fare very well. He was ridiculed by the press and the public, and became obsessed with wanting to see the Visitors again, to get proof that he was not a liar. Within a few years his wife died. His daughter moved to Canada to get married, and never saw Tibor again.

What astounds is that Tibor's 1954 film of the Moon's surface, taken 15 years before we first set foot there, is very similar to those taken by NASA's fly-overs and landings. As the camera reaches the horizon, you can see the blackness of space and the (iconic) Earth rising beyond.

"The Assessment"

Many early contactees describe the Visitors as being so much like us they could live in our society without being detected. This brings to mind comments by US researcher Bob Dean, whom I respect, and met while he was in Australia.

Bob had been a professional soldier, a Sergeant Major in the US Army, seconded to the Supreme Headquarters Allied Powers Europe (SHAPE) in Paris in 1963. There, he learned of a top secret study called *"The Assessment"*, which focussed on strange craft – large, unidentified, metallic, disc-like objects, often flying in formation, seen all over Europe. On several occasions these put both Allied and Soviet forces on full alert, with the very real risk of all-out conflict.

Bob admitted he was sceptical at first. It was only during this study that he and his colleagues became aware of information about aliens and UFOs which the US had not provided their NATO allies. They concluded the objects did not appear to be a military threat, and they had been here for a very long time. Repeated demonstrations of technology far beyond anything we have, indicated that if they wanted to harm us, they would have already done so.

US authorities were troubled by one incident in 1963, when a plane belonging to the Turkish Air Force disappeared without trace. While being tracked on radar, operators detected an unidentified craft following it. Both objects disappeared from their screens, and wreckage or remains from the Turkish plane were never located.

The Assessment took several years, interviewing witnesses and contactees from all over Europe, including military personnel. Bob reported that a 30-meter disc which crashed on a Baltic beach in Northern Germany in 1964, was retrieved by British forces. The twelve bodies examined were similar to what we now call 'little Greys', and autopsies indicated they were similar to biological robots. (This, in some part, explains their normal reported role as 'workers'.)

They were also aware of three other species – all humanoid. One rarely-seen group was extremely tall, white and pale, with no body hair. Another was what we refer to as 'Reptilian'; still basically humanoid, but up to six feet tall with scaly type skin and vertical pupils in their eyes.

What excited everybody in the study was the third group which looked *exactly like us.* They were not Nordic in the way some researchers describe them. Not all had blond hair; some had brown or black hair, and their eyes varied from blue, to green, or brown. They varied in height, and this made them less distinguishable from the rest of us. Along with many contactees from the 1950s, Dean said some of these Visitors are living and working incognito among us. These upset the US Military more than any other species. They were very concerned that infiltrating aliens, "who looked so human, they could walk down the corridors of their own HQ, even the Pentagon, or White House, without being detected."

Bob and his colleagues discovered the US Military had already reached the same conclusions in a secret study in 1948-9. Russia's own investigations had concluded just as much. They all decided to keep it way above top secret, and still have, reasoning it could have an enormous impact on all facets of human society. The fact is that most authorities, for various reasons, want to discourage all interaction between extraterrestrials and normal humans.

Bob Dean did not make details of *The Assessment* public until the early 1990s, and named the generals involved in the study. Their report is so secret only 15 copies were ever made. (An account in *Unicus* suggests Bob did not actually participate in *The Assessment*, but was allowed to study the report after a SHAPE Operations Center (SHOC) controller took it out of a vault for him to read.)

UFO researcher Mark Birdsall later reported that Timothy Good and Lord Hill-Norton tried to get a copy of the report, or at least confirmation of its existence, but without success. While most participants in *The Assessment* were either dead or very elderly, some of the names provided by Bob were verified as genuine staff of that unit at the time.

In 1994, Bob went a lot further in his disclosures. *Flying Saucer Review* reported that at a conference in Florida he said the US government was hiding the presence of four species of alien, one of which looks just like us, on the Moon. Dean had said: "We were told to get off the Moon, and stay off. Every Apollo mission we had was monitored and followed, and US astronauts were forced to "keep their mouths shut."

As expected, there have been several attempts to discredit Bob Dean. It has also occurred to me that since there was a great deal of espionage in Europe at that time, *The Assessment*, while genuine, would have made an ideal diversion. While spies thought we were still struggling with the extraterrestrial problem, scientists in the US were making enormous progress in advanced, yet covert, technological projects.

Therefore, while western governments are expert at keeping secrets, one cannot be entirely sure of the accuracy of the information. On the other hand, similar reports of human-looking aliens integrating and assimilating with society, have come from many countries over the previous 60 years. It only stands to reason that the authorities would want to quietly investigate. However, they would also wish to silence or ridicule any details which might become public knowledge – better that people think of 'little Greys with big black eyes'!

The humanoid aliens have always been careful to keep a very low profile, and usually make contact in secret. They are careful with whom they communicate, and refuse to have their photograph taken, for fear of being recognised while mingling with human populations.

Timothy Beckley wrote about several cases from the 1960s and 1970s where normal people had chance meetings with these undercover aliens: In 1967, Michael Montecalvo, a young student at Maryland University, came across a 30-foot diameter disc, landed across a highway as he travelled south toward Washington

D.C. A man, with short light brown hair and blue eyes, dressed in a light blue coverall approached him. During their 15-minute conversation the man told him his name was 'Vadig' and he was from another planet. He was leaving, but would be seeing him again 'in time'.

In 1968 Michael was working nights in a restaurant, when Vadig came in, sat down and smiled at him. He was wearing conventional clothes, and could was indistinguishable from anyone else in the cafe. The following week Vadig came in again at about 8.30 p.m., and said if Michael wished he and his associates would pick him up after he left work.

Michael later joined Vadig in his old sedan car. There was another man in the front seat, "who looked just as normal as anyone I was used to waiting on." Michael said they looked so human, the only thing that convinced him they weren't a couple of hoaxers, was when they took him for a ride in a UFO that was identical to the one that he had seen landed on the road.

There are other times one cannot be sure. One woman, 'Mrs B', was driving towards a local town in the US Midwest one afternoon. She stopped when she saw a strange, elliptical craft near the road, resting on tripod legs, with two men and a woman next to it. They appeared to have a conversation, and then walked over to a parked car and started to drive off.

Mrs B. wanted to know what was going on, and tried to block their vehicle. They swerved around her, nearly forcing her off the road. Some months later Mrs B was in the local supermarket, and saw the woman from the craft. Mrs B. followed her to the checkout, and when they were standing in line, she said: "Haven't I seen you somewhere before?"

The woman bolted from the queue, leaving her shopping behind, and ran out into the street and disappeared. Mrs B. never saw her again.

It stands to reason the authorities would try to locate and identify alien infiltrators who have blended in with the human population. They would naturally be concerned about those who may have access into government departments and agencies. There is little information to be found regarding such covert detection missions. Some whistle-blowers on the internet have released details regarding the capture and interrogation of a couple of Nordic-type aliens. Some of what they reported seems plausible, but I doubt many of these claims.

Several investigators assert that Visitors met with President Eisenhower at Edwards Air Force Base, California, in 1954:

In his book, *Extra-terrestrial Friends and Foes* George Andrews states the meeting did take place. He claims the 'Good Guys' reiterated their message about our errant ways in caring for the planet and each other. They would not assist with any armaments, but offered to show us how to produce free energy without polluting the environment.

Eisenhower's Chiefs of Staff advised against any agreement. They did not wish to relinquish their nuclear weapons, and feared disruption of current religious dogma. Furthermore, they did not wish free energy to upset the economic system. Andrews says that after their offer was refused, the Visitors left. Later there was an agreement made with a different race of aliens in return for new weapons and other technology.

Sometimes too much knowledge or understanding can be a dangerous thing, and most sensible investigators do not divulge all the information they unearth. There is a very long list of scientists and researchers who have died suddenly in unexpected circumstances.

Tony Dodd

Tony was a British police officer for 25 years, and exceptionally well-trained in standard investigation procedures and psychological profiling. Completely trustworthy, he served in the Diplomatic Protection Squad. When he retired, Tony Dodd relentlessly pursued information on humanoid aliens, and the reasons for, and intention of, their activities. He had previously helped with research on the Holy Grail and been in contact with British contactees such as Elizabeth, Lydia, and Vera (see chapters 8 and 9). He once claimed researchers and those who got too close to the truth often meet with fatal accidents or suspicious deaths.

His research was always thorough and meticulous, and he was not a person to be fooled by hoaxers, or fanciful witnesses. He supported genuine contactees, and once commented: "Instead of conducting a witch hunt, sceptics and debunkers would be well-advised to remember there are more things in Heaven and Earth than perhaps science will ever be allowed to understand."

He once commented; "Out of the four different groups, all humanoid, one group was so human looking, they could sit next to us in a restaurant, they could sit next to you in a theatre, and you would never know."

One of his contentions was that the humanoid aliens were who they said they were, and had been associated with us for a long time. He considered that a more malevolent Reptilian type had formed a liaison with some 'authorities' and were trying to locate, capture, or eliminate those with Visitor connections. He had ignored warnings not to continue writing about these activities and infiltration of our society.

(Tony Dodd researched many facets of ufology, and I do not know if it was this, or some other aspect he disclosed, that upset US officials. Graham Birdsall, in an article, *The Watchers,* detailed the intense pressure and threats Tony and his wife were subjected to when attending a conference in Tuscon, Arizona in May 1991.

In 1994, when attending the annual UFO Congress at Mesquite, Tony was again threatened by a couple of men who told him: "You are a very dangerous individual ... and don't think we can't get at you when you're back in England ... we can and we will." In 2009 Tony was diagnosed with a rare and aggressive form of brain cancer and died six weeks later.)

"Allow modern science to evolve and take its course, albeit through a narrow field of vision. Let us at least respect those who are not scientists, who display an open mind to the amazing possibilities and probabilities all around us.

"We all arrive on this Earth with nothing, and we all depart with nothing, except the learning of a lifetime. Before we can begin to understand the truth of who we are, and where we come from, we must first begin to know ourselves. In truth, we are all alien to this planet, our real home is amongst the stars."
......Tony Dodd.

Levitation

I knew one elderly gentleman born in Sweden, who was very intelligent and spiritual. He had an incredible understanding of UFOs and aliens, and I always suspected he had experienced contact and communication. He had been in the Swedish Navy during the War, and admitted that his ship often sailed over to Nazi Germany. He later migrated to Australia, and was very knowledgeable about matters our science couldn't currently replicate.

After he died, his wife confided one of his strange abilities was to 'move' enormous objects, despite his small, frail stature: "I never saw how he did it. One day there were some huge trees we had cut down in the backyard. He insisted I go inside and make a cup of coffee. He didn't even have a wheelbarrow, but when I came out a few minutes later, the trees were neatly stacked in the front yard."

How did this frail man master the art of levitation? It may not be connected, but the Nazis were supposed to have research facilities in Sweden, and were intent on discovering mystical secrets from the Himalayas. Two Swedish scientists visiting Tibet, had reported 'the art of ritual levitation.' Henry Kjellson travelled through the Himalayas in the early 1930s, and saw Tibetan monks using drums, trumpets, and chanting priests to raise massive blocks of stone. In 1939, his friend Dr. Jarl visited Tibet to treat a High Lama, and made two films of the ceremony. However, these were confiscated by his employers, The Oxford Scientific Society.

Around the world there are ancient structures made of stones weighing 150 tons or more. Some of these massive rocks were quarried up to 200 miles away, then transported and set in buildings so carefully, our modern technology cannot replicate it. This brings to mind the mystery of just how the Egyptian pyramids were built; it has been suggested that a form of levitation was used to raise the massive blocks of stone, both there and with the other ancient monuments. Some researchers believe these structures were built with the help of advanced alien technology.

Many years ago, *Fate* magazine, published an article on *Coral Castle*, in Homestead, Florida. This structure of massive coral blocks, some weighing 30 ton, was partially constructed by Latvian immigrant, Edward Leedskalnin, between 1920 and 1936. He worked alone and in secret, between dusk and dawn. Teenage witnesses, who were never believed, claimed they saw him 'float coral blocks through the air like hydrogen balloons.' The building has many astronomical alignments, and complex features.

In 1936 Leedskalnin bought a property ten miles away and transported his building, block by block, to the new location. Again, he worked in secret when re-erecting his 'Castle', which was eventually completed in 1940.

Leedskalnin died in 1952, and never revealed his secret. He did say he had discovered how the Egyptians and other ancient cultures raised and set in place blocks of stone weighing many tons. He was never very specific about his methods, referring only to 'the laws of weight, measurement and leverage used by the Ancient Egyptians.' He alluded to a method of natural magnetism and electricity. Some experts postulate that 'anti-gravity' or 'earth energies' were involved. Whatever the principles applied, they remain unknown.

I wondered if this were the case with my Swedish friend? Certainly, our society has not mastered any technology such as this. So how, and from whom, did Leedskalnin and my friend from wartime Sweden learn this feat?

In 1979 scientist John Hutchison discovered that exposure to focussed, coherent electromagnetic fields could levitate extremely heavy objects. This has led to Beam Weapon technology and may also explain how UFO abductees are 'taken up in a beam of light'.

Sometimes too little knowledge can also be a dangerous thing. Most people are not aware that by the 1960s it is likely we had some secret prototype flying discs of our own. This could cause confusion in a population who were sometimes encouraged to believe in alien visitation, rather than our own technological advancement.

We may never know the complete truth regarding the following episode -from *True* magazine's *Flying Saucers and UFOs Quarterly* #3, 1976:

Investigator James Bonham interviewed a hunter with a guilty conscience about what he had done in the winter of 1961. He and three friends were returning late one Sunday night from a hunting trip. It was a miserable night with sleet falling, and they were all very cold.

Suddenly, they saw a fiery object coming down from the sky. It landed about 150 yards away. They stopped at the side of the road, and could see an object sitting in mud on the other side of the railway track. It seemed to be leaning slightly off-centre, and they thought it might be the tail section of a crashed plane. The craft was 'lit' and they could see four 'people' walking around. As soon as they turned a spotlight on the area, the light from the object went out. They could still see what they thought was a small plane crash.

They drove back to a township about twenty minutes away, and persuaded the local police officer to return with them. When they arrived back at the site, despite a search, there was no evidence of any wreckage. The policeman left, and the four hunters continued on their way.

Not long afterwards, they saw the craft descending slowly from the sky. It seemed to be in flames, but they all saw it land in a small clearing close to the road. It had a lighted top, and a reddish glow seeping from underneath. They stopped the car, and watched two men who were outside the object. They were about 5 foot 6 inches tall, wearing white coveralls.

Two of the hunters stayed in the car, holding a searchlight, while the other two men circled around the two UFO occupants, who were heading towards the woods. Nobody will admit who fired the shot, but one of the stalkers fired his rifle, hitting one occupant in the shoulder. The other 'creature' ran back to his wounded colleague, helped him onto his feet, and yelled out in clear English: "What the hell did you do that for?"

The hunters' intention had been to capture one of these 'aliens' to prove what they had seen. Now they suddenly realised it may have been an experimental aircraft, and that the wounded figure was a US Air Force Officer. They ran back to the car, and sped off as quickly as possible. They were sure they would be arrested, and agreed they would never mention the incident.

Their fears were partially realised the next day. One of the hunters was called into his supervisor's office, where some men were waiting to speak to him. They asked him about the clothes he had been wearing on Sunday, and went to his home, carefully examining his muddy boots. After they departed, the hunter was left totally confused and scared.

It may be never known whether these trigger-happy citizens had accosted a genuine alien Visitor, or shot an Air Force officer on a covert saucer-prototype operation. They were lucky, that either way, the government would not want the publicity of a court case!

Chapter Eight

Elizabeth

After World War 2, odd things happened to the children of many British ex-servicemen and women. Due to my British heritage and contacts, most of the early contactees and their families that I liaised with in the 1980s, were mainly from England. Some of them were associated with a little-known abductee support group, and I got to know them well

Elizabeth lived in Australia, but often returned to Britain to stay with her mother's family.

Childhood

Elizabeth recalled her childhood: "We lived on an isolated farm near The Wrekin, an ancient mountain in central England. It was a sparsely-populated area in those days, and the frequent mists made you feel isolated in a mystical way. There was no gas or electricity – no lights, radio, electric cooking, or heating. It was hard, with coal for heating, a wood cooker and oil lamps. We were not well-off. I had few toys, and there were no distractions except for bonding with all the animals and Mother Nature herself.

"My father was discharged from the Air Force some years after World War 2, and every night he would take me out and show me the stars."

She paused rather thoughtfully, "He instilled a wonder and awe into me as he explained about the vastness of the universe, and how one star was in fact a whole galaxy of millions of suns and planets. I refused to go to bed until I saw Orion's Belt, and in my childish way wanted to know who and what was up there in the dark expanse of space. It was only much later in life that I connected his comments about encounters with foo-fighters during missions over Europe, and his own connection to outer space.

"We would be snowed-in during winter, and it was so cold when you went to bed you stayed there, with a chamber-pot underneath. My mother once commented that I used to sleepwalk on the farm, but it was too cold and dark to go wandering – even to the bathroom. There is only one instance that I can recall. One night, when I was only about three, I remember suddenly finding myself downstairs, in that cold and dark, all alone and crying.

"My parents came with a lamp, asking; 'What are you doing here? How did you get downstairs?' I didn't know, I had suddenly found myself there. Certainly, it wasn't something I could have physically done in the pitch dark at that age. It was only recently, a lifetime later, I had a sudden flashback that quite frankly left me in shock. I was standing in the night, outside the front door, looking across the garden.

Taking up almost the entire field on the other side of the fence, was a huge white saucer-type craft, with windows all around the bottom of the dome.

"It's only recently I've had time to reflect on my early childhood. At about the same time I had that strange experience, my mother was pregnant again, but had an early miscarriage. She was always psychic but once, when we were on the best of terms, she told my best friend that I was a changeling. Much later in life, when she was becoming a little confused, she started asking me where my sister was ... but I never had a sister. Had something also happened to her on that isolated farm?"

Elizabeth continued: "While I did have the usual childhood illnesses, about that time I had a very bad case of measles, which left me in a temporary coma for about twenty-four hours. I don't remember much of it, of course, but apparently, my parents kept me in a warm room with the fire going, and the doctor was so concerned he stayed in the farmhouse, by my bedside, all night. My mother tells me I suddenly sat up, without warning, and demanded a drink of water. The doctor was amazed, as this spontaneous recovery is not the norm in such cases.

"I then developed what they thought was a bad ear infection, as a result of the illness. I remember screaming with the terrible pain in my ear, and my father took me to the local hospital in a nearby town.

"I had always associated that with a vivid memory of being wheeled down a white corridor, with large round bright white lights passing overhead. Then I'm lying in a white room. Everything is bright white, with one big light beaming down on me from above. There are three people gathered at the bottom of my 'bed'. They are all looking at me – white gowns, head coverings and masks, just like you would see in an operating theatre. Their size and eyes looked human. Then everything went blank."

She suddenly reflected: "In later years both my parents told me that did not happen; there had been no trip to theatre. My doctor assured me I did not have any operation, and no drainage tubes were ever put in my ears for the infection. I'd forgotten until now, but I do remember being very upset around about that time when I had a few inexplicable nose bleeds.

"You know for a long time I did not connect my later health problems with those memories. When I was nine I started getting pains in my lower right side. Initially they thought it was just growing pains or a grumbling appendix, but it became apparent it was connected with my reproductive system.

"When I was 16 they discovered my right ovary and fallopian tube were badly damaged. My body had grown lesions which would have taken many years. They couldn't find any cause, but noted an ovarian cyst, which one doctor suggested was replacing 'missing ova eggs' – but it made no sense to him.

"During my late teens and early twenties, I had irregular and often painful periods. On a couple of occasions doctors thought I was definitely a few weeks pregnant, only to find a short time later that there was nothing there."

Schooling

"I was sent to nursery school from the age of two, and could read and write before I was five. My father was always encouraging me to do better, and used to make me show visitors and family how clever I was. When we moved to a nearby town, I wasn't allowed to play with the neighbourhood children.

"In primary school I got unusual attention, although I didn't understand the significance of it at the time. From the age of six, every so often I would be taken to the headmistress's office where there would be nice 'Men from the Ministry' in dark suits. I would sit there drinking tea from her best china, read my books out loud, do little tests, and answer questions. The headmistress always paid me special attention, but my own teachers were aloof. They seemed to keep their distance and showed neither affection or anger where I was concerned.

"My parents were unaware of this for a long time," Elizabeth recalled. "However, when my father found out about the 'Men from the Ministry' his whole attitude changed. He had wanted to migrate to New Zealand, but he became desperate, almost paranoid, about leaving Britain. He contacted his old commanding officer, Chris, from the RAAF – an Australian who had served with him in a joint British-Australian-US unit. Since then I have wondered how much Chris knew about those wartime years, as they had been involved in US-UK controlled SAS secret missions and activities together. I know they had been dropping supplies, spies and Jedburgh saboteurs into Europe. Had Chris also encountered the foo fighters along with my father?

I asked her what kind of aircraft had her father and Chris flown when together in 1944-45? Elizabeth replied: "I think I heard him mention Sterlings and Lancasters," then paused and looked a little perplexed. "You know something has suddenly occurred to me. On the day of my father's funeral, Chris cornered my mother, and demanded she give him all Dad's wartime logs and records. I was furious when I found out. She had given them to him because he was so insistent, and she was in a fragile state having just buried her husband.

"I tried to get them back, but all the Australian War Museum would admit to was one of his log books from 1944-45. Other British RAF records from 1939-1943 were unobtainable, so what had happened to them? In later years, I spoke to an elderly man who had been a very senior officer in the UK during World War 2. He dismissed any chance of seeing the records, saying there were 'things' they didn't want anyone to know about."

As Elizabeth thought back I realised Chris, who often flew on joint missions with her father from 1944 onwards, must have also seen, or been aware of, some of the obviously classified matters, plus any other associated experiences. He was very much a 'government man' in later life.

"There was also something else I have never been able to find out. Dad joined the RAF in 1939 as a Flight Engineer, and after two years was sent to the Isle of Man, between Britain and Ireland. There are absolutely no records regarding his time there or the name of the place or establishment. There was one photo of him in the Fleet Air Arm from that time. He never spoke about the period 1941-43, but I knew he had also 'been to sea' as he taught me how not to be seasick. What was he doing on the Isle of Man, and later on, where did he go to from there?

"There was another thing", she recalled. "Dad apparently suffered some form of amnesia or 'blackouts' after 1943 – not only when he was flying with Chris in 1944-45, but also occasionally in later years. He would be conscious and active but have no memory of anything he'd said or done during that period. Chris 'covered' for him, and when I asked him about a pocket map I found, where Dad had noted different Bases and dates in 1944, he said; 'Your father could do things nobody else could do'. – What did that mean?"

Elizabeth continued on about her childhood; "Chris was certainly able to pull strings, and within months we were on a migrant ship to Australia, having jumped the queue and been given a cancelled passage on a cargo ship, of all things, with just two weeks' notice. Mum never wanted to migrate, but was old-fashioned in her belief that she should accept her husband's wishes. I can remember also being very unhappy about leaving England, but as a nine-year-old, I had no choice.

"Once in Sydney I attended the local primary school, and for the first ten weeks my interaction with the teacher was much 'warmer'. Then more men in suits came visiting. I did further tests for them and next thing I was moved into the headmaster's class. He was a brute of a man, but for some reason I was teacher's pet and he was always kind to me.

"When the Education Department transferred me to a special school for bright kids Dad was not happy, and later when I qualified for a classic education in a top selective high school, he tried to prevent it. All my life he had been a total control freak, and pushed me into home studies, even to the extent of supervising his own lessons for me on the migrant ship. Now he was actively discouraging my advanced, special education, saying that domestic science and typing were sufficient for me. I often wonder if the visits from the Men from the Ministry had affected his bragging about his intelligent daughter, and pride.

"My father himself was no longer the happy, pleasant person he had been in earlier life, and later openly admitted he secretly planned to return to England within a few months, leaving my mother and me stranded 12,000 miles away. Somehow Mum became unexpectedly pregnant, very late in life, with my young brother and he stayed, but it was a tense, unhappy home with Dad becoming very morose and openly having affairs with other women. In hindsight, I think he was suffering some form of post-traumatic stress, but whether it was from the war itself, or something more sinister, I'm not sure.

"I was also becoming very disturbed, and was probably close to emotional and mental breakdown. I eventually left school at fifteen and home soon afterwards. I took the English and Maths exam for entry into the Public Service and came top of the State. At one stage when I considered going to night school, the principal told me I was already up to matriculation standard in these subjects.

"Several years after I left school my cousin kept urging me to join Mensa. I missed the exam, and they asked if I could get something from the Education Department on previous intelligence tests. When I inquired, they said; 'Oh no, we don't keep records that long – wait a minute, for some reason we still have yours.' I received a letter saying my intelligence score was in the top two percent of the population. I recalled the Men from the Ministry and thought 'forget Mensa' – I did not want to be special or tracked anymore."

The 'Men from the Ministry'

Elizabeth was in contact with British researcher Ken Phillips, his support group, and other experiencers such as Lydia (see chapter 9). Ken investigated the 'Quantock Case', where the witness was not believed when he claimed secret visits at school by Men from the Ministry; Elizabeth told him of her experiences.

Ken was involved in several British cases where children had been visited by these men during school hours. One quite complex case involved witness 'Elena' at a Catholic boarding school in Buckinghamshire, from 1978 to 1982.

Elena often had trouble sleeping there, and one night in 1980, at about 1 a.m. she remembers looking out the window and seeing 'sort-of stars and things'. The next thing it was 3 a.m. and she was sitting up in bed with one of the other girls asking if she was all right. The next day the convent's grass tennis court showed a very big circle, all burnt to a crisp, with at least one three-inch hole in it. The following day a lot of police arrived and were checking out the tennis court and surrounding area. All the girls were forbidden to go near it.

She didn't tell anyone what she saw. However, about three months later, Elena was sent to a private room to meet two visitors she had never seen before. All they told the nun was that: 'We've come to see Elena'. When Elena asked who they were, they claimed her doctor had sent them. But their arrival was unexpected, and the doctor later said she knew nothing about it. They also drank the cups of coffee the nuns had provided, and asked Elena various questions, in a scenario very similar to those experienced by Elizabeth.

Elena described them as being middle-aged, clean shaven, creamy-coloured faces, and short black shiny hair. She noted their brownish-grey eyes and black suits, shoes, socks and ties with a white shirt. They looked almost identical, and seemed to move in unison. They didn't have a briefcase, or a watch, as they asked the time before going. When they shook her hand upon leaving, she felt their flesh was icy cold. They asked how she was getting on at school, but they kept going back to asking if anything strange had happened. She knew what they meant, but kept avoiding them, answering only in the negative. They persisted, but luckily the lunch bell went.

The men had to leave, and as they did, commented they would return to see her. She watched them wait outside, then get into an unusual black car, with a similar man as the driver. Elena went in to lunch, feeling fuzzy in her brain. As she stirred her coffee, her stainless-steel teaspoon bent in two.

After her sighting, Elena's artistic abilities were greatly improved. She did not have any hypnotic regression, but had dreams and very clear visions of being in a flying saucer, although she denies it actually happened: "It seemed so real – as real as I see you – I walk up a slope into a funny looking round room with coloured, flickering lights all around. I pinched myself and could actually feel it. I also dreamed about bumping into those same men in the street, and they asked me the same questions, and I kept running away."

What she thought was another dream was verified by her fellow boarders. She was 'flying' (just like many other contactees report). Her colleagues recalled seeing her airborne, and remonstrated with her, telling her to 'come down'. In 1986, while working as a computer operator in Harrow, she and all the girls in the office saw a huge metallic saucer through the office window.

Encounter in the Blue Mountains

It was the Australia Day weekend 1976, and Elizabeth said she scrambled along the rough track down the side of Mt. Victoria, wondering why on earth she had ever agreed to come on this mad expedition. When they had discussed it at the Bushwalking Club meeting, nobody mentioned to her the route was the Navy's Jungle Training Course. Someone had said the Grose Valley was very beautiful, with wild brumbies in Blue Gum Forest. Strange unidentified craft had recently been seen from the lookout at Govett's Leap, north of Blackheath, and everyone wanted to spend a couple of nights, sky-watching at the stars and hopefully any visiting aliens.

"I was glad my partner, Gunter, had decided to come along. He knew I had been to a couple of UFO meetings, and bought a couple of books and magazines. I was always intrigued with astronomy and the possibility of intelligent life 'out there'; something he did not relate to or believe in. I was reasonably young and pretty then, and I suspected his real motivation was his unease at my going on a camping trip with other men. Our relationship had been on rocky ground for some time, and he knew I was thinking of leaving."

Gunter had already grabbed Elizabeth's rucksack, and hauled her to safety, when the narrow path crumbled, and she nearly fell into the ravine below. They both gave a sigh of relief when they reached the valley floor. Dusk was falling. Surely, they would rest and pitch camp soon.

The gathering around the campfire was convivial. "Not a UFO in sight, but I felt strangely peaceful. It felt as if we were a million miles away from civilisation, with a huge moon and brilliant stars lighting up the white cliffs of the surrounding National Park. I thought how silly I had been at that initial planning meeting, when I had sensed some unseen presence in the room."

"Sunday was much tougher than I could have imagined – rough hilly tracks full of brambles, prickly obstacles, and slippery creeks we waded through waist deep. I didn't even want to think about the snakes and ticks lurking in the undergrowth."

The hot summer sun was tiring, and Elizabeth had fallen way behind the rest of the group. Gunter was just in front when she spied a well-dressed man up ahead.

"He was about 5 foot 10 inches tall, blond and good-looking, wearing an immaculate three-piece brown suit with a white shirt and tie. As I got closer I noticed his highly polished brown shoes, and thought to myself; 'Thank God, we must be close to civilisation.' As we passed by we politely greeted him – 'Hello', 'Hi', and got identical responses back from him.

"As we rounded the next corner I felt a strange compelling force to return and speak to that guy – it was almost physically 'drawing' me there. It was so strong I had to resist the urge to go back. Gunter was disappearing up the track, (with all my willpower) and scared of being left alone, I scurried after him.

"It was late afternoon when we caught up with the others resting at Blue Gum Forest. It was a beautiful wooded area, with a sparkling creek and wild horses grazing in the grassy clearing. 'Did you see that man about two miles back?' I asked them. 'How could he get there dressed like that? The track is full of mud and brambles and we've waded through two creeks since then! It's like he was dropped out of the sky into that spot!' The others looked rather bemused and made no comment. Then Jasmine, the only other female in our group, admitted noticing him."

Elizabeth continued; "It was time to make the ascent back up the mountain to Govett's Leap. Nightfall would make the climb, sometimes on narrow tracks, a little dangerous, so Gunter and I made the effort to stay fairly close behind the others. I could see the rugged cliffs and waterfall ahead. 'Not much further, thank God,' Gunter said, 'then home to a hot bath and comfy bed – so much for your bushwalking and useless UFO spotting!"

Elizabeth described how she was wading through the last creek, when her whole body seemed to collapse, as if she had been struck down by some unseen force. She called out: "Gunter – I can't walk, help me." He half carried her to the narrow track at the side of the cliff, and Daniel came back from the party ahead: 'Better stay here for the night. It's getting dark. I'll get the Park Ranger to come down for Elizabeth in the morning.'

"I can remember Daniel and Gunter setting up the tent and boiling the billy for a hot drink. I remember crawling into my sleeping bag then everything faded into the blackness of exhaustion …"

The early rays of the Monday morning sun brought Elizabeth back to reality; "I felt so good – energised with a sense of physical satisfaction that only another woman could understand. I felt like I'd had the best sex of my life, but couldn't remember it. 'What happened' I thought, 'on the edge of that cliff?' Gunter was still asleep in the tent. It certainly wasn't him – he never made me feel like this! I struggled to understand, but couldn't get past the fleeting memory of a blue light coming towards me from the gorge down below. Then I suddenly realised I wasn't in the tent. I was outside, lying on top of my sleeping bag!"

(At this stage I asked Elizabeth if she thought that handsome, blond stranger was responsible? – She wasn't sure. If he was would she want to see him again? She looked at me and went quiet, then gave a telling, naughty grin: 'Next time I would want to remember it!')

"I literally bounced towards the waterfall and up the tracks and ladders to the top of the cliffs. Gunter stared at me in slight bewilderment and then went strangely quiet. That energetic elation lasted for about three hours. By the time I arrived home, in muddy, tattered clothes, the extreme exhaustion and sore muscles kept me in bed for the next two days."

I paused for a moment after Elizabeth told me about the unusual man. I couldn't tell her, at this stage, but I had heard of this happening before. A Blue Mountains woman had been telling me about several unusual craft in the area, including a long cylindrical object with windows. She then added, more as an aside to the same conversation: "My brother once saw a man, deep in the thick forest of the Grose Valley, wearing a suit. How strange is that?"

(One of my BUFORA colleagues had also mentioned to me that an attractive, blond-haired man, in a three-piece brown suit, had been described in similar situations from several different countries.

I had also spoken with another woman who, when nine years old, also in 1976, had an experience with 'blond aliens' near Govett's Leap. She was later to experience further contact with 'blonds' and 'little ones' who were 'not so pleasant'. When older, she was five months pregnant when the doctor found the baby was 'gone', with just the placenta and umbilical cord left in her womb. She used spiritual faith-power to stop the experiences, and is now clairvoyant and quietly helping other abductees.)

Back to Elizabeth. The next few months were confusing for her. Gunter was a lot older, but up until then it hadn't made any difference. Suddenly he became morose and introverted, retreating into himself. He spent more of his time alone at the local club, drinking and losing his money in the poker machines. Elizabeth couldn't understand it. Despite her attempts at reconciliation, he barely spoke to her, and since that trip to the mountains any physical relationship was long gone.

Their landlord, Roger, on the other hand suddenly seemed to be smitten with Elizabeth, and pursued her whenever Gunter was out. She resisted his advances, and by the end of the year could not stand the tension any longer, and decided to move back home to her parents.

"Gunter was devastated. We had been together for several years. He then announced he was going back to the Mountains 'to go away with them!' This totally floored me. I had tried to put that trip behind me, and he had always dismissed all thoughts of UFOs or extraterrestrial beings. I tried to ask him what had happened that night below Govett's Leap, but he just wouldn't talk about it.

"I confided in our neighbour Renee, and was startled when she told me she had seen unusual craft over our home on several occasions. As a psychologist, she was intrigued to know more of the incident in the mountains, and everybody's subsequent behaviour. Renee persuaded Gunter to have hypnotic regression, and when he came back he was very subdued. Renee told me that while ethics prevented her divulging details without permission, she confirmed Gunter and I had been abducted by extraterrestrials that night in January."

Elizabeth refused to undergo hypnosis, even though Gunter had already revealed something untoward had happened. She was still in denial, and given the fleeting memories of sexual arousal, felt it was all too embarrassing. Instead, Renee attempted a mediation session with Elizabeth, Gunter and Roger. All three confided that over the previous few months they had experienced an unseen influence over their out-of-character thoughts and behaviour. Regardless of the details, all relationships were over. "It wasn't easy for me," Elizabeth said. "The matter was closed for Gunter and Roger, but the insidious, powerful unseen control over my thoughts, behaviour and emotions continued."

Although she remained friends with Gunter, Elizabeth was on her own to rebuild her life. "It was strange that despite several romances of his own since, Gunter remained friends with me and my family for the rest of his life – almost like he was keeping an eye on my wellbeing. He once told me he had made a promise to make sure no harm came to me.

"Gunter himself altered radically. He came from Prussian aristocracy, and after his childhood in war-torn Germany, didn't believe in God. Suddenly he started not only attending church, but also sang in the choir and helped with charitable work. Up until then he had been essentially selfish and self-centred. In many ways, after the few months of depression, his whole attitude had changed for the better. I also noticed he wasn't wearing his glasses any more, which he had always needed for reading and driving.

"He told me he didn't need them now, and had dispensed with them for good. He said; 'I met two of *those people* while driving in the country. They told me I wouldn't need glasses anymore!' He added this had been done to verify their powers and bona-fides." No amount of persuasion or pleading would get Gunter to reveal what had happened, either in the mountains, or on his eventful country drive.

Elizabeth hadn't recalled any more flashbacks, but had experienced strange dreams: "When I was young I used to have nightmares about running away from a tidal wave, and sure enough there would be an earthquake somewhere in the world within 24 hours. Perhaps I was just picking up small vibrations in the earth. My mother could always tell in advance when there would be an earthquake or volcanic eruption. She was very psychic, and what worries me most are her predictions of World War 3.

"In the years following that night in the mountains, I had dreams of 'flying'. In fact they were so vivid I can remember them today. I know they were only dreams, but they felt so physically real. In one I soared up into the night sky. It was all black with beautiful stars, and I was scared I wouldn't find my way back."

Post Experience and the Security Agencies

Elizabeth took leave from work, and fled back to England to the long-remembered safety of her mother's family.

"One day my aunt and her husband sat me down, saying they needed to talk to me. They spoke of their days during World War 2, when they worked as a team for MI5, posing as a butler and maid, infiltrating the homes of aristocrats who may have been collaborating with Nazis. I was astounded, but they provided confidential details which convinced me they were telling the truth.

"They then continued to explain that one never really leaves the security services, and they had been asked to talk to me. Their masters were aware that I had just become interested in UFOs and had been going to a couple of meetings. The message they had to pass on was that if I had any problems in Australia to come home, and 'they' would protect me – adding that 'they' would like any data-knowledge I had regarding extra-terrestrials and their craft. He then said; 'Now I've done my duty. As your uncle, please forget about UFOs and those organisations.'"

Elizabeth was quite perplexed as to the British government's interest in her. "There were lots of other intelligent children – so why was I singled out for those previous visits from the 'Men from the Ministry' when at school in England? And why were they now wanting to ask what I knew about UFOs when I wasn't even an investigator?"

I was also intrigued. The British government was, at that time, officially denying the existence of UFOs, stating that they were all misidentifications of conventional objects.

Elizabeth had to return to Australia and her job. The split with Gunter had left her with some financial problems. When she left she had paid all the outstanding bills, which had accumulated from his drinking and gambling.

"All I really wanted to do was to crawl into a corner and cry, but that powerful, silent mind control pushed me on. I became a vegetarian and started joining all kinds of scientific and political-ecological-activist organisations. Every night after work I would trudge the streets delivering pamphlets to make extra money to pay off the debts. Sometimes I would look up at the black starry sky and just about beg;

'Leave me alone – leave me alone!' but this invisible 'power' or control was unrelenting.

"My previously-limited social and intellectual life widened enormously, and despite one fleeting relationship for a year, I remained single with no new romance to hinder my upward progress. Within five years I held senior positions both with voluntary and political groups, and started night classes at University towards a business degree. I was still craving answers to what had happened, and what was still happening to me, and kept contact with a couple of UFO groups and their meetings. I was like a little speeded-up robot and my mental and physical health were suffering.

"It was about that time I experienced what I think was another underhand approach by a security agency. I don't know which one. I was secretary of a volunteer organisation, and one of our members, who was a naval civilian employee working on the Jindalee 'Over-the-Horizon' radar project, arranged the donation of a very large, cumbersome word processor-computer. We couldn't get it to work, and he said he knew someone from the manufacturing company who would come to sort it out, for free, one afternoon.

"I waited in the office, and when the technician arrived, he quickly turned the conversation to UFOs, as if he 'knew'. He was very skilled at getting me to chat, and when he started mentioning the Grose Valley my inner alarm bells went off. As I avoided his probing, I was literally getting a headache trying to ward off what seemed to be almost a psychic penetration of my mind.

"A few days later I asked another volunteer, who had a friend in the Federal Police, to check out the technician's manufacturing company. Despite having a large building, I could find no record of its actual existence. He got back to me a little shaken: 'My friend started a search on the Federal Police computer, and had to log-out really quick! The computer's security program threw an 'alert', and started tracing back to the originator of the query. That meant it was a 'front' for something else that even an officer of his rank shouldn't have been asking about."

Elizabeth paused for a moment: "There was another strange development. My father and I were more-or-less reconciled, and he started encouraging me to actively participate in campaigns promoting environmental reforms. He was aware of my interest in UFOs, and while not commenting, never once tried to debunk the issue."

The Island

I was glad I asked Elizabeth about her parents and ancestry, and when I discovered her mother was *fleur-de-lis* (Flower of the Lily) bloodline, it started me on the realisation that there was a definite connection between several of the women contactees.

"My father was a Flight Engineer in the RAF and he met my mother in about 1940. They saw each other for a couple of years, until he was posted to the Isle of Man. He later wrote Mum a 'Dear John' letter. He never once spoke of what he did there. I know it was not associated with the Radar School or internment camp. It was probably *RAF Andreas,* as I think it was associated with some combined Allied operation and the type of planes he was familiar with."

(I later discovered some of the other contactees' parents were also on the island at that time, as British or US Air Force – hardly a co-incidence.)

"He never said a great deal about what he did during the War, except to talk about fellow servicemen, and that they were involved in special SAS missions. He mentioned to Mum about encountering foo fighters while flying. He was an aircraft flight-engineer, and said that there was 'no way' they were plasma balls or any other natural phenomenon.

"I know he didn't stay on the island the entire 1942-43 period, because I found some photographs, hidden in an old wallet, showing him in Navy Fleet Air Arm. He never talked about what he did during that couple of years, or if he went somewhere else after that. I never made the connection before, but after he returned, he started getting those blackouts in the form of bouts of amnesia. Mum and I had always connected it with some form of shell-shock, but now I wonder if it came from something more insidious.

"He suddenly re-appeared in 1944, and was posted to *RAF Shawbury*, near The Wrekin. He went to see my mother, insisting that she marry him. He was like a man possessed, and rushed her into a wedding in less than two weeks. Much later, after I was born, it was as if whatever spell he was under had gone. He was certainly not happy, and while not a womaniser, had at least four affairs on the side that I know of, and possibly more."

Unusual abilities

Elizabeth didn't mention any bedroom visitations or similar phenomena so often reported by contactees. When I asked about this she said: "No, but then I cannot sleep in total dark and quiet. I never go to bed without a small light, and the radio or television on in the background."

Knowing this special category of witness usually has heightened abilities in various fields, I then asked Elizabeth about any 'hidden' talents; "I think I'm what is called 'kinetic'. At work, I could unintentionally affect photocopy machines, computers, fire alarms and other 'electricals' if I was too close to them. In fact, I was officially 'banned' from some areas. Sometimes if I'm close to computer devices, such as in supermarkets or banks and so on, they will suddenly freeze, and I have to walk away before they will function again! I have friends and other people actually witness this.

"One time I was visiting a patient in a locked psychiatric ward, and the computerised door lock refused to open. I was trapped inside along with all the medical staff! Again, I had to keep my distance before anyone could get out! I always get nervous when I get into those modern elevators which 'talk' to you. It often happens when I'm agitated, stressed, or rushing to go somewhere to do something. In fact, I have been 'naughty' on a couple of occasions, and deliberately set off security and fire alarms just by concentrating on them.

"I am sometimes scared about what I can do with my mind. One colleague ended her friendship with me, saying my energy levels were so high that she got sick if she stayed too close. In fact, she had been shouting at me a lot during a joint project. I was angry, but didn't show it. Perhaps I was subconsciously retaliating. It is an ability I have tried to control and suppress by consciously taking deep breaths and trying to relax. Tony, my first partner before Gunter, was Greek, and his family and friends claimed I had the 'Evil Eye'. Some years ago, I was furious with a couple of very nasty people, who had hurt someone close to me. They both became seriously ill soon afterwards.

"I went to a very good Russian psychic, who was recommended by friends. He gave me some astoundingly accurate predictions of future events in my life, so I asked him about my alleged 'Evil Eye'. I'm actually scared of getting angry, as I don't want to hurt anyone. He looked very nervous, and said 'he wasn't allowed to say much, but it wasn't me, it was the powers around me'!

"I occasionally get bouts of precognition, although I think we all have inherent psychic abilities. When I have these periods where I'm 'driven' to do certain things, it is not my own ability. Something or someone gets into my mind and exerts a lot of influence – it's not me. Also, sometimes I just 'know' things. It's not really like any telepathic communication – more like I have a time-capsule in my brain which suddenly downloads certain information, usually about events or political figures in the world."

When we progressed to discussing any paranormal events in her life, there were only two or three that she could recall. "When I was about 18 and Tony and I were together, I felt really tired and lay down in the spare bedroom one hot afternoon. I fell into an unusually deep sleep. When I woke up there was an ethereal figure of an older man in the air over me and the bed. He was just looking down kindly at me, and I remember his long white hair and beard, and a sort of old flowing robe. I will never forget. He was as clear as can be, and after about 30 seconds just faded away. I was quite religious in those days. I still am, and always thought he must be my guardian angel.

"The only other truly astounding incident was in the mid-1990s. My car was in the driveway and I was loading some things on the roof-rack for a trip away. Suddenly this male voice said in my head; 'You'd better stop – there's a storm coming.' I jumped and looked around – nobody there! The sky was clear blue, and at first I thought I was going barmy. As I kept loading the car the voice insisted again, telling me to take the cat inside. It sounded like it came from behind my ears, inside my head, like when you have a hearing test and they put something there on the side of your skull.

"I looked again, and there was some narrow cloud on the edge of the horizon, about ten miles away out to sea. I picked up the cat and walked to the front door.

As I got there this massive bolt of lightning shot straight across the top of my car and hit the house across the road, setting it on fire. Talk about a bolt out of the blue! I thought it must have been my guardian angel again, but now I know more about good and bad aliens, it scares me. I wonder if it was something more sinister. Was someone or something evil trying to kill me?"

Elizabeth pondered on how on earth she could have heard that voice in her head. She wanted a conventional explanation. She had never had any X-rays of her skull or neck, and wasn't about to follow my suggestion; "The doctors will certify me if I think I have an implant!"

The later years

By the 1990s Elizabeth's life had become calmer. Although she was still actively involved in several volunteer organisations, she thought this weird paranormal-alien influence in her life was now in the past. Once, in 1991-92, along with some friends, she saw a UFO going across the sky – but that was all there was to it; nothing untoward happened.

In the mid-1990s she inexplicably became extremely nervous, even distressed, about living in Sydney. "I just had to 'get out'. I don't know why. I remember walking home from the shops one afternoon, crying the whole way.

"I felt drawn back to the Blue Mountains and Govett's Leap. Within a few months, I uprooted everything and moved to Blackheath. I wonder if it is connected to that episode over 20 years before. Sometimes at night, in the quiet mountain air, I can almost feel 'Their' presence – just out of touch and sight."

Elizabeth's life in the mountains remained fairly stable. Her work with voluntary organisations, mostly helping the environment and others less fortunate, increased. "I thought my urge to return to the mountains was perhaps associated with my mother's and my premonitions about some type of future disaster, and that was all! It was just the first of several uncontrollable compulsions that started to permeate my mind, and very being. I thought; 'Oh no, here we go again!'"

At first Elizabeth was a little hesitant to go into further detail, and I wondered if her reluctance to be hypnotised was due to fleeting memories of a more sexual-type encounter. Other female contactees have confided a strong, irresistible impulse towards a specific, previously-unknown man, as if the Visitors still control their hormones, thoughts and emotions. I asked Elizabeth if she ever had a similar experience?

She jumped, and started to blush. "How did you know? I've always been shy and reticent where members of the opposite sex are concerned. Yet a couple of years ago I suddenly experienced the strongest attraction to an entertainer I didn't even know. It was ridiculous – he wasn't even my 'type'! It was totally consuming, as if that old uncanny mind control had got hold of me again.

"I thought 'they' had finished with me, and I could live my life in peace. But no ... there I was having a crush – 'in lust', with some unknown bloke like a silly teenager. Powerful as it was, I did manage to keep it to myself. I must admit, in various ways, this sudden awakening of hormones and desire did lead me to make several beneficial alterations in my life. Once I made those changes the spell wore off!"

A sudden thought occurred to me, and I checked his surname. Sure enough he was a direct *fleur-de-lis* bloodline, and his father had been in the military! While she was now very much single and unattached, I knew she had few relationships in the past, and had been with Gunter and one other partner, Tony, for many years. I asked if there was any other man or relationship in her life that stood out above all the others?

> **Fleur-de-lis (Flower of the Lily) bloodlines?**
>
> This old, iconic 'heraldic device' goes back to ancient Egyptian and Babylonian times.
>
> It has been assimilated many times since, for many uses – by European royalty and Baden-Powell's modern Scouting movement, for example. Traditionally, it is very closely linked to French Royalty.
>
> However, European states and their ruling classes have also advertised their kinship to validate their power and influence, by adopting this device.
>
> Therefore, the *fleur-de-lis* has become closely connected with positions of power and influence throughout European history
>
> This 'kinship' could also be reflected within the Abducted community, which suggests an alien focus on specific human bloodlines.

"Yes, I never really went on dates or out to clubs, but I was very attracted, physically and mentally to a man I worked with for a long time. For months, I resisted his attempts to get closer, as he was married. I eventually succumbed and believed his lie that he was separated and getting a divorce. We had a clandestine affair, but when I discovered he had a young child he had 'forgotten' to tell me about. I ended the relationship and changed jobs.

"It was the hardest thing I have ever had to do. He was like a soul-mate. We were connected in so many ways. I had never felt this way about anyone else. I still have his photo! I haven't had another man in my life since then, and it was a long, long time ago! Years later he was 'free', and mutual friends said he was trying to contact me. I knew the minute I saw him again I would crumble, but I couldn't forget the previous lies and heartache, and decided not to renew the relationship."

Elizabeth thought for a moment: "You know I had stayed in that job for quite a long time because of him. It actually did advance my career to the next step. It's as if an unseen force or intelligence is interfering with and controlling my very being and life!' I asked, in confidence, the name of her secret lover. Lo and behold! – he was also a direct *fleur-de-lis*, and had spent some years in the army! Both men who had attracted her so much were of her own bloodline with military backgrounds!

A 'Eureka' moment was growing in my mind. What if some of these inexplicable attractions were somehow connected to mutual genetic vibrations or frequencies? Could a highly-advanced intelligence Puppet Master be using unknown technologies to manipulate their hapless victims on multiple levels?

I was extremely interested in not only Elizabeth's experience with compulsions, but also that of Leesa, Patty, and other experiencers, as discussed in the following chapters. Elizabeth had always stressed that while she was helpless to prevent some occurrences in her life, she always had the choice as to whether she should follow the compulsions or not: "I am not anybody's 'mind-controlled' puppet."

Compulsions

The enlightened and qualified researcher, Dr Karla Turner, who died several months before Ken Philips, investigated many cases of 'compulsions' which occurred after a consciously remembered alien contact, and affected the abductee's life in a number of ways. While the cases I discuss do not involve the nefarious Greys Karla had been researching, I felt that advanced scientific methods used to control peoples' minds could essentially be similar.

In the *UFO Times* (Jan-Feb, 1996) Turner discusses the experiencers' sudden impulses to go to a certain place, or to open windows or doors, indicating that these particular Visitors do not make bedroom visits or spirit people away from crowded environments. She noted many experiencers make drastic changes in their lifestyle, careers and personal habits, including moving to another geographical location, especially a more mountainous area. In most cases, the contactees are not sure *why* they do these things. Karla felt, on the balance of probabilities, that experiencers were being programmed for some future scenario.

Since Karla and I had been involved with entirely different contactees – a world apart – some of her findings left me gob-smacked, and with a better comprehension of the nature of my subjects' experiences.

Karla highlighted some of her observations: "For the most part, unfortunately, these compulsions often cause disturbances of a very intimate nature in their lives and thus, like the sexual aspects, are rarely made public as part of the overall data record ... for some abductees the compulsions have focused on public figures or celebrities. Most don't take it to the stage of 'fan obsession', and worship from afar. It does however, distract them from regular relationships."

Dr. Turner bravely confided her own personal experience of this, and the compelling 'dream encounters' which gave some credibility to those recounted by Elizabeth. When Karla noted that her musician 'idol' was also the same obsession of three other abductees, I wondered if there really was more than a co-incidence to Elizabeth's attraction to men with the same bloodline and military connection. There is no way of knowing the details of Karla's musician.

(Apparently, if these close-to-home 'sexual obsessions' are realised, sometimes resulting in a pregnancy, other relationships are affected disastrously. I must admit to a private giggle where celebrities or others, many not that attractive or famous, are totally unaware of contactees privately fantasising about them.)

Chapter Nine

Lydia, Vera and Ronda

Elizabeth had come from England, and one of my colleagues in BUFORA suggested I contact Ken Philips, who ran a witness support group. There was a second 'private' group for a certain category of experiencer. It was through Ken that Elizabeth met 'Lydia', (pseudonym), and they formed a very close connection. They even discovered that Lydia's great-grandfather was Elizabeth's great-great-grandfather.

Lydia

I became acquainted with Lydia in the early 1980s, and our firm friendship has lasted well over 30 years.

Once we got talking I discovered Lydia, like Elizabeth, had strange experiences as a child, although at that time she was living at Weymouth in the south of England: "I was outside playing with the other kids, and although there was one of the parents keeping an eye on us, I suddenly went missing. Everyone was searching, and the police were called. Just as suddenly they found me back in the same place I had been over twelve hours earlier. It is strange that I can remember every detail of my mother's kitchen in those days, and have no recall of those missing hours.

"I can also remember one evening, when I could see a fairground across the park, and kept asking if I could go. I could see the Ferris-wheel, all pretty with coloured lights. I thought Mum was lying when she said there was no fair. If it wasn't a Ferris-wheel – what was it?"

Lydia also mentioned that her mother's youngest brother, Daniel, was only six years older than her. There was another day – she was four and he was ten – when they had a strange 'missing day' experience together.

"When I was about eight or nine years old I remember waking one night and seeing two men at the end of my bed. They were upright and motionless, just staring at me. At first, I pulled the eiderdown over my head, and then sat up and looked. They were human, one fat and one thin, and had very white skin. Their clothes were old fashioned, like early 20th century, and they reminded me of Laurel and Hardy – I think they were wearing bowler hats! They looked luminous, almost like an 'electric glistening', but I have always told myself it must have been a dream.

"My mother was also psychic, and my husband Tony, never quite understood when she started rambling on about something to do with aliens and 'flying carpets' in the early 1940s. She said one didn't want to meet them – it was worse than war! I later wondered if she was talking about the time she spent in the military on the Isle of Man during World War 2."

Out of place and Time

"I will never forget an incident on my birthday in July 1972. Tony and I were still courting in those days. He bought me a bunch of flowers and took me for a night out in his brand-new E-type Jaguar. It was about 9 p.m., and we pulled up at a red traffic light. I remember seeing a light behind us, which I thought was a police patrol, and told Tony to be careful as they targeted sports cars.

"It was a clear starry night, and suddenly the car seemed to be 'spinning' just like those ones at the fairground do. Next thing we were still sitting at the red traffic light, and we both urgently wanted to go to the toilet! Tony drove to the pub, but it was closed – everything was closed! We looked at our watches in amazement – it was 3 a.m.! What had happened for six hours? We couldn't have been stationary at the lights all that time – other motorists would have done something. When I picked up the bunch of sweet-peas they had grown! It may not be connected, but two months later I discovered I was pregnant, but subsequently had a miscarriage."

Another strange episode occurred in 1978, when Lydia and Tony took her daughter Annie to stay at their nearby caravan, where a relative was holidaying. After they dropped Annie off, they can't remember 'travelling', but found themselves in South Wales!

"We regained our composure, and made our way home. Both Tony and I rushed upstairs, both vomiting. Our son young Martin, who had also been in the car, remained unaffected."

Lydia and Tony's strange experiences in the car are not isolated. Others have experienced similar phenomena.

On the other side of the world, in Kallangur, Queensland Australia, a nurse was driving home from her shift at the local hospital on 14 February 1990. UFOR(Qld) reports how she stopped at a red light near the shopping centre. There were no other cars or pedestrians to be seen, and about 150 metres after driving on, she suddenly found herself 5 kilometres further along the same road, but travelling in the opposite direction.

She pulled her car over to the side of the road and stopped, wondering what on earth had happened. To her, it seemed to have occurred in a split second, but she later realised that her trip home had taken 30 minutes longer than normal. She felt extremely nauseated with a throbbing headache, and rapid heavy breathing, and later suffered gynaecological problems.

Family encounter

Lydia's next experience, in 1979, when she was 36: "My friend James had been over for the afternoon, and the kids and I walked along with him through the fields as he cycled home. It was dusk by the time we left him at the road on the other side, and as we were ambling back, about a ten-minute walk from home, my son Martin claimed the Moon was coming down out of the sky.

"Of course, I thought he was being ridiculous. I looked, and got quite a start when I saw this bright spinning object coming down out of the sky towards us. I initially thought it was a plane about to crash, and made the children crouch down in the tall grass with me for protection. When we didn't hear any impact I looked up and saw this object pass overhead, then drop silently and vertically behind a nearby embankment.

"Everything all around was eerily silent and still, like some unseen barrier had suddenly eliminated all background noise. Thinking it might have been some kind of a small plane crash, I had a compelling urge to go and look behind the embankment, and the children and I took a few steps closer. Everything seemed safe so we hurried up to the top of the rise.

"We all stood there and stared. It was a crescent-shaped object, about 60 feet across, hovering a couple of feet off the ground. It was hard to see the details – the massive white light around it was so bright. At times, it didn't appear to be totally solid, it was like a dark grey, intricate lattice, and I could still see the field through it. It was pulsating, moving backwards and forwards. It seemed to disappear, then reappear, then disappear again.

"I was mesmerised, transfixed. It must have come back into view because I could see this separate white light above it, which still seemed to be part of the overall structure. I felt drawn to it – like a moth to the flame, and it seemed to get brighter as I moved closer. A slowly rotating orange ball of light came from the far side of this 'thing', and began to move towards me. I still kept walking towards it, as if in a trance.

"My daughter Annie started screaming at me to come back, and she jolted me back to reality. It was weird, I had this strong feeling of fear and déjà-vu. In hindsight I wonder if this was somehow connected to previous 'episodes'? I grabbed Martin and Annie by the hand and started running down the embankment.

"Poor Martin was having trouble keeping up, and Annie was screaming that the 'thing' was now at the side of us. I scooped five-year-old Martin into my arms, and ran like hell, dragging poor Annie along with me. Everything seemed to be in 'slow-motion' as Annie called out again; 'Look Mum – there are two of them.' I was close to exhaustion but told Annie not to look back – just keep running.

"We were now running along the riverbank path, and the surrounding area was starting to look surreal. The grass was folding flat upon itself, as if being pushed down by some strange force from above. We kept running until we reached the house, and I was surprised to find my Tony was home from his evening shift. It was well after 10.30 p.m. – there was over an hour and a half I couldn't account for since we saw the strange object at 9 p.m.

"While he did not mention the two previous episodes in the car, I'm sure he must have recalled it when we told him what had happened. He got us all to draw a picture of what we had seen. Tony also made me look in the mirror – the skin under my eyes was all red and scaly. Also, Annie and I both had violet scars on our left legs.

"Tony was also very understanding, because a few years before his younger brother (now deceased), had a sighting on the Yorkshire Moors. He was with his kids, and there was some missing time. His one son is very intelligent.

"It's strange, and rather worrying that of my two kids, now adults, who were also there, remember everything quite clearly. Martin can talk about it privately, but is so terrified, he always sleeps with the light on."

I asked Lydia about Annie, who was 15 at the time. "She just totally avoids the subject, and I can't ask her what, if anything, these 'beings' did to her. What nobody else knows is that they apparently got James and his bike as well. He also suffered physical side-effects, including to his pineal gland, but didn't want to come forward."

In 1979, about a month after their experience, neighbours a few doors down the street, mentioned previously seeing a large, silent, orange 'ball' bobbing up and down over Lydia's roof and the house next door. Three different neighbours confirmed seeing a 'thing', through their windows, about the same time as Lydia and the children's abduction. Their descriptions were similar – a 'dark grey disc'.

"We hardly told anyone about it, but a friend persuaded me to have a couple of hypnotic regressions, which I found so disturbing I couldn't even watch the tapes afterwards. Later I started to get more conscious recall and flashbacks and knew that sooner or later I would have to face what happened to us and come to grips with it.

"I recalled that at the point of turning to run away I saw, and bumped into, a person – a human figure – standing next to the main object, then everything 'blurred'. It was like I was in a dream, and I felt myself 'floating'. The next thing I was in a room and six people came in. They were human, but Oriental in appearance, with yellow-olive skins, very dark hair and slanted eyes. They were all dressed the same, wearing dark suits but with high necks.

"I recall being laid on a table, with very bright lights shining in my eyes. Someone was examining me and something cold, like pieces of ice, was being put on my legs. I don't want to know or remember what was done to me on that examination table.

"After that my periods stopped, and a few weeks later I had a slight 'show', and a waxy discharge which I took to my doctor. He told me I'd had a miscarriage. I was flabbergasted. I'd not been pregnant. I couldn't have been, and there was no blood loss or any sign of a miscarriage. What was happening to me?

"My menstrual cycle did not return, and I was referred to a gynaecologist who ran a series of tests. He said my fallopian tubes had scar tissue, which may have been caused by an ectopic pregnancy. Of course, he said he was only speculating at a possible cause, but I knew I'd never had an ectopic pregnancy or anything like it.

"Of more concern was his inquiry as to when and why I had my ovaries removed. **I hadn't!** What was he talking about? How could he say that 'somehow they were *gone*?' Then it dawned on me. I hadn't had a period since that encounter in 1979! What is even more inexplicable is that, at the age of **60,** in 2002, I started to menstruate again – at least that's what I thought.

"Later, in 2005, the specialists said 'something' was lodged in the lining of my womb. They weren't sure what it was, but it had been there a very, very long time. They wanted to investigate, but for some reason I was not only terrified of anaesthesia but also 'needles', so I still don't know. I couldn't tell them why I was scared of 'not being in control.' They would have thought I was nuts."

After the encounter, in 1979, Lydia also noticed strange marks would appear on her body, only to vanish the following day. Seven years later in 1986, she was required to wear a plastic name badge at work, and within hours her name just disappeared from it. After this happened three times they were tested by a scientist who felt the anomaly may have been caused by 'radio waves'.

There had been strange 'happenings' before on the riverbank from which Lydia and her children were abducted. The houses, in the street where she lived, had fields going down to the river at the back.

"One of my neighbours told me that during World War 2, he was walking out there with his wife, and saw massive lights up above, like bright spotlights. They thought it must be some form of film set, and saw some people on the ground. Thinking they must be actresses, as they were wearing robes, similar to 'nuns', they went up and asked them what was happening. They got no reply, and after walking away they turned and looked back – everything was 'gone'!

"Another odd thing occurred when I was a teenager. I used to go to a dance across that field, and I'll never forget one summer's night, when this unusual man turned up. He didn't seem 'normal' and had pale white 'baby' skin. He looked about 23, older than the others, and his clothes were at least 20 years out of date. He was not wearing a suit and tie, and nothing matched. He didn't speak much. In fact, nobody has seen him before or since.

"He didn't seem to be able to dance, and made a clumsy attempt to emulate the others. He ignored the other girls and immediately sought me out. He asked me to sit on the seat outside, and suggested we go for a walk – to exactly the same place our abduction occurred. This guy really spooked me! I went back inside, and when I left I avoided the fields and took the long way home.

"There was a woman, who used to mind my son, and the first time I met her she said: 'I've seen you before.' It transpired that as a child she had lived much further down the same river, and used to also cycle along the bank. On several occasions, she had gone out in the morning, and the next thing it was dark and she was coming back home on her bike with no lights. She also made vague references to aliens."

A continuing phenomenon

One night, in 1988 Tony and Lydia were driving across the Pennines, in the Peak District National Park. (This region is high in quartz crystal content, and considered a 'window' for UFO sightings and other unusual occurrences.)

The area was deserted, and their headlights started fading in and out making it harder to see the road ahead. "We pulled over into a lay-by, to let what we thought was another car pass, and the electrics in the car seemed to fail. Things are a little vague, but our next recollection is we were in a field, several miles further on. We were standing outside the car and Tony was pointing to a large bright circular craft directly overhead. At first it was slowly rising, and then suddenly shot upwards until it was just a dot in the sky."

Lydia said they got back in their car to continue their journey. She then realised she had no recollection of getting out of the car when they'd pulled over at the lay-by. When they did get home, the journey had taken one and a half hours <u>less</u> than it should have taken!

Lydia was naturally concerned about other 'altered or missing time' episodes: "I know I wasn't suffering from what you could call 'amnesia', because on more than one occasion I was physically missing.

"One nice sunny day in 1992 I went out into the garden, at about 1p.m. I sat down and relaxed at an outdoor table. Tony had dropped in for lunch and returned to work, and I was expecting a friend at 1.30 p.m. My mother, who lived with us was expected back from the Day-Care centre at 3.30 p.m. The next thing I knew I was still sitting at the table, but it was **7 p.m**.

"I thought I must have fallen asleep, but the thing is – I wasn't there during the intervening time! My friend had called and left when she couldn't find me. The assistants from Day Care had brought Mum back, and finding no-one home had left her at the local hospital for us to collect later. After we picked her up I looked at my bare arm – it had a round area of tiny pinpricks of dried blood, similar to an inoculation site!

"Another time I was visiting some relatives in Somerset. It was 9.30 p.m., in winter. When I went out into their backyard, half of it lit up like sunlight. I ran back inside, recalling that a similar thing had happened at home in the West Midlands."

It was another 20 years before an implant was discovered and removed from behind Lydia's ear. No-one was aware of it until her body began to grow a protective membrane around it.

Later years

"In the mid-1990s Elizabeth rang me in a frantic state: 'He's dead – now we'll never know!' she cried. I couldn't understand what she was talking about."

Ken Philips had been travelling between two UFO meetings, when he collapsed suddenly, and died.

Elizabeth confided: "Lydia and I get on so well, mostly on the telephone. We also have physical similarities. Lydia says it's like we're 'two peas in a pod', and that is what led us to check our ancestries."

I rang Lydia and she explained that the connection between her and Elizabeth was uncanny, almost as if they were twins: "We are somewhat alike in appearance. When we talk on the phone, sometimes for hours, we find ourselves simultaneously saying the same things.

"We discovered we had similar habits and personality traits, and thought, given our experiences, this might be more than co-incidence. I remembered that Ken Phillips mentioned he thought we had a 'connection' when he first put us in contact with each other. He also made reference to the Grail bloodline, which I didn't think about at first. When Elizabeth and I realised we had a common ancestry, we checked our family coats-of-arms, and would you believe, both our mothers were *fleur-de-lis*.

"It was much later that we explored our family backgrounds and found another coincidence. During World War 2 and before we were born, our parents were involved in some 'hush-hush' operation on the Isle of Man, between 1941 and early 1944. My mother, and my father – an American pilot, were there, as was Elizabeth's father, who was a flight engineer. In both our cases all documentation was 'gone', although we had a few photos and other bits of substantiating paperwork.

"My father was killed in the War before I was born, but I have been able to trace some of his family. After my mother died officials removed all of her records from the Isle of Man, and documentation about my parentage. My biological father's friend – a military engineer on the Isle of Man, married my pregnant mother after he died. He was always very protective of me.

"I was born near The Wrekin, where my mother's family lived. Then (and this is uncanny), I am friends with two other experiencers, Vera and Ronda, who were abducted near The Wrekin, and near where Elizabeth had her first experience as a child. Would you believe both Vera and Ronda had parents with connections to the military and the Isle of Man? What's more, all four of us, seem to share a common 'psychic connection' which we can't explain.

"Further, both of our fathers had been on the Isle at the same time, involved in secret activities. They had then returned to immediately marry *fleur-de-lis* women, and we were both the first-born of their unions. I was so excited, and thought we were really 'on to something'. Ken Phillips had been so supportive of us all, and never tried to exploit us like other researchers did. On the Thursday, I rang and told him the news.,

"Ken was intrigued by this information, and I got the impression that it confirmed some unspoken theory he had. He said he was preparing for a conference, and would get back to me. I never got the chance to find out what it was he suspected or knew. He was only in his fifties, and seemed fit and healthy. He had been to a UFO meeting, where there had been a lot of witnesses and he suddenly collapsed and died on the spot. They said it was a 'heart attack'! Elizabeth and I have been so worried that it could have been connected to my phone call two days earlier. Other researchers have died because they 'knew too much,' and one of his fellow speakers at the conference was struck by a hit-and-run driver the same night, but luckily survived."

I felt my blood run cold when I heard this news. Was I, as a researcher, dabbling in a dangerous line of enquiry? I discreetly asked a couple of contacts in the UK, but they preferred to believe Ken's early death at 54 was purely due to natural causes, as he did have a hectic schedule. However, one close colleague, who claimed to be an experiencer - but extremely right-wing in his views, told me differently. He said: "I had a really bad feeling about that conference, and begged him not to go, but he didn't take any notice of my premonition."

Lydia admitted that three months earlier in 1996, a 'psychic' friend had warned her she was in danger if she spoke at a particular conference. She arrived late and missed giving her talk, but asked Ken about it. He confirmed hearing a warning for both Lydia and himself, but kept in mind it was only a 'psychic' who gave a list of people in danger; he'd not said anything to Lydia as he didn't want to frighten her.

I have given Lydia a pseudonym, although from publicity at the time some may realise who she is. Originally, she never reported any of the incidents, and it was a concerned relative who advised a professional. From there she was referred to an English researcher and later hypnotic regression. The hypnotherapist who assisted with the initial and ongoing investigations, participated in documenting her experiences, with others, in a book. She never wanted any exposure. Unfortunately, when the initial press releases were sent out, Lydia's true identity was revealed.

"I had no idea," she bemoaned: "One morning I opened my front door, and there on my doorstep, front path and out on the street, were journalists, photographers and television crews. It was all so confronting, and there was no way I could retreat into anonymity! After that I agreed to give interviews and speak at meetings, but I also attracted unwanted attention and even threats and stalking. In hindsight, sometimes I wish I had never told anybody what happened to us all. I was just so glad, for James' sake, he hadn't told anyone else that he had also been abducted from his bicycle that same fateful evening in 1979. At least he was spared all the unwanted publicity."

Lydia has developed an increased psychic ability, but only uses it privately, and not for commercial purposes. She now has five grandchildren, all very intelligent – one could write and draw before the age of two. Amazingly, she still remained close friends with the hypnotherapist. Perhaps he was one of the few confidents she could talk to, now that Ken was gone. He still rings her frequently. Unfortunately, due to dementia, he was not really able to assist with any further follow-up.

Vera and Ronda

It was after I got to know Lydia for a while that she put me in contact with Vera, whom she had met through a private experience support group, run by a couple of UK researchers. "I have met a few people who've had experiences, but Vera and Ronda (pseudonyms) are different. It's really bizarre," Lydia said, 'but we are so much alike – me, Elizabeth, Vera and Ronda. We look alike, and have similar behaviour, especially in the fact that we are hoarders – always coming home with bargains from the charity shops! I don't know why we have houses full of 'goodies', and we discovered we all have ridiculous stashes of non-perishable food. You would think we were all stocking-up for some big disaster! And we are always on the same 'wavelength', and say the same thing at the same time – how weird is that?"

Vera did occasionally have precognitive dreams and premonitions. She was also very good writer, and artistic. Just like Mary, (see my Chapter 9), she had a 'gift' for painting flowers.

Vera didn't know whether she had an implant, but it was possible, as she often experienced a high pitch buzzing or humming behind her right ear. I immediately thought of Lydia and the implant she'd had removed from the same spot. Vera also had experienced the telepathic 'control' over her actions and life, similar to but not as severe as Elizabeth.

Childhood

Vera had also lived close to The Wrekin, and in some ways her childhood memories were similar to those of Elizabeth. "I have always preferred to remember this as a dream. I was four and I was floating down the stairs with my two-year-old sister. We 'floated' through the door. It was like going through a 'cobweb'. The next thing I knew we were sitting on some benches up the top of the road. I think my mother came and got us.

"I also have a strange memory of being carried down a white corridor to a white brightly lit room. There were people in white gowns at the bottom of where I was laid down." (She was not aware of an almost identical memory, shared by Elizabeth.) I asked about any problems with her reproductive systems, and she outlined irregular periods from an early age, one of the most common complaints made by the women.

"As a child, I used to experience a form of precognition/premonitions, and both my parents were psychic. When I was fifteen I saw a strange object in the nearby sky, and got the distinct feeling it was watching me."

The Abduction

Vera was with Ronda in 1981 when they shared an experience they will never forget. "We had been out for the evening, and set out for home in my car at about two in the morning. About an hour before we had noticed two men, strangers, near the bar, who appeared to be looking at us. They came over, and asked if we could give them a lift to Wellington, on the way to Telford. After we said 'no', we turned around and they had literally 'vanished into thin air'. How could that be? How did they know where we were going?" (I didn't tell Vera about the other cases of these 'people' vanishing into thin air!)

"We were nearly home, fairly close to The Wrekin, come to think about it, and there was hardly any traffic on the road. Although we had not been drinking any alcohol, at that stage we were all fairly sleepy and anxious to get home. We saw some lights in the distance, but didn't take much notice, until Ronda became excited at spotting a strange craft, very low, ahead of us. I leaned forward and looked up to see the round, circular bottom of a very unusual craft, about 200 feet above us. The 35-foot, dark grey, metallic base of whatever it was had two red lights in the middle, and four very bright yellowish-white lights spaced evenly around the circumference. It certainly wasn't a helicopter or anything like that, and didn't make any noise.

"We were curious, but also very frightened. As we tried to speed up away from it, everything seemed to be going in 'slow motion'. At first the craft was before and in front of us, and we were looking at it through the windscreen. We were sort of confused and dazed, as if in suspended animation. The next thing we could see the craft low down over a field to the side of us, and it was at that stage we noticed it had a dome, with windows around.

"We were all confused, not recalling seeing the craft move over to the field, and the intervening time to the next memory of it rising up into the sky, when the white lights seemed to dim and it vanished.

"We drove to the local police station and reported the object, but they said it must have been a helicopter from *RAF Shawbury*. To that stage, the trip had already taken 30 minutes more than usual. I didn't arrive home, quite excited, until about 3.25 a.m. I told my family and neighbours, but didn't really welcome the publicity that followed. At that time, although we didn't relate to any missing time, we both felt that somehow, we had some contact with the beings in the UFO, and that we would see them sometime again during our lives. In fact, we both felt elated for several weeks. Then we experienced a feeling of depression, but that could have been due to events in our personal lives."

Ronda had contacted some UFO investigators, who persuaded them to have some regressive hypnotherapy. Under hypnosis the women recalled both themselves and the car being 'floated' up through a door and into the craft. Ronda felt herself floating out of the car and was then on a long table on a stand in a semi-circular room. She remembered four 'beings' coming in, the first looked like a 4-foot tall metallic robot. She thought they seemed friendly, but could remember no more until she was back in the car.

Vera's recall was a little more detailed: "Inside the object I could see windows, lights and what resembled banks of computers. I think I was 'scanned' – and there were some men; dressed in green. They were all about four feet tall, but very ugly, with strange looking noses and thin arms. I also saw that one of them was a female.

They all seemed fascinated by my clothes and hair, and were also putting their hands inside my legs and feeling my bones. The next thing I remember is being carried to the car which was back on the road.

"It is probably co-incidental but the next day Ronda and I were joking about what those aliens wanted with us, and I said: "Perhaps it was for breeding purposes". Now I think it was a misinterpretation on my part. Perhaps it was to do with 'spiritual evolution'.

"About two months after the encounter both Ronda and I discovered we were pregnant. We both had partners, so it was not necessarily connected to the encounter. I had a miscarriage after about seven weeks. Poor Ronda was not so fortunate. Her baby was stillborn at eight months, and very deformed, without legs."

Later thoughts

"I have had a lot of time to reflect upon what the beings said they wanted with us, but they also thought we would not understand. It involved the 'higher' mind, and could not be understood by the slower physical mind.

I feel strongly that there is life in other dimensions which can be contacted. Personally, I think it is important that in order to understand and communicate with UFOs, it is necessary to learn more about psychic, esoteric and spiritual matters."

Vera has gone on to develop her psychic abilities, and used them to help a lot of other people.

Certainly, our scientists have recognised the potential existence of other dimensions, and her words reminded me of the thoughts of Professor John Wheeler. He claimed that consciousness is a form of energy - a basic and crucial requirement of nature, which it needs to ensure its continued successful functioning.

Our world, which teams with consciousness on varying levels, may be of much greater cosmic importance than we have ever realised.

If everything in the universe is an interconnected whole, then both humans and aliens are part of that existence. Perhaps, as many experiencers claim, the Visitors are leading us to a higher standard of enlightenment.

I was naturally curious about any generational link involving experiences and intelligence. All Vera's children have seemed wise beyond their years, and did very well at school. One daughter and her nine-year-old son are both very psychic, and another musically gifted.

I needed to confirm some of the common denominators which Lydia had mentioned the women shared. Elizabeth had lived near The Wrekin, where she'd had experiences, and I wondered if they had anything else in common. As an afterthought I asked Vera if she or Ronda had any connection with the Isle of Man?

"Oh, yes! How on earth did you know that? My mother-in-law is related to one of the oldest 'line' of people on the Isle of Man. Ronda and I have both traced our ancestry. Her mother's people were the ruling family on the Isle of Man from the 11th century, and my own grandmother came from, and had relations there, often wishing she could return."

Chapter Ten

The Wrekin and Isle of Man

Where some of the British born contactees were concerned, there were two places which seemed to be consistently connected to the events – the Isle of Man and The Wrekin.

The Wrekin

The Wrekin is an ancient and mysterious mountain, which rises out of the plains of England's Midlands. On the summit are the remains of an iron-age fort, and it is only a short distance from the ancient Roman city of Wroxeter. It is reputed as having been a favourite location for Wiccan ceremonies for many years, and co-incidentally has two *fleur-de-lis* on its coat of arms. There is a supposed fault line running west from The Wrekin to Craven Arms on the Welsh Border, and many believe it sits on a ley-line. I wondered if this ancient mountain had a high magnetic energy that was being tapped into, both now and in the past.

My friend Rosemary had mentioned ley-lines on several occasions: "What was the purpose of the ley grid in Britain? Certainly, not to make roadways for travellers – many of them leap cliffs or pass across lakes. While some mystery remains, at least one important purpose is now known. The lines are energised by magnetic earth currents, which are strengthened when straightened. These energies can literally 'charge' stones and even plants, as demonstrated by Havelock Fidler in his book *Earth Energy*."

In 1975, a transmission station was erected near the top, with part of the facilities underground. The locals claimed that it was honeycombed with caves, some of which were utilised during World War 2. Little is known about military activity around or within this ancient mountain during World War 2, however it is said the authorities still maintain a covert presence in the vicinity.

The Wrekin kept cropping up in my continuing research. The abduction of Lydia and Vera, and the earlier experiences of Elizabeth were only a couple of the many incidents which have continued to occur in the area. Further, Elizabeth's father had been stationed at nearby *Shawbury RAF Base* when he rushed her mother into marriage. It was perhaps more influential than anyone realised. Elizabeth had once commented her mother seemed to have some affiliation to the area, and mentioned they had both climbed it in their younger years. When Elizabeth's mother took her there as a child, she warned her not to stray from the path, as there were 'hidden dangers'. Elizabeth thought she must have meant caves, although she never saw anything.

Nearby Contacts

There are surprisingly few reports from this part of the West Midlands, but they are country people, not that far from the RAF base, who tend to keep things to themselves.

Paul Stokes advised the *Encounter* researchers of a perplexing event which occurred in 1952, when he was a young airman at Cosford Air Base, near The Wrekin. At about 7 p.m. his fellow servicemen called him out to observe a strange craft which was silently moving and hovering over a nearby field. It looked like a bright white light, shaped like "two saucers placed face-to-face" – an elongated disc.

He climbed on top of an old air-raid shelter to get a better look, and recalled the others running back to the billet shouting: "Quick, get out of here ... Get away ... Run!" He was fascinated, and stayed put, trying to mentally communicate saying: "Over here ... Come over here."

He recalled later returning to his billet, but his memory of the next few hours was totally erased. The next morning, he suddenly found himself on the parade ground. He didn't know how he got there, or what had happened. Totally confused he looked up and down the ranks of airmen, until the others shouted at him to get into place.

On 21 October 1954, in the late afternoon, Mrs Jennie Roestenberg was with her two children in their home at Rampton, near Shrewsbury, not that far from The Wrekin. They all watched an aluminium-coloured disc hovering, at a tilted angle, over their house. It had transparent panels, through which they could see two men who appeared to be Caucasian, with white skin, and long hair. They could not fully discern their features as they seemed to be wearing transparent helmets and distinctive turquoise body-suits.

In his book *Alien Base*, Timothy Good researched an encounter, at Church Stretton, not a great distance from Elizabeth's farm, and an area near The Wrekin. In November 1957, Hubert Lewis was cycling into town to get the paper early one wet, windy morning. He was feeling cold and miserable, and stopped when a man appeared on the road in front of him. To the side, and hovering above, was a circular object, approximately 60-100 feet in diameter. It made a slight whistling sound, but seemed to dispel the wind around them.

The stranger, who spoke English, seemed to know details about his life, and counselled him on his current difficulties and unhappiness. They spoke for about 30 minutes, and after the visitor wished him well he just 'vanished into thin air.'

Lewis found he had enhanced psychic abilities after the incident. In May, the following year, he received a visit from a senior police officer and another gentleman, who asked him a lot of questions, and told him to get on with his life and forget 'certain matters'.

A few weeks later he saw a different Visitor, whose craft was way across in the fields. He must have walked some distance to contact Lewis. His message was somewhat different, in that we should not be afraid of our 'friends', who could impart great knowledge and abilities if mankind would guarantee their safety, and that they would not be exploited or imposed upon.

The Visitor made arrangements for him to go to London, and soon after he met a contact at Paddington Station, where he and a woman of similar appearance took him to a flat for the evening. At times the couple conversed in an unintelligible language. The two were both tall and very healthy looking, with a slight Southern Mediterranean appearance. He met with them over several days, during which time they imparted much information, including the fact that many of them are living among us, and he should be careful whom he told.

BUFORA investigator David Pointon documented a report from 1996 when two men – MM and CL – were travelling from Telford to Wolverhampton. At 8.45 p.m. they saw a bright, rectangular shaped light which appeared to be above *RAF Cosford*. It was divided into three sections by two 'pencil thick' lines, and whilst very bright did not illuminate the surrounds.

A second object approached, at a very low altitude, going NE to SW. When overhead, it stopped, and the two men could see it was triangular, matt black with green lights on the points and each side. The underside appeared to be a transparent dome containing a white light, which flashed on and off in a ten second cycle.

They slowed to 10mph and the object stayed with them for about two minutes, before slowly moving off towards the first object.

Five hours later, when they were returning to Telford, a beam of light shot down from the sky in front of them, and then to the right. Although it did not hit the road, CL was so affected he could hardly drive. His legs 'felt like jelly' and he was violently ill three hours later, and again later in the week. MM was also sick that night, and has recurring dreams of a triangular craft crashing.

RAF Cosford advised there were no aircraft present any time that night. MM gave details to the military police, and several days later two unidentified callers rang him requesting more details.

It is not known what these objects were or where they originated. It cannot be said, with certainty, what caused the illness and dreams of the witnesses. The craft, whilst unidentified, were in the proximity of the mysterious Wrekin and couple of Air Force bases.

Nearby is the town of Telford, and Global Investigation Systems, based in Manchester, have an ongoing interest in the area. Staff from a Telford hotel which lies at the foot of The Wrekin, have all witnessed strange events. In 1996 they had several sightings of a large, black, triangular craft, which hovered over the mountain for an hour, before flying towards *Shawbury* base, descending slightly as it went.

There appeared to be an increase in military presence around that area during this time, and investigators found damage to trees and the ground, consistent to where witnesses suspected the unusual craft may have landed.

The Isle of Man

The main connection for some of the contactees was that their parents or ancestors were associated in various ways to this mysterious place.

The Isle of Man is situated in the Irish Sea, off the west coast of Britain, and is almost an equidistance to England, Scotland and Northern Ireland. With an area of 572 square kilometres, it has several small offshore islands, its highest mountain being Snaefell at 620 meters. Its capital is Douglas, and it has been inhabited since before 6,500BC. Over that time, it has been subject to invasion and settlement by several cultures, including the Vikings and Celts. It is not really part of Great Britain, and is classified as an internally self-governing Crown Dependency, not even being part of the EU when Britain joined. English is the usual language, but some people still speak Manx, which is similar to Gaelic. Mann has a useful geographical isolation, and a legal and political situation which could work to the advantage of less than orthodox activities.

Reputed to be on the intersection of several major ley-lines, Mann is steeped in mythology and superstition, regarding the 'little people' and 'Manannin' the King of the Otherworld. The locals have always talked about strange lights, mists and time slips, but they never reveal who or what 'may lie below'.

In 1937, knowing hostilities were imminent, the first military airbase, *RAF Jurby*, was established. It was followed by *RAF Andreas*, which was in the most 'paranormal' region of Mann, where strange energies and powers seemed to exist. Reports of ghosts, fairies, goblins and aliens had been legend there for centuries. Also established were the Voight-Sikorsky Chesapeake under the 772 Squadron Fleet Air Arm and the 811 Naval Air Squadron. During World War 2 the island also housed a radar school, a couple of internment camps, and an air-sea rescue unit.

In recent years, while reports are rare, there has been some UFO activity in the area. One night, in the summer of 1977, several witnesses on the promenade at Port Erin, saw an orange oval, dumbbell-shaped object in the sky. It moved steadily over the bay, and stopped and hovered on several occasions. It emitted a beam, like a 'silver rod' with no diffusion of the light, for a moment or two. Afterwards, it would move, suddenly and quickly, at a sharp angle in the other direction. It repeated this manoeuvre several times over a five-minute period before flying away to the north. One witness claimed that about a year earlier she hadn't believed her elder brother and his friends, who claimed they had seen a UFO while fishing in the harbour.

On Sunday 14 January 2000, there was great publicity given to several reports. At about 4.30 p.m. a 25-foot triangular-shape UFO had crashed into the large communications mast on the summit of Snaefell. While there did appear to be some damage to the mast, the RAF and the entire emergency service authorities of the Isle of Man could find no evidence of an accident of any kind. Witnesses found this odd, as they had seen dense black smoke, red navigation lights were damaged, emergency service radio links impacted, and fire alarms in nearby buildings activated.

Locals are used to drones and some military aircraft flying over the island, but claimed the object they saw was none of those. One witness said that the object definitely had the "terrific sound of an aircraft engine", but it didn't look like any of the images of UAV, UCAV or RPVs he was later shown for identification. There was apparently a security clampdown with the local media pulling all coverage. A resident claimed that Royal Navy officials confiscated footage he took of three mysterious red lights, close to Snaefel's summit, shortly afterwards.

Later, other witnesses came forward to suggest the object was in fact a new black triangular UAV drone, 30 feet in length, which had crashed into the sea, obviously hitting the communications mast on the way down. In fact, one report stated an American craft exactly matching that description, had been badly damaged and sent for repair with faulty navigation and directional capabilities.

While it was obvious that some form of military operation was what was observed on the Isle of Man, Graham Birdsall and British researchers were quick to investigate the situation. They reported that a week later, when witnesses in Lancashire reported an unusual large light, blue and red with a white corona, local police advised the Ministry of Defence had tagged it to a report from the Isle of Man. A similar report had been made by witnesses in Cumbria on 14 January, a few hours before the accident.

If the January 2000 incident was indeed a military operation – was it merely an exercise gone wrong? The white lights remain a mystery. Were they what the drones were after? Given that UFOs can affect electronic controls, one can but wonder. An island, surrounded by sea, is always the ideal location for alien contact, experiments and covert activities. We will never know what, if anything, occurred on the Isle of Man either then or before and during World War 2. The ancestors and servicemen and women are all dead, and their records and log books confiscated long ago.

Chapter Eleven

More British Cases

There were so many common denominators with some of the British-born or descended contactees, that I thought it had to be more than a coincidence. All were looking for answers, but could only quietly contemplate their own startling theories.

Mary

Mary also lived near the Welsh border, although she had spent part of her childhood and younger years in Northern India before World War 2. She was 15 when her family returned to England. I met her through Ken Philip's abductee support group while on a trip back to the UK. She was born about 1932, and was extremely intelligent and psychic. She alluded to many sightings of UFOs, but only ever divulged a few, remaining very quiet and secretive about most. I later realised she had much in common, and was also very similar in looks to the other women in this category.

She was vague about any experiences as a child, except that as a boarder in a convent school in the Himalayas, they used to go out to watch "the incredible meteor showers". While she was well versed in astronomy, and did not confuse natural phenomena for UFOs, I suspected that more had happened during those early years. She admitted to many UFO sightings, but was reluctant to divulge any details.

In 1955, when she was 21, she was confronted by a metallic UFO which landed in front of her car in broad daylight. A dark shadow had appeared overhead, her brand-new car spluttered and slowed, eventually coming to a halt.

"I got out, and about 18 feet above me was a solid grey 'cloud', with a well-defined oval perimeter which covered the entire road. It came to a halt, and seemed to solidify into a bell-shaped craft. Three ball-bearing type wheels came down from the smooth underside. They retracted again, and it started to spin and hum, flipped on its side, levelled up, and 'set down' on the road just ahead. There was a common nearby, and bystanders (including children) and my two passengers all stared in disbelief. We could see a classic domed flying saucer – with three spheres set into its base - a shining black/pewter colour, like polished metal, and about 35 feet in diameter. The centre was still and the outer rim slowly spinning with flashing white lights. There was a humming sound, and it had what appeared to be moulded concave glass tinted windows, so nobody was able to see in.

"We just stood there gawking as the craft rose about five feet above the road and hovered for a good five minutes. As some of the locals went closer, it tilted and hovered overhead. After moving slowly to above the local school, it hovered for another minute and then went high up into the sky with a sudden swishing sound. My family and friends were very sceptical until the County Newspaper published reports from different witnesses, including a local policeman."

Over 20 years later, in 1978, Mary and her neighbour were gardening and chatting through the wire fence: "We looked up and saw the weirdest thing. There was a patch of red sky with thick black streamers of smoke coming from it. We thought a storm was coming, and went inside. Although the sky looked blue, when I saw a flash I got up to close the curtains, and realised it wasn't lightning. This silver object was slowly coming across the sky. It split in two, with one half shooting off in another direction, and the other hovering just above the house opposite."

Mary raced outside with her binoculars and alerted her neighbour. "We watched as this 'blob' turned into a giant umbrella-shape cobweb of little silver twinkling lights, which tumbled, twisted and turned over the rooftops until it hovered about 800 feet over a local park. For one and a half hours it twisted, turned and rotated, with a growing gathering of locals watching on.

"It was getting late, the sky had darkened, and just after a small passenger plane passed overhead, a 'long black cylinder' slowly came into view. It gradually positioned itself over the spherical cluster of lights which stopped moving. That entire area of sky became as bright as daytime, and only darkened again after the cylinder and lights moved slowly away in unison."

Many other witnesses in the area had seen the same phenomena, and some reported that earlier that afternoon they had seen a strange cloud-like object in the sky. An egg-shaped silver disc had flown into it and then re-emerged and continued on across the sky.

In 1999, it was a clear sunny day, and early one afternoon Mary was shopping with a friend in North Wales: "I saw a police helicopter hovering in the blue sky just above the buildings. It was only about 500 feet above the ground, and the noise it was making was what first attracted my attention. I was startled to see, about 25 feet above it, a white cigar shaped craft, about 35 feet long. I watched for some time, until it flew slowly across the road, and hovered over a park for a few minutes, before rapidly flying off towards the coast. It was impossible to tell if this craft was making any sound because of the racket coming from the chopper.

"Again, one night in October 2001 my husband and I were driving north along the Welsh Coast and admiring the stars in the dark sky over the Irish Sea. Suddenly an 'oblong' of red and white light dropped, and then vanished from a large patch of stars. At first, we thought it must be the lights of a helicopter turning, but then, to our amazement, that whole cluster of about 30 bright stars started moving about. They went up, down, sideways – all changing positions quite rapidly. I wanted my husband to stop, but he said there was too much traffic, and when we came to the end of the motorway I lost sight of them."

Connections

Mary is short and fair haired, similar in appearance to the other women. She is highly intelligent, loved and cared for animals, an author of several books, and like Leesa a gifted artist, known for her watercolours of flowers. I asked about her ancestry - she said it was a mixture of English, Irish/Jewish, German and Norman. She could trace her family tree back to an Archbishop of Canterbury around about the time of Queen Elizabeth 1, and certainly had the requisite blood-lines.

When I asked Mary about her father I got a bit of a surprise: "He was a scientist but also worked for MI5 – it took us to several parts of the Far East up until the War, when we returned back home." (I was reminded of Gordon Creighton and Patty's Grandfather, who had also returned from Northern China when the Japanese invaded.) I was curious as to what Mary's father had been involved in, and she replied: "I would like to have known that myself, but within a few hours of him dying two people arrived at the house and went through his files and paperwork, taking it all away with them. My sister and I were still in a state of shock, as he died suddenly of a heart attack. I wondered who they were, and the powerful network of the British secret services – how they could know so quickly that he had died. She had no way of knowing if he had been on the Isle of Man during or before the War."

I immediately recalled Elizabeth's memory of her father's records being taken on the day of his funeral, but said nothing to Mary – What was in all those records that was so important to merit almost immediate devious confiscation?

It was far later in our friendship that Mary, now in her 80s, decided to confide her own interest in Earth's immediate future – her own thoughts and related prophecies and predictions.

She listed many prerequisite events as foretold by various seers, astrologers and other sources that would lead to World War 3. It was bone-chilling that most of these have now come to pass. She alluded to the many visionaries who described a huge object suddenly appearing in the sky, and commented that ancient astrologers always interpreted comets or similar objects as harbingers of disaster – usually war or plagues.

She advised if the information was correct, a large object will travel around the sun just before World War 3, which will have started by the time it returns on what seems like a collision course. She thought the first close orbit would be presumably a warning, and the second a judgement of our actions. She wondered if, in the past, these were really just comets etc. or rather large mother ships passing by.

During her life, Mary had seen many UFOs from a distance, and managed to photograph a few. She also was a little distressed that once a friend, on the way to visit her, was abducted from a quiet road en-route.

Charles

While most of the 'connected' contactees were women, it didn't necessarily mean there weren't any men with similar experiences and family history. I just hadn't found them, or they hadn't contacted me.

One exception was Charles who was born near the crop circle areas in England in 1965. He certainly had travelled the world by the time he was 30, when we first met. Up until the age of 18 he had lived in various parts of Sussex. During his schooling there, although he passed all his exams, he was never really singled out for anything. He tended to be a dreamer, a thinker and rather introverted – yet in later life he was sought out by psychics.

In 1983, he moved to Papua New Guinea for three years, and in 1986 went to New Zealand for another 12 months. In 1987 he arrived in Melbourne, and permanently relocated to Randwick, Sydney by 1988.

Childhood

We discussed his childhood. He had always been interested and 'believed' in UFOs, and while he had no scars or conscious recollections, there were a few odd experiences and strange dreams. He started with an often-common denominator: "I was an only child. Both my father and grandfather were in the British military for a while, but neither ever mentioned unidentified flying objects."

I asked his mother's maiden name, and after telling me he commented: "I was in some museum in Winchester, it had something about a 'round table'. I was surprised to see a stained-glass window of a coat-of-arms with my mother's maiden name underneath – I took a photo."

Having ascertained that his mother's maiden name was indeed *fleur-de-lis*, I went on to ask about childhood memories: "I used to have dreams of 'colour' going up the side of the wall, and would get so frightened my parents would have to calm me down. I would talk in my sleep, and thought it was my father I was having conversations with."

"I have vivid memories of a recurring dream. I was being dragged into a planetary system by some gravitational force I couldn't fight – it was very upsetting. I once woke up and was very scared to see an old lady at the side of my bed. She seemed to be 'tickling' me of all things! For some reason the bald-headed figure at the end of the old '*Star Trek*' series used to frighten me."

(Although I suspected there may be more to his childhood than he realised, I did not consider regressive hypnotherapy advisable at this time, as he indicated he would rather 'not know.')

Michael

We then started discussing more recent events: "One afternoon in 1994 I was having a nap, and had an out-of-body experience – it was not a dream! I was at the front door and a man was there. He was smiling – but said nothing. He was about

35-years-old, Caucasian, about 5 feet 8 inches, with broad shoulders, curly blond hair and blue eyes. I knew I was astral travelling, and tried to get back into my body. I heard the front doorbell ringing, but could do nothing. It was my flatmate Nigel, who had forgotten his keys, and eventually had to climb through the window.

"I thought no more about it until three days later. My friend Grace rang and said I just had to meet a man she knew in the Blue Mountains. Grace and Alice were working at a Spiritual Retreat in Katoomba. They had met a man called Michael who said he had been 'waiting for them.' He drove them to the edge of one of the cliffs, where they all sat on a rock and played their guitars. After a while a UFO appeared. When they returned to the Retreat, they spent the night playing music and discussing multi-dimensional beings.

"I met Michael in the city a few days later, and was astounded to see he was the man from my out-of-body/dream experience only a few days earlier. He told me he was also from England. He was travelling and needed a place to stay. I offered him free board and lodging, and he actually stayed a month."

(Many years later, when I was going through my research notes, I realised Charles' description of Michael was identical to that given by Leesa – see chapter 15 – of the man who followed her around Nowra in July 2000!)

"I got to know him well. When he played his guitar, Michael's music had an ambience I had never heard before. About 10 p.m. one night my friend Paula and I were in the lounge and Michael was playing his guitar. There was no window in that room, and he insisted we go outside with him as he 'wanted to show us something'. The sky was covered with clouds, but as we looked above the building they slowly parted.

"We saw the black sky and stars, and suddenly an object came down and hovered about 200 feet overhead. It seemed to 'ripple into being' rather than just 'fly in'. It was about 25 feet in diameter, and the round bottom was all I could see. Michael told us he was in communication with these beings who were multi-dimensional.

"I thought to myself; 'Am I really seeing this?' and mentally said; 'If you are there – do something!' The craft flashed about 10 very bright lights, which went on and off and beamed down onto the ground. I continued to watch, and when I deliberately kept a calm, quiet mind for a while the flashing stopped, only to start up when I directed my thoughts back there again. The craft stayed for a few minutes, then 'rippled back' into nothing.

"Michael came from somewhere near London. He told me a lot of things, but at other times would become quite aloof and vague about his past. He claimed he had been in Canada before Australia, and was smoking an unusual pipe which he said the Hopi Indians had given him. He said he had visited them with a message from the 'multi-dimensionals'. It was a prophecy regarding the return of the *Bird Tribes* (ET craft), and that now was the time for them to start emerging and making themselves known."

Charles continued: "I often wondered about Michael. He had been working with chakra balancing and spirit guides at the Retreat, and I must admit the craft which had appeared over us seemed benevolent. One night we were walking past a park in Randwick when a schoolgirl stepped out of the bushes, which was rather odd. Michael said she was not a schoolgirl, but another 'multi-dimensional being' doing special work on Earth.

"I thought this was a bit far-fetched, however another event had also left me shaken after the sighting over the house. I introduced Michael to another friend Edwin. Edwin's father was dead, and a much older family member, Adam, was a sort of 'surrogate guardian.' Adam had been in the Navy all his working life, and apparently was involved with some form of top secret project. He once spoke of laser guns and other technology used when he served in the Vietnam War.

"When Adam heard of Edwin meeting Michael he became very concerned. He claimed 'someone' in the military had been investigating Michael, who was told to 'stop interfering with this planet – the governments didn't like being manipulated.' He was ordered to 'go', and left Australia soon after. I haven't heard from him since, but an acquaintance received a postcard saying he came back."

(As a researcher, I wondered about the other reports of the infiltration of our society by these Visitors. Was Michael one of them?)

Back in England

In 1995 Charles returned to England to see his parents. One day his uncle picked them up and drove them to see a nearby crop circle. They didn't think the researchers knew about it, as the farmer had deliberately taken the tractor-mower over it. The outlines were still there, and strange things had been happening near the area. He stood in the middle and took photos, but didn't know if the energies had any effect on him.

"In August 1996, I had another strange dream. It was as if somebody was talking to me. The only thing I can remember were the actual words I heard as I woke-up. They were something about everyone's 'mind machinery' soon being connected to a cosmic grid around the earth.

"About a month later, in September, I was carrying my shopping through a local park at about 4 p.m. one afternoon and sensed something overhead. I looked, and could see an unusual craft in the sky. Being near to the airport, I took no notice until suddenly this object was only 35m away, and about 10m above the grass.

"There was nobody else around, and I couldn't believe what I was seeing. It was oval, silver metallic, about 25 feet in diameter with no windows. There was a small white light underneath, which didn't seem to be attached, and was hovering with its own motion. I couldn't decide if this was military or ET as I could only see it from the side, and not from underneath as in the 1994 sighting.

"Remembering the 1994 incident, I consciously sent feelings of love to see what would happen. The craft responded by emanating beams of white light, which flashed out and back about six times. I realised a small aircraft had passed, and was now circling overhead. The object started moving slowly and steadily upwards until it became a point of light high in the sky."

Charles had been away from home for several hours, and it was difficult to determine if he had experienced any missing time. There were several factors in common with other similar witnesses and their contact with humanoid type beings. Perhaps this was just one more piece in the jigsaw puzzle.

John

John was also born in the UK in 1971 and lived in Worcester, not that far from The Wrekin. It seemed his mother, born about the end of World War 2, had also been affected by this phenomenon. His first memory was from the age of four, or even earlier.

"I used to see 'ghosts', or at least that's what I thought they were. Once I suddenly woke up in my cot, and realised I was tucked in the wrong way around. I sat up with a start and could see a white light – like a soccer ball with a blue tinge – hovering outside the bedroom window. My ten-year-old brother Bruce was also asleep in the room, but he didn't stir or see anything. Bruce did tell me that he once saw a thin, black spindly being come out of the wardrobe, but he may just have been dreaming – I don't know!

"During the 'Warminster Flap' something happened to my mother whilst my brother and I were asleep in the car. My father was also there, but apparently unnaturally drowsy. My mother is very reluctant to talk about what happened that night, but has mentioned seeing a shooting star which came across the windscreen. She said it was slow – rotating and changing colour. It came down low, and she saw something at the side of the car. I don't know how much time elapsed until she saw the craft go behind a nearby barn, and she quickly drove off. My parents seemed to have an interest in UFOs since this event."

(This report reminds me of other cases where only one passenger in a car is targeted, while the others remain in an unnatural drowsy state.)

John and his family migrated to Australia when he was twelve. Before they left there was another disturbing event: "A tall female being, with long blond hair walked through my room, and the next night my mother slept in the bedroom with me. We had a bad experience and Mum was saying the Rosary. She told me that 'something was on her back but it went away'. I know she had more troubles later, but she wouldn't tell me about it."

John went to the local school, excelling at some subjects. Thinking of Elizabeth's experiences with the 'Men from the Ministry' I asked John if any special interest or attention had been shown in him.

"I'm not sure what you mean," he replied. "That question has made me start to shake, and I'm not sure why. When we arrived in Australia I was visited by some sort of officials who assessed me and moved me to a school with older children."

Generational

By this stage, and given his mother's tell-tale signs, I was suspecting another generational scenario. John, like several of the other special experiencers in the following generations, was very talented – artistic and musical. In 1986, when he was 15, he was sitting under a tree in his uncle's garden in Brookvale, Sydney.

"I was sneaking a cigarette, and trying to think of words to go with a song I was writing. Suddenly I saw this bright light zig-zagging in the sky, towards the sea. My parents arrived and we all watched as it came closer. It looked like a huge diamond, and then we could see it was a huge, dark V-shaped object. It had to be the size of two football fields, and had a large light at the front, 2 small lights at the side, and a medium light at the back."

John paused: "In 1995 I got a 'bump' on the head and X-rays verified a possible implant. My brother and I both used to wake up with inexplicable nose bleeds, but these became less frequent as we got older. I often wonder whether they were connected with the strange electronic beeps we sometimes hear in our heads."

I asked John more details about his family: Yes, they were the 'right' bloodline. Was this another generational family of contactee/experiencers? John said his mother had gone back to live in the south of England in 1993, and has told him that the phenomena has still followed her. She sees balls of light and 'things' in the house.

It seemed his mother had certainly been singled out. Her father fitted the profile – he was in the military. They lived near The Wrekin, and as a child, John had seen the blonde humanoid type woman in his bedroom. A further similarity was that his paternal grandfather had been in Government Service.

Louise

In 1977 Stefan Spencer discussed several very intelligent people who had highly-developed ESP telekinesis and psychic abilities, including telepathy. This particular group, now adults, some having graduated university, had one thing in common. They had all been raised in orphanages, some were left as babies on the doorstep. There was absolutely no paperwork or records accompanying their arrival. Every attempt to identify or trace their parents had proved fruitless, all were child prodigies with a blank background.

I am good friends with one of these 'prodigies', Louise, born in Britain in 1945, obviously from wartime parents. She was adopted from the orphanage soon after. Louise is exceptionally intelligent, with an interest in UFOs, science and ancient history. She wishes to retain total anonymity, and consciously recalls an event when she was in England, and only twelve years old:

Louise was taken aboard a small craft, which she recalls had 'seats that went back', and some controls and screens. It could move instantly from stationary to an incredible speed. The occupants were human, with medium colour hair, blue eyes and wore bluish-grey zip-up suits. She wasn't sure exactly what they did, but heard one say: "She's too young", before taking her back.

She grew up in Britain, studying at university, and acquainting herself with ancient traditions and teachings. She had travelled to the Himalayas, and was familiar with the hidden knowledge the Nazis and many others were anxious to possess, but never found. She told me: "The monks in Nepal and lamas of Tibet will die rather than reveal the repository of this ancient knowledge." She had been friends with author John Michell, who said it referred, in part, to aliens and their spaceships and technology.

It wasn't until her later years that she moved to Australia. She was also interested in the aborigines and the Wondjina culture, and is aware of a very powerful 'portal' area, which is a closely-guarded secret. One of her friends, Tony, who lives there, is also well informed regarding the power of vibrations, and the reality of the portal. He considers if its existence was known to the wrong people the consequences could be disastrous.

He once received a strange visitor, a man with bare feet, who arrived wearing shorts and T-shirt in the dead of winter. He was an 'alien' and had apparently been given appropriate clothes for the 'time and country' – but the wrong season! He said very little, and merely drew many pictures of spaceships and their technology. Tony looked away for a moment, and when he turned around to speak to his guest, he had just 'vanished into thin air'. Tony and his wife also had visions of bad times to come, and had stocked-up on provisions and become self-sufficient.

Louise considers that certain people are repositories of ancient knowledge, and that it is retained through genetic engineering and certain bloodlines.

Rosalind Reynolds

British researcher Philip Mantle extensively investigated the case of Rosalind Reynolds, which had many common factors with some of the other experiencers.

On an evening in September 1982, Rosalind and her boyfriend Philip were driving on the outskirts of Sudbury, in East Anglia. Suddenly, a set of fast moving horseshoe-shaped multicoloured lights approached them and swooped low over their car. A flash of blue electric light illuminated everything around them. The windows were open, and the radio on, but she could smell a 'foul, rotten egg' odour as it passed, and noticed a silence and stillness that seemed to surround them.

They drove through Sudbury and onto the A604 at Haverhill. Soon afterwards, another oval ball of light headed towards them, drew level, and started pacing the car. Philip kept driving, until the car's engine and electrics cut out, and the car came to a halt in the dark. Philip sat staring straight ahead, as if in shock, while Rosalind looked at this 'big, bright round ball', 60 feet away.

The next thing she recalls is they were outside, looking at the car's engine, when the headlights suddenly came back on. They jumped back in, the ignition started up first time, and they sped away leaving the UFO behind them. When they arrived at Corby, their destination, they were three hours late, suggesting a large amount of missing time.

As with the case of Elizabeth and Gunter, Rosalind and Philip, who had been together for six years, parted company a few months later; "He developed mental problems, and was a different person, not the Philip I knew," she said. In a similar pattern to the other women, Rosalind's behaviour changed. She looked after her health, and became very creative, speedily writing complicated scientific papers.

Eventually she sought help to discover what had happened that summer's evening. The first hypnotic regression, in her own home was a debacle. A bright beam of light came into the room, all the clocks stopped and the video recording was wiped. A later hypnosis session was to a certain extent more successful, and she remembered the fateful night at the side of the road.

She recalled four or five small beings forcing her into a craft, undressing her, and placing her on a clear perspex-type table in an 'examination room'. She underwent some form of gynaecological procedure, but there the hypnosis session had to be terminated prematurely when she became distressed, and sat bolt upright in the chair screaming: "No I don't want any babies."

Like the other women, she suffered irregular and missed periods. Although she later married another man, she has been unable to have children. In 1999 she was advised, after changing four doctors, that some of her reproductive system is 'mysteriously missing'. She also developed a buzzing in her head, and has recalled other periods of missing time in her past, which she did not relate to any kind of experience at the time.

Certainly, she appears to be an intelligent person, who has developed a thoughtful and spiritual attitude once the shock and depression wore off. She learned to rise above the unethical behaviour of some of the media and sceptics.

As with most abductees, she has always asked: "'Why me?" It was only much later she discovered the *generational* aspect to her experiences. As a child she was quite spiritual, and had written long passages, well beyond the aptitude of a normal seven-year-old. Much later she found out that her mother also had experiences: "These were backed up, as just before my father died, independently, and not knowing of my experience, or that my mother had told me hers, he told me of his and his brothers recollections which occurred just before my conception."

Chapter Twelve

Genetics

DNA – Deoxyribonucleic Acid

The human genome contains 23,000 genes and our scientists are beginning to realise that we are just at the beginning of the Genome Era. There is still much to learn about genetics and human DNA. In fact, it's not what we know, it's what we don't know. Research is still in its infancy.

One pioneer, Francis Crick, co-discoverer of the shape of the DNA molecule, posited the *Theory of Directed Panspermia*. He was reported as saying, 'an advanced civilisation transported the seeds of life in a spacecraft!' He is not the only scientist to quietly entertain the same viewpoint. There are many who do not totally agree with the Theory of Evolution, citing 'missing links'. Recent research indicates that 223 currently-identified unique human genes do not come from our genomic evolutionary tree. So where did they come from?

Except for identical twins, every human's DNA is unique. Some scientists suggest our DNA contains more than just the physical blueprint for who we are, that it serves as a communication and biological data storage computer.

DNA is a nucleic acid made up of millions of nucleotides, and is found within the nucleus of every cell in the trillions of cells within our bodies. Two strands of nucleotides are strung together into a long ladder-like structure, with a hydrogen bond between the bases. The strands themselves are twisted around each other to form a double helix. (Some scientists consider that a form of quantum entanglement helps the DNA maintain its helical structure.) Each nucleotide comprises a sugar molecule, a phosphate molecule (which is identical in every nucleotide) and a nitrogen base, of which there are four different kinds – A(adenine) – T(thymine) – C(cytosine) and G(guanine). These are often referred to as the building blocks of DNA – of life.

The double-stranded DNA provides the code for assembly of proteins in ribosomes in single stranded RNA, forming a string of 146 animo acids, in an infinite variety of sequences. The subsequent proteins are many, varied and complex, and make up what we are. They are so minute they must be magnified a million times for us to even study them. The strand of DNA which provides that basic code is referred to as a 'gene'. However, only 2% of our DNA is used to produce these proteins. The other 98% of our DNA has functions we have barely begun to research.

A large part of our 'junk DNA' has historical significance. By comparing the genome of different groups of humans throughout the world, we are better able to understand various milestones in human history.

There are three billion 'letters' in our DNA code, which creates a very complex system. So far, most research has investigated where common code variations correspond to known diseases and medical conditions. It is not just the mixture we inherit from our parents.

Our DNA can be modified naturally by learning, experience and the environment. There is ongoing research into the 'adaptive' genome which creates 'cognition' and reprograms genes during our lifetime, so adaptations will continue to be inherited by the following generations.

Jean-Baptiste Lemarck (1744-1829) first contended that the experience or intelligence of an individual was passed on to offspring in transgenerational inheritance. 'Lamarckism' was controversial and completely superseded by Charles Darwin's (1809-1882) theories. However, recent epigenetics research suggests RNA (ribonucleic acid) can sometimes act on DNA in reverse, rewriting some DNA master code, using a chemical process and methylation. RNA can also replicate itself without using DNA.

Professor Marcus Pembrey conducted similar research and provided compelling evidence of the biological transmission of memory – a transgenerational inheritance. Dr Brian Dias of the Emory School of Medicine in Atlanta also stated that the chemical changes to DNA, before conception, can influence the structure and function of the nervous system of subsequent generations.

Russian researchers have likened our DNA to a 'biological internet' and contend that it can be 'influenced and reprogrammed by words and frequencies'.

One may ask why this research is of importance to UFO, alien and other research? It suggests that our genes can not only be altered by our RNA, but also how the offspring of a genetically-manipulated parent can inherit, or acquire paranormal abilities and advanced intelligence. It also gives us some insight into the later accounts of those children being further augmented or having reproductive material removed from their bodies.

Of more importance is the discovery that most (98%) of the messages our DNA sends to the RNA are not to produce proteins at all. Initially scientists referred to these codes as DNA- or RNA-'junk' merely because they lacked any protein coding. Other experts consider these unencrypted codes the key to the evolving complexity of who we are. One interesting finding is that molecules of guanosine, a building block of RNA, behave like tiny transistors.

One of the most important questions we need ask is does this 'junk' DNA have functions of which we are still unaware, or is it lying dormant, ready to function or be activated? Bioengineers, including an international collaboration of research groups, ENCODE, are working to unravel and define the mysteries contained within our genes. Cosmologist Paul Davies has suggested a 'biological SETI' to find a mathematical or semantic code, buried within our DNA, which could indicate some form of alien genetic manipulation – a message to us from some ancient alien visitor.

Recent studies at Harvard University have found that our state of mind and thoughts can switch various genes on or off. Even more revolutionary are theories, partially based on Quantum research, that our DNA interacts with both our own and other bio-electromagnetic fields. The current thinking is that humans are a complex electromagnetic and chemical interaction, and our genes can act as quantum objects displaying quantum bioholography.

Genetic Interference

In the case of the families I have followed through several generations, it seems as if some form of reproductive genetic enhancement was possibly performed via the sperm of the original male ancestor (often when he was in the military). Since individual male sperm has a limited lifetime it makes sense that it appeared to be only the child, conceived a relatively short time after military service, who was affected. But the vast majority of these children, besides being intelligent and gifted, possessed a telepathic ability between each other. Leesa more aptly termed it synchronicity, often over long distances. This is normally only found in some identical twins.

One could surmise that besides having mothers with a similar ancestry, they possess a similar or identical genetic component which enables them to resonate with each other. Dr Vladimir Poponin, a quantum biologist, experimented to show that DNA can communicate by non-local energy.

We know from times gone by that the persistent gene of succession is carried within the mother, mitochondrial DNA. It is of concern that most of the original female offspring of abductees have presented with damage to their reproductive systems, and missing ova, from a very young age. Many recall an associated abduction experience, often on more than one occasion throughout their life. Perhaps genetic augmentation requires more than one stage – a gradual implementation. Conversely, this doesn't always seem to apply to the next, or third, generation, although the offspring and descendants, of these alien encounters are often endowed with high intelligence or paranormal abilities.

I have investigated a relatively small number of cases. There have been many similar encounters reported from all around the world. The vast majority of these contacts were mostly benign in nature, although some definitely involved the forcible taking of genetic material, sperm and ova, obviously for some purpose involving reproduction.

One must ask who is responsible for this, and why? Is it aliens, humans, or a combined project? All of the women I work with, had parents or grandparents involved with the military, diplomatic corps or secret services, and in addition a common ancestry and/or bloodline. I had initially concluded that some fathers had been part of a secret genetic augmentation project on the Isle of Man, where their sperm was initially altered, and their desire for, and union with women from the *fleur-de-lis* bloodline was the planned outcome. (Alternative historian and author, Sir

Laurence Gardner stated that in ancient Sumer the key females of the Dragon succession were all venerated as 'lilies' and given like names.) Were these new genes to be introduced in gradual stages, making the progeny of these unions suitable for stage 2?

Then I realised there would be hundreds of thousands of suitable women with the same ancestry, and possibly others with a suitable genetic makeup. Maybe an enormous amount of men had been tampered with. It is one thing to abduct a man from his home or street, but how advantageous war is to an alien or even a human program.

Widespread battles and military action provide an ideal situation to quickly scoop-up and interfere with hundreds, probably thousands of men, and interfere with their biology. any suffering stress and fatigue would not remember – others reluctant to ever report such an event to their commanding officers. The British Army had unexplained 'disappearances' of two groups of soldiers in 1898 – an entire platoon in the Sudan, and a Company of engineers in the Khyber Pass area. (And what of the foo-fighters – were they not as inconsequential as we thought?)

The few abductees I had liaised with, who were possibly the result of 'stage 2', were all concerned with the state of the planet, and worked towards 'improving the fate of mankind', if only in a small way. The Woodstock movement in the 1960s, preaching love, peace, and harmony, was motivated and fuelled by young people, many of whom would have been conceived during or just after World War 2. Due to their passion for sex, drugs and rock and roll at that time, possibly many members of the next generation were also conceived during those hippy festivals!

Although I have concentrated on families who were exposed to the humanoid aliens, there are others who indicate that definitely more than one alien species is practising genetic manipulation. Simon Parkes, is a British contactee, whose experiences involve other beings with a similar agenda involving bloodlines etc. It may be more than co-incidental that both his mother and grandfather worked for the security services.

Genetic Experimentation

The Nazis, during the first half of the 20th century, were obsessed with genetics and creating the perfect Aryan race. They were reputed to have conducted some appalling experiments, some of a genetic nature. Why? Was this precipitated by some form of alien liaison? Right throughout history there is evidence of various societies and nations being discouraged from marrying, (ie. reproducing), outside their own race etc. It is also suspected by many that the Nazi eugenic scientists and their experiments were one of the sought-after prizes at the end of World War 2.

Since World War 2 there have been cases which suggest that abductees are being carefully chosen, and subjected to some form of genetic enhancement or alteration. In some cases, governments seem to be aware of this and monitor subjects from an early age. In other cases, no interference is apparent. I have wondered about the organisation Mensa, which encourages highly-intelligent people to join, therefore bringing them to the attention of the establishment.

Many years ago, the United Nations authorised the investigation and cataloguing of genetic variations within the human race, but it is speculative to suggest they had any joint project with alien entities. Initially most testing of people's origins were concentrated on blood types, but as our knowledge of genetics increased it concentrated on the Mitochondrial DNA (mDNA) haplogroups, which altered some of the earlier beliefs of anthropologists and historians.

Many years ago British researcher Graham Birdsall was highly critical of the Icelandic Parliament's agreement to supply Roche Holdings with the country's entire genetic, medical and genealogical records for £123 million. Blood samples were to be collected from all citizens who didn't object. Apparently, Iceland's few hundred thousand residents have a remarkably similar DNA due to their geographical isolation, making it ideal for medical genetic research.

It is curious that the vast majority of Iceland's population are born blue-eyed and blonde, and Icelandic lore records countless rumours and myths regarding alien visitation and interaction!

Also of interest was a Freemason initiative; MasoniChip, introduced some time ago in the US and Canada. While the project has government support, it is funded and owned exclusively by the brotherhood. The stated purpose of this program is an identification system to facilitate the recovery of a missing or abducted child. In addition to normal details, modern technology enables authorities to record digital imaging, video, fingerprints, dental impressions and DNA. This will eventually give them the ability to identify the bloodline of massive numbers of individuals.

I have considered the work of Laurence Gardner and his 'grail bloodline' theory, and don't feel qualified to comment either way. The Freemasons' roots date back to the legendary Knights Templar. They were apparently interested in the search for the Holy Grail. Does it even exist, and is it a small chalice or a particular bloodline? I honestly don't know. There had to be an enormous number of descendants, worldwide, with this heritage. I couldn't help wondering about the close similarity in the ancestry of these particular experiencer families I had been liaising with and researching.

I remembered Elizabeth telling me of a visit she once received from a rather officious representative, from a government department well-known for its large Masonic contingent. "He suddenly stopped and stared at my mother's *fleur-de-lis* coat of arms on the sideboard. Changing the subject completely, he asked me about my family. Three months later he returned with an entirely different attitude, and all my problems solved. He then mentioned to me that he had been to Britain 'to buy some stamps'. (On his salary?) He had visited Mum's small rural home town, and mentioned confirming some of the details she had given him."

Some people think that the government is doing secret advanced genetic research, and lead the public to mistakenly believe that extraterrestrial entities are conducting animal mutilations. Others believe that it is to frighten the general public from initiating any contact with extraterrestrials. The circumstances in each incident vary, and there could be arguments for and against either human or alien involvement.

Could there be human involvement in unethical advanced DNA experimentation? Unfortunately, it could be a possibility. There is great controversy among scientists as to the ethics of genetic experimentation. It is one thing to isolate genes carrying inherited health defects, and another to introduce genetic modifications to produce designer babies. In the late 1990s many countries passed legislation prohibiting human germline engineering, or any kind of human cloning. Other major countries only forbid the use of government funding for such projects, allowing private corporations a free hand.

There was legal opposition by some individuals when medical biotech corporations tried to claim patent rights on their genes. Human and other genes have become a commodity to be patented, bought and sold. We may well ask why would they want to do this? While initially the programs incorporated the legitimate need to identify the cause of many medical conditions, it has gone way beyond that. The ownership of genes, and who may or may not benefit, is indicative of the greed of big, powerful organisations and their apparent wish to dominate the entire planet and everyone in it.

One answer may lie in a book, *Remaking Eden: Cloning and Beyond in a Brave New World* by Princeton geneticist Lee Silver. His view, on the desirability of reprogenetic technologies which will create a separate class of humans, is that these will be superior, in every way, to the normal population and therefore more suitable to rule the planet.

One has to ask the obvious question, is this de-facto continuation of the eugenic experiments begun by Nazi Germany many years ago?

Mysterious, unmarked black helicopters are often seen when mutilated animals are discovered by their angry owners. Human agencies could easily obtain animal genetic material in their own covert establishments, so why do the perpetrators leave a carcass behind, instead of permanently removing their specimen to a secret location, where they could perform their gruesome work well away from human eyes? I'm not so sure, but solving the mystery of animal mutilations, (and it is not just cattle), is so important. It could help unravel the truth about the UFOs, their occupants, and any possible secret government participation as well.

It is not so simple to allocate blame for human reproductive genetic experimentation. While it could be suggested ova and sperm could be covertly harvested through hospitals or by unethical doctors, it seems specific people or families are required. We can only speculate as to the ultimate purpose for these ongoing procedures.

There is another aspect of human/alien genetic experimentation which few seem to consider. Our own medical scientists have successfully implanted human tissue from a donor to another patient. For example, foetal stem-cells transplanted into another person's brain can successfully grow and produce dopamine etc. But wait ... there's more! Recipients of heart transplants have been reported as 'inheriting' personality traits of the donor. They used words unfamiliar to them, often developed the same dietary and music preferences, and in extreme cases their behaviour changed to reflect the sometimes-undesirable characteristics of their deceased donor.

Neuropsychologist Paul Pearsall, who has been researching 'cellular memory', also discussed the amazing case of an eight-year-old girl who received the heart of a murdered ten-year-old. Following nightmares about the murder, the eight-year-old was referred to a psychiatrist and then the police, who were able to identify and convict the culprit due to the transference of cellular or other 'memory' contained in the victim's heart.

Discoveries relating to quantum physics affect our perception of *everything*. Recently scientists have embarked down the road of quantum biology and the existence of 'biophotonic energy' transmitted from living cells within the body. Some have postulated that it is processed by the DNA within the nucleus of each cell, and others consider that it is associated with molecules in the body's connective tissues.

In Russia, a body of scientists conducting research at the Quantum Genetics Institute, is just beginning to unravel the quantum, holographic and fractal properties of previously little-understood 'junk' DNA. Most experimentation in this area is still in its infancy, and co-ordinated by the National Human Genome Research Institute. We cannot really conceive the progress and capabilities of an advanced intelligence. Have alien cells been transplanted into human 'guinea pigs', or vice-versa, and for what purpose?

Nature 323 in 1986 reported that doctors at the Department of Genetics at Churchill Hospital in Oxford were analysing chromosomes in prenatal amniotic fluid, when they found a minute object which looked like a 'fragmented crossword' in appearance.

There are many and varied reasons given for the Visitors taking human sperm and ova, none of which can be verified. Who are these humanoid beings – where do they come from, and why are they here? Although I certainly don't have the answers, the claims that we are related in our distant past do make sense. Scientists suggest that evolution on another planet is unlikely to provide an identical life-form to us, due to our own circumstances, and unique genes, often altered by mutations. If these beings are close enough to make cross-breeding or genetic enhancement a worthwhile possibility, then perhaps they are telling us the truth about their connection to us.

Some experts claim that it is unlikely that humans could be 'crossbred' with aliens, due to a total incompatibility between species. Since no-one really knows the biological make-up of these strange visitors how can anyone be sure about the ones who look like us – or do we look like them? Basically some reports state that they are so similar to humans, they are virtually indistinguishable.

In 2001 MUFON Los Angeles reported an interesting lecture given by clinical psychologist Dr Christianne Quiros, who claimed she was asked by aliens to write a doctoral dissertation on adult Earth-living alien-human hybrids. In 1997-98 she interviewed six female subjects who believed they had one human and one extraterrestrial parent. They ranged in height from five feet two inches to five feet nine inches, and while not having any distinguishing physical characteristics, were all slender to medium build, with fair skin. Their eye and hair colour varied, and they ranged in age from 37 to over 65.

They had varying explanations as to why they believed they were hybrids. Some claimed on-board UFO experiences, some had night-time visitations by aliens and others were informed of their lineage by a parent. One described her mother's deathbed confession that she had seen UFOs and was impregnated by an 'angel'. The only thing that surprised her siblings was that she hadn't been told the secret earlier.

Doctors discovered one subject had unusual blood pressure and brainwave patterns, and all had extraordinary, and powerful, psychic related abilities.

While dogs basically have the same physiology, they come in a wide variety of sizes and features, yet they can still interbreed, and produce mixed progeny. They are all genetically compatible. Why should it be so different with humans and visitors who appear more similar to us than some dogs are to each other?

One victim was told by his abductors that 'Their People' had been all but annihilated in a disaster on their home planet. There were comparatively few survivors, and they did not wish to risk the pitfalls of inbreeding. In order for their species to survive, they require our DNA which is similar.

It is not just the aliens who should be regarded as being responsible for forcibly taking genetic material. There were the Nazi genetic and other experiments, and their obsession with the perfect Aryan race. Were those scientists also seconded by the major powers to continue research after World War 2? Anyone who considers our own authorities would never sanction unethical research is gravely mistaken. Ethics can be very controversial.

Nexus magazine recently reported that London scientists can create genetically-modified human beings. All that is preventing this are laws in both the UK and US which prohibit transgenic embryos living longer than 14 days. Veteran embryologist Robert Edwards created the world's first IVF baby in 1978. Years later, Cypriot-born Panos Zavos, who ran a clinic in Kentucky, claimed to have cloned the first human embryo, but his work was completed outside the prohibitive jurisdictions. At the same time, a competitor, Italian gynaecologist Severino Antinori, boasted he was weeks away from the birth of the first truly-cloned baby – and we have come a long way since then!

In December 1998, the Kyodo News Service reported that Chicago physicist Richard Seed said he was about to participate in a Japanese-based project to develop genetic technology he hoped would eventually make human cloning routine.

Recently, scientists have developed a gene-editing bacterium, CRISPR, which has broad applications. Despite their obvious enthusiasm, opponents fear the technology could fall into the wrong hands, and be used for nefarious purposes. Some had already expressed the wish to create a superior class of humans to reign over the less-gifted majority!

'Grow your own Humans'

I have contemplated another possible scenario – potentially more troubling. A close workmate once confided in me that she was still distressed over what she witnessed while a university student in the mid-sixties: "There was a secret experiment in the basement. We created a test-tube baby, but it didn't turn out 'right'. It was a sort of a 'blob' and made strange noises. We fed it, and it 'eliminated', but no-body knew what to do. If we 'killed' it, that would be murder, but we couldn't let it continue." I asked her what happened – she didn't know and had fled from any further involvement.

Our expertise and technology have progressed over the years. If male sperm and female ova are being harvested, are they being used to create test-tube babies which are totally human? If there is a 'Create Your Own Humans' project; we must ask by whom, and for what purpose?

Aliens have repeatedly and systematically harvested human sperm and ova, as well as foetuses from victims' wombs. Successfully creating and raising test-tube babies should be no problem for them with advanced technology and knowledge. It is worth considering that humans bred, raised, and educated by these Visitors could join us on Earth without raising any suspicion at all. While they could assist their alien parents in hopefully beneficial tasks, one must consider that the nastier aliens could also implement a similar program. There have been cases of human experiencers insisting aliens are their parents, rather than the family they have grown up with on Earth.

Although we blame these activities on those with less than ethical motives, there is also another possibility we must consider. We have a massive seed-bank in Scandinavia – a Noah's Ark insurance policy against possible world cataclysms. Do we also have similar animal and human genetic and reproductive material secretly stored away?

Investigator Kathleen McErlain discussed the case of French astronaut Dr Claudie Haigneré who was studying human adaptation in space, after two missions; MIR in 1996 and the International Space Station in 2001. Part of her research was apparently human-alien DNA experiments and in 2009 she attempted suicide screaming, "Earth must be warned!" Within hours, her laboratory was destroyed by fire.

In *Contact Down Under* I reported the case of Penny, who had an encounter as a child in Roma, Queensland. When she discussed the incident with us, as a mature adult, she took some time to reflect on her memories and thoughts. I have a feeling there was more Penny wasn't sharing. Despite her lack of adequate formal education, part of a letter she later wrote to me contained the following profound and thought-provoking statement:

"While scientists search for life on other planets and pose questions of whether we're down here alone or not, the alien has encroached on mankind in a very obscure and non-intrusive way. This form of invasion cannot be fought by our military. We are not equipped to defend ourselves.

"Invasion and adaptation go hand-in-hand. Genetic engineering is very high on the alien agenda. We hear about abductees seeing hybrids and having eggs taken from them, not to mention their embryos being removed. It is ignorant on our part to assume that they need us or our DNA to survive, or for that matter that they are the hybrids. Dipping into the human gene pool might give the alien the genetic make-up to adapt and multiply.

"In other words, you might say the alien has landed, genetically speaking. Who knows, maybe the microscope, and not the telescope, will be the first to discover the alien in all his glory and wonder. It is not a few of us who are chosen, it is all Mankind. This would account for the elusive and insidious behaviour by the so called 'Greys'. Most people would laugh at such an idea, but it is human nature to laugh at what we fear – the truth."

Penny made a very pertinent observation. With our current technology, we cannot travel the galaxy ourselves due to the vast distances. However, robots could go in our place. Perhaps the same applies to other intelligences way out there in the great beyond. Whether robotic or biological, or a combination of both, the visitors are taking tissue and genetic samples of most living organisms on Earth. Are they also leaving their DNA with us?

This possibility has recently attracted the attention of the scientific community. *Icarus* journal published a paper titled *The Wow! Signal of the Terrestrial Genetic Code*, by astrobiologist Maxim Makukov and mathematician Dr. Vladimir Cerbak, suggesting a biological SETI project. They noted that genomic DNA is already used on Earth to store non-biological information, and considered that since some features in the human genetic code defy natural explanation, could they possibly contain an intelligent embedded signal? They stated that the code is a flexible mapping between codons and amino acids, and artificial modification can occur because of this flexibility.

I have also given a lot of thought to suggestions that mankind today could be a product of genetic manipulation of our race by aliens far back in our past. It is perhaps significant that many contactees are motivated to research our ancient history, especially as it relates to the ancient Egyptians and Sumerians. They all point out that ancient Sumerian records show depictions of their Anunnaki creator holding snakes in a perfect representation of what appears to be the DNA double helix, something we have only recently discovered!

In this book, I do not address the many reports regarding abductions by other types of aliens, such as the Reptilians and taller Greys, and their alleged hybridisation programs and half-alien offspring.

Let us then go back to the present issue of aliens and their possible program of genetic manipulation of some humans. Alan told Dan Fry that his ancestors were a group of survivors when civilisation collapsed on this planet. Radiation levels had been raised to such a level that over the succeeding generations of those left on Earth, there was a progressive degeneration of mental and biological functions, and a large number of genetic mutations.

This explanation would certainly account for the reports of some extraterrestrials resembling humans, and perhaps their attempts to rectify some of the genetic damage we have inherited from our past.

If these cases are added to current accounts of humanoid-alien behaviour, we are presented with a seemingly massive amount of incomprehensible activities and motives for these activities. We cannot really know the answer to all the questions and varying hypotheses.

Chapter Thirteen

Implants and Microchips

I have pondered for a long time as to the synchronicity among this group of contactees. They are telepathic with each other, even over long distances. Are their abilities due to a genetic link, implants, or a combination of both? Leesa, Elizabeth and Lydia 'knew' things, and didn't understand where they acquired such knowledge, especially in advance.

Some describe our bodies as biological computers, with the brain as the central processing unit. It is well-established that we only consciously use ten percent of our brain power, mainly processing sensory and other input. So what is happening or is contained in the other ninety percent; can that also be accessed and manipulated? During sleep, or an altered state, the neurons in the remaining 90% of the unconscious synchronise all data into meaning. Combined with its stored memory and recognition, which it can cross-reference, the brain decodes and converts this information into instantaneous reality patterns.

This can provide an over-simplified explanation of the forgotten experiences of abductees, and the probability that they were calmed down to the extent that their consciousness was suppressed giving access to the subconscious. This also correlates with the methods described by James in New Zealand when they were initiating contact with aliens. It takes our short-term memory about 20 minutes to transfer information and experiences to our long-term brain facilities. Even if this can be successfully blocked, information is still stored in the short-term memories of our minds – hence the more reliable flashbacks some witnesses experience – or the access provided under hypnosis.

Recently I had an unexpected 'Eureka' moment, when I downloaded a massive file of data from one computer hard drive to another. Of course, of course, why didn't I recognise what had been blatantly obvious all along? Enormous amounts of information and knowledge could be transferred into a person's mind in just a few seconds! Experiencers have often reported this.

Just as our DNA and fingerprints are unique and individual, no two human brains are identical in their cognition and perception. They are constantly in a state of re-adaption, and dependent not only upon the correct chemical balance, but also the interaction and effect of our hormones and genes. This has made me consider if the alien program requires both the genetic augmentation of the subject, combined with a synchronised implant?

I also devoted some thought and research into implants and microchips. Lydia had just had hers removed, and Leesa and Elizabeth still had theirs; I was not sure about the others in this particular group. I know of many contactees and abductees who have detected them. Some had been removed and others not. In one instance, in 1996, a witness gave me a small device which had been removed from her leg. An ex-colleague had arranged to get it analysed in the US for us. Silly, trusting me! We never saw him or the implant again, and the next week he was awarded a lucrative three-year government agency contract!

Many researchers discuss implants and microchips a little flippantly, without realising the infinite complexity and variety of technology required to alter the recipient's behaviour or thinking. It is one thing to track someone's movements, alter their mood, or transmit auditory messages, and quite another to input memories or knowledge.

The Brain

The human brain weighs about 1.5 kilos and is one of the most complex natural organs known. Comprised of wet 'jelly-like' material, it has hundreds of billions of cells and a quadrillion connections. Different species on Earth have different brains, and we do not really know the mental capabilities of an alien race.

The human brain is divided into two hemispheres, joined by the *corpus callosum*, a bridge comprising 200 million nerve fibres. Every fibre can 'fire' 20 times per second, which equates to about four billion impulses per second. Each hemisphere is capable of taking over functions usually performed by the other, and recent research suggests that learned abilities seem to be holistically dispersed throughout the brain, rather than confined to a specific location.

Our own senses are quite limited to biological receptors. Our eyes can only detect the wavelengths of the visible spectrum of light, a fraction of the electromagnetic spectrum, most of which we are unaware. The brain itself is certainly like a computer and depends upon 'input' from our sensory organs. It receives information regarding sight(visual), sound(hearing), smell, taste, touch, temperature and other perceptions.

Once sensory input is received it transmits as electro-chemical signals to an incredible number of neurons in our brain cells. Almost instantaneously, hundreds of electrical pulses are sent to thousands of other neurons. (We have 15-20 billion in all which are constantly encoding information!)

The brain constantly changes and adapts to all experiences. It is the brain's interpretation of all inputs, existing data and memories, which creates our unique personal reality. It is a most complex 'biological computer', the interaction of the neurons, via electrochemical signals, continually modify our thoughts, emotions, memories, and reasoning. During our lifetime our thoughts, emotions and knowledge can affect our genome and be passed on to our offspring.

Since 1933 Soviet, US and UK scientists have sought to harness the capabilities of mind control, telepathic communications, telekinesis, bionics and other phenomena. They are aware of the effects of oscillating electrical fields on human behaviour. They discovered that microwave radiation affects the central nervous system and also learned that low intensity modulated (ELF) waves affect the rhythm of our brainwaves. They could achieve resonance with specifically-tuned lengths to the desired 'waves'. In the human body the cells and nerve fibres resonate simultaneously as antennae in tune to the electromagnetic centimetre waves.

Implants

Implant technology was apparently developed by authorities and corporations after World War 2. As early as 1948 Norbert Weiner wrote the book *Cybernetics*, where he outlined research into neurological communication and control, arising from a group of scientists formed at Princeton in 1944. In his book, *Crosscurrents* Dr Becker notes that Northrop Space Laboratories were also involved in that area, and that 'Weiner had been involved in a German experiment in which human volunteers were unknowingly exposed to a low-intensity, 10 Hertz electrical field. The subjects reported feelings of unease and anxiety when the fields were turned on, confirming the belief that the internal rhythms of the brain affected behaviour, which could be altered by pulsing external fields!'

We have perfected the art of brain frequencies. Our bioelectrical resonance is as unique as our fingerprints and DNA – meaning that implants and other technological devices can be tailored to an individual target. More advanced species and some highly-evolved humans can 'tune-in' to the unique resonance of another person and communicate telepathically as if using an individual radio frequency. *Defence Electronics* July 1993, reported that the Russians were researching a 'computerised acoustic device ... capable of implanting thoughts in a person's mind without that person being the source of the thought'. If humans can achieve this, no wonder contactees experience 'compulsions' and other phenomena at the hands of more technologically-advanced species!!

Neuroscience is one of the most highly classified fields of study due to its military and population control potential. Behaviour modification using brain implants and electromagnetic energy has been researched and developed by less-than-ethical scientists for at least 70 years, with both animals and unknowing human subjects.

The Veri Chip has been around for some time; a 12mm by 2.1mm radio frequency device inserted in people and often used, quite ethically, in conjunction with implanted medical devices. Developed by Applied Digital Solutions, the medical benefits are obvious, but other ramifications became disturbing. It has developed into a radio-frequency identification device (RFID) which can operate, via a scanner, in conjunction with other security technologies and biometric devices.

Bar-codes are utilised to great advantage by the commercial and retail sectors, and that is highly beneficial to society. In 1984, a series of patents was granted in the US for *implant* technology, variously described as a 'passive integrated transponder' (PIT), with an identifying code, inserted into a recipient. It would then respond to a separate interrogator-reader. The PIT was injectable, and manufacturers in the US claimed they had up to 34 billion pre-programmed unique codes. These are sufficient for the entire population of the world and all their pets!

Microchips have advanced society in many positive ways; they identify lost pets, and most people carry bank and credit cards. The technology has been extended to payment or identification for drivers' licenses, passports, medical records, insurance, transport, freeways, clubs and many other purposes. Of course, the stated reasons for the more insidious implantable technology were originally made to sound innocent ('merely for identification purposes, such as entry to restricted areas, personal identification, and financial, security and safety applications.')

In the 1950s miniature depth electrodes were developed to receive and transmit electronic signals. Project MKULTRA was instigated in the 1960s, when the 'stimoceiver' was developed. By 1967, primitive design implants were attributed to Sweden and Canada. Sweden was originally in the forefront of implant experiment and implementation. The 1972 Swedish State Report *Statens Officiella Utradninger* revealed that the brains of implanted human beings could be remotely monitored by supercomputers and their behaviour altered by changing frequencies. It has been claimed that in 1973 Sweden legislated to allow prisoners to be implanted, then nursing home patients some 10 years later.

In 1997 media disclosures referred to a supposedly confidential 'Security Division within IBM' report regarding the use of the 20/20 Neural Chip, which had been tested on security risk prisoners in three US States, (Texas, California and Massachusetts). Their primary use had been as a surveillance monitoring device, but they can also promote lethargy and sleep, to minimise aggression, when set to a frequency of 116 megahertz.

We have come a long way since then, tracking people and altering their behaviour and mindset. Hallucinations can be induced and memories can be changed or suppressed. All manner of thinking processes and emotions can be affected – hostility, passiveness, sexual behaviour, and the loss of a sense of time. Electronic stimulation of specific cerebral structures of the Brain (ESB), is a perfect invasive mind-control system, with little regard for the recipient. Later developments allow for remote control by satellite over implanted microchips linked to supercomputers. When microchipped, the body's communication traffic is literally hijacked. It is claimed that the Tetra and HAARP programs in our satellite networks perform this task using low-frequency electromagnetic and microwave radiation.

This technology is understandably of great concern to the security agencies of all governments, and much information is classified as 'top secret'. It has the potential to create 'Manchurian Candidates' and also fanatics who were normal people a short time before. A couple of years ago *New Dawn* magazine published an article on this very subject, claiming that electromagnetic weaponry, based on new physics principles, has been researched and developed by the US and Russia since the 1950s, and forms part of arms procurement programs.

Initially, implants were quite visible on X-ray, but by the early 1980s catscans could detect small spherical, oval or flat devices, as small as three mm. Some revealed an interior with a crystalline matrix embedded with what seemed to be micro-electronic circuits. Soon implants were reduced to the size of a grain of rice and later to five micro-millimetres, making them almost undetectable and impossible to remove.

Tiny microcircuits, nanotechnology chips, and more sophisticated biological implants, are almost impossible to detect, and require a microscope to see them. It is claimed they are so tiny they can be implanted in the human body without us even being aware. This knowledge has caused some unwarranted scare campaigns against vaccination programs.

This presents a conundrum as to why, if any of the contactees' implants were alien, were they large enough to be detected or analysed? A visiting alien society would be far more technologically advanced than us, so it is very possible many contactees could be totally unaware they contain such a device. (One contactee claimed he was told by aliens that some implants are from a 'less advanced species'.)

The contactees themselves report many varied reactions to their implants, and their thoughts as to the reason for them. Obviously, they feel it is not only a tracking device, as their thoughts and emotions were being manipulated. Information seems to be sent to their brain and they can have telepathic contact with these beings. On the downside, they can be put in a state of paralysis or suspended animation, and their conscious memories altered or erased.

In 1989 D. Pritchard (PhD, Physics) analysed an implant which had a crystalline core with appendages. Sceptics at that time insisted it was something natural, and if not, certainly no alien device. While we did not have the knowledge and expertise at the time, scientists are now developing 'photonic crystals' in order to realise their dream of super-efficient photonic circuits and microchips. 'Chips' using this molecular technology will be minute, and would replace the silicon chips used in computers and many benign and invasive modern technologies.

In 1995 L. Fenwick, a Canadian investigator, had a 1 mm implant analysed by a laboratory at the University of Toronto. It had been surgically removed, at the local hospital, from behind the left ear of an abductee. She had reported hearing 'signals', like Morse code, and sometimes words in an unknown language, for years following her third abduction in 1961. Three main elements were found, aluminium, silicon and titanium. The conclusion of one expert was that "such a device would be a transducer and can be used to transmit or receive signals."

At the same time investigator Derrel Sims was analysing X-rays of some experiencers, which indicated they may have implants within their bodies. In one case, similar objects were seen in X-rays of the one witness's mother and brother.

Simms also felt it may indicate that abductions may run in families and along genetic lines, as many other researchers believe.

Dr. Roger Leir assisted with the investigations. Along with medical staff, witnesses and a video camera 'rolling', he began removing implants from abductees and sending them for meticulous analysis. He noted that in each case they were covered/protected by some form of dense membrane, composed of proteinaceous coagulum and keratin which could not be cut with a scalpel. The membrane seemed to be composed of the recipient's own body tissue, and was capable of absorbing iron and oxygen from the host's blood cells. Its composition seemed to prevent the rejection of the implant, which is body's normal reaction to a foreign body.

Some of his preliminary findings were that they were highly magnetic and contained 'isotopic ratios consistent with non-earthly isotopic ratio numbers.' Some were composed of eleven complex elements, and most were located where the recipient had a high quantity of proprioceptors – small nerve receptors. Leir couldn't definitively say why the nerve endings were there. Others have suggested they could be attached to the nervous system as some form of monitoring device, however this would require some intricate insertion. (Although I have no idea how this can be achieved, I have considered the possibility that the implants incorporate some component that encourages the brain itself to form and connect new neural networks.)

Later analysis of one of these chips showed a core of the hardest known magnetic, iron carbide. Eleven different elements comprised a complex cladding, complementing the soft carbon magneto-conductive core. Ultra-magnification showed a band of crystals completely circling a portion of the object. Scientists postulate these tiny objects have been manufactured with purpose and precision, but by whom?

(What is of interest was the occasional discovery of 'crystals' in these microchips. It was the initial use of a crystal to test electrons, that revealed an interference pattern, which led to the discovery of 'superposition', and the beginning of quantum mechanics and 'wave function'. Tesla always considered crystals as something special, not just rocks. He said: "in a crystal we have clear evidence of a formative life principle. Though we cannot understand the life of a crystal – it is none-the-less a living being.")

Publicly Dr Leir says he is unsure of the actual purpose of these devices. It is assumed they were extraterrestrial/alien in origin due to the circumstances reported by the subject. He also raised several questions including:

1/ What was the nature of the strange electromagnetic fields surrounding these objects while they are in the body?

2/ How is the functional metallic structure produced and what is its connection to the body's neural energy system?

3/ What was the nature of the very strange biological membrane that surrounds the metallic objects, and how does this tissue eliminate the body's natural rejection and inflammatory reaction? He also queried how messages are relayed, and who is monitoring them.

Dr Leir would have been aware of our own development of microchips and implants, and it is not known how much consideration he gave to them being a product of our own human agencies, with less-than-ethical intentions.

Over 20 years ago Budd Hopkins, who specialised in abduction research, puzzled over the fact that he had seen the analysis results of ten purported implants, and each device was composed of entirely different elements. No two were identical, making any clarification of their origin and purpose very difficult.

Implant technology has always been of vital interest and importance to the military and intelligence services of all major powers. There have been claims that experiments were also conducted on prisoners in Utah State Prison. Further claims were made that 'Rambo' chips were implanted in soldiers during the Vietnam War, and an IMI – (Intelligence-Manned-Interface) - during the Iraq war. Medical researchers have established that while very young, our neurons form numerous new connections. The brain can reshape its anatomy and is continually changing, often diverting connections for alternate purposes. It is known that 'memories' can be naturally inconsistent, or manipulated, altered and induced by external means. Is it possible that either we, or an alien intelligence, have discovered how to actually create and exploit specific connections in an individual's brain? Neuro-impulses can be transmitted to and from the brain of the unfortunate victim, who can be manipulated from afar.

It is also interesting that many years ago, it was reported that reverse engineering the crashed discs indicated that the alien himself was the 'craft control'. It was thought that the craft itself was conscious, and had an artificial intelligence which the beings on board connected to. Scientists researching neuro-compatible interfaces, have been developing similar technology using EEG signals from a pilot's brain (i.e. thoughts and consciousness) to interface directly with the craft.

Similar medical technology is being tested to help patients with various disabilities. This is the more beneficial and altruistic component of the technology. By 1996 the boffins had designed chips to be inserted into the brain and connected to the neural cortex. A team of university scientists in Atlanta, Georgia, developed a brain implant for severely disabled people. This let them communicate their thoughts directly into a computer. Two small hollow, chemical-covered, glass cones, each the size of the tip of a ballpoint pen, are placed in the brain's motor cortex. The chemicals encourage the growth of nerve cells, which once they reach the cone's interior, attach themselves to the tiny electrodes inside. When the patients have mastered the technique, they can move a cursor around a computer screen using their thoughts.

For several years scientists have been developing the neuroscientific and signal-processing foundations of synthetic telepathy, which would benefit stroke and paralysis patients. This could have immense benefit during hostilities, and nearly ten years ago the US Army invested in research to produce a more cumbersome 'Thought Helmet', enabling silent communications on the battlefield. The device harnesses a soldier's deliberately concentrated brainwaves, transmits them as radio waves, and translates them into words in the headphones of other soldiers and commanders.

Advanced technologies already enable direct links between chips and the government or corporate satellites orbiting the earth. Mobile phones, the internet, global positioning and many other digital devices incorporate similar technology. Where and how did our own governments, military and big business originally obtain this expertise? Did they have alien or other assistance with its development?

We still find sceptics ridiculing experiencers who claim implants, even ones they can produce or show on X-rays. The question still arises as to who inserted these devices and why? In 1970 NASA initiated a report to the Office of Technology Utilisation – *Implantable Biotelemetry Systems* – which also included transmissions from inside the body. They are clearly a violation of human rights, a crime against fellow beings. I don't think this overly concerned the agenda of covert agencies either then or now. Already it is mandatory to microchip our pets and more and more of earth's population are being persuaded to accept a microchip for a variety of reasons that seem plausible. Some have been implanted without their knowledge. All are in a vulnerable position.

One disturbing report was made in the British *Daily Mail* and *Daily Telegraph* in July 1996. They claimed that scientists working for British Telecom, had an 'Artificial Life Team', headed by a Dr. Chris Winter. They were developing a new microchip called the 'Soul Catcher 2025' ready for use by 2025. Designed to be implanted in the skull, just behind the eye, it would record the recipient's experiences, thoughts and sensations, which could be played back on a computer.

Dr. Winter enthusiastically explained that by combining the information with a record of the person's genes, they could recreate a person physically, emotionally and spiritually. He likened it to the black box of an aircraft, and said it would enhance communications beyond current concepts. When challenged about the ethics of using this implant, he admitted the implications, but said British Telecom needed to remain at the forefront of communications technology!!

Investigator Mike Adams claims that 'trans-humanism', which advocates uploading our minds to a computer, and 'living forever' through machines and robots, is a dangerous form of quackery, which fails to encompass our consciousness and very 'being', or soul. What is of concern, is that the high-profile expert pushing for this technology promises it will be a reality by 2045!

This leaves George Orwell's *1984* looking like a kindergarten picnic. It is not the technology itself which is the problem, rather its inevitable development and application. The potential for misuse could have far reaching consequences, too horrendous to contemplate!

I have often thought about other rarely mentioned possibilities, which should be seriously considered by all of those responsible for our safety and well-being. For example, what happens if some unfortunates end up with two competing implants from separate technologies? If a natural or military occurrence destroys or disables the controlling satellites and digital technology, all control of the hapless victims would be lost. Further, our sophisticated modern lifestyle, dependent upon artificial intelligence, would come to an abrupt halt. What if an enemy, either human or alien is able to commandeer the controlling facilities and technology?

Of more concern is the alien factor, their motives and intentions with regards to the use of implants and the manipulation of humans. I am undecided regarding the claims of some experiencers that there is a federation of galactic species, somewhat similar to our own United Nations. It is said they have a law prohibiting the interference with another planet, such as Earth.

Somehow many of our own governments and powerful corporations have been convinced we should willingly insert implants and microchips into the population. Having done the job for them, an alien intelligence would certainly possess a superior technology which could override our own primitive control mechanisms. What then...?

As with all new discoveries, implants and microchips have both a dark and light side. If our best scientific minds are still grappling with the concepts, ethics and problems, how are mere mortals expected to adapt to this new technology? Their ethical use for medicine and society could prove a true blessing. How can we protect ourselves mentally, physically and spiritually from unethical intrusions and abuse by Earthly or alien powers? It is this new facet of scientific progress which causes me great concern in the 21st century.

Quantum Biology – Quantum Thinking

"Science cannot solve the ultimate mystery of nature. And it is because in the last analysis, we ourselves are part of the mystery we are trying to solve." - Max Planck, Physicist.

Our new scientific discoveries in physics, have revealed that while explaining many mysteries they raise far more questions, and the possibility for developments both beneficial and detrimental to mankind.

Known as 'Bell's Theorem', particles at a sub-atomic level, once connected to each other, retain that connection and influence upon each regardless of how far apart they are, be it a few inches or millions of light years. They remain entangled on a 'non-local' basis and can interact via a quantum wave function. This can occur naturally, or be engineered by an advanced intelligence.

A human being, and indeed every member of the animal kingdom, is an extremely complicated living entity. Every cell of our body, brain and nervous system are interconnected on many levels, including the influences of hormones, genes and many other factors. Scientists call this continual interaction which creates and maintains life; 'phase-conjugate quantum resonance'. They have determined what many mystics already knew; that our bodies are not just a biochemical/bioelectric system, they are akin to a macroscopic quantum computer.

This has led scientists to postulate that the entangled neurons in our brains are also entangled beyond ourselves, and able to resonate and communicate to 'connected' recipients. On a basic level, this certainly explains the synchronicity between some sets of identical twins. Can it also relate to telepathy and comparable phenomena between contactees who either have similar ancestry or bloodlines, or have been physically manipulated or implanted?

Chapter Fourteen

Further Cases

Two cases I document in *Contact Down Under* are relevant to the cases I discuss here. Valerie's experience, whilst partially inter-dimensional, comprised several contacts, a probable implant, and communication with a humanoid.

In Jackie's case the contacts affected three generations of her family, starting with her father, and involved possible implants and mysterious 'blonde haired' people often described by other witnesses.

Valerie Maxwell

Valerie lives in a caravan in a country area of South Australia, which is isolated in terrain comprising flat limestone. People in caravans and tents seem to be more prone to encounters, perhaps because they are more accessible. (Sometimes solid houses do not seem to prevent a second or subsequent event.)

During the 1980s and 90s Valerie had several encounters over a fifteen-year period. Until she finally contacted me, she had tried to persuade herself that it was all in her mind. She sought help from a psychologist, but this did not prevent the phenomena re-occurring. She needed to talk to someone as she felt this would be therapeutic.

Whilst Valerie had several encounters and interactions, she only discussed the two most significant with me. I wondered if this particular intelligence had utilised some form of inter-dimensional technology in their visitations.

"It's happened on several occasions; the animals get restless and the atmosphere takes on a strange quality. If it's dark or twilight there's a clear blue glow, and looking up I see almost the whole sky filled with a blue, glowing UFO. It is faint, but cannot be ignored, and seems to be associated with my unnaturally tranquilized condition and usually short episodes of missing time.

"It was round and domed overhead. The dome looked to be high, but the base seemed to be all around me, and no higher than treetop level above the ground. It did not move, merely hovered, but stars, clouds, trees, the distant ridge etc. were visible through it and distorted, as if through a lens. The ridge appeared to be about one km away instead of three km, and the horizon, all around, appeared much closer than it really is.

"After the missing time, I would seem to experience another abrupt shift in consciousness, and continue on with what I had been doing. It simply wasn't there anymore, although the blue light persisted. I would have a temporary feeling of being unwell, and changes in my apparent 'gravity'. Sometimes there would be metallic and other substances in my mouth. They seemed benign except for the telepathy and implants."

The second incident was the first time Valerie feels she was fully conscious when she saw an alien being: "I was lying on the bed reading, when I glanced up from my book – distracted by flashes of clear blue flame-like light to my left side. Although the wall was only a foot or so away from me, it appeared to have dissolved, and I was looking into a dark space. The lights were actually a couple of metres away, about the size of tennis balls, and they silently exploded, as if to get my attention.

"On my right, instead of the body of my caravan, was a large room. It was round, with a high ceiling which curved down to meet the floor, which curved up. There were a few geometric shapes in it. The clear blue light became stronger and filled the room, which I now saw was bigger than my caravan. There were lines indicating structure, and every so often a vivid yellow-white flash. There was no atmospheric change as there had been on previous occasions.

"Beside my pillow was a man, human, average build, with dark hair. He was wearing quite ordinary street clothes, and had an almost humorous expression on his face. Thoughts were passing through my mind, although I felt tranquilised to an unnatural degree. I was thinking 'maybe it is space people', and the man replied, as if I had spoken out loud: "They're not all <u>that alien </u>looking," and pointed to the end of my bed. Standing there was a being who answered the description of the tall Greys in the abduction reports I've read.

"I was aware of being given some injections, and being assured that an implant would be removed from my head. Apparently, it was responsible for intense, intermittent irritation I'd been suffering for some months. I then went (was put) to sleep and woke up at the usual time the next morning. The irritation was somewhat relieved, although a trace remains even now.

"Up until this fully conscious experience, the previous incidents seemed to be submerged and only vaguely remembered, so I was inclined to be sceptical, and even self-ridiculing."

Jackie Hayes

Jackie rang me mid-2003, and whilst traumatised by her own experiences, was more concerned regarding three generations of her own family, especially her young children.

Her father, a quiet man, was born in 1949 and married early, becoming a father at 21. He worked as a farm manager, and the family lived on various properties over time.

"In 1982, we were living near Grafton on the NSW North Coast. Dad went missing for three weeks, and when he came home, genuinely believed he had only been away for a week. He had no memory of the other fortnight. Around about the same time, he also used to talk about several occasions when he met a six feet blond haired man with blue eyes. Once he had his wife with him, who looked almost identical, except she was female. They had weird powers. One night the horses went missing, and the man told him where they were - several valleys away!"

The next year her father and his mate were in the truck with the dog and noticed unusual noises and strange lights. They got out of the truck, saw a UFO, and remember nothing else until they found themselves back in the truck. An hour had passed!

Jackie continued: "In later years, Dad confided in me that when he was 19, he was on his motorbike, just out of Sydney. It was a very cold day, and he pulled over into an area where it felt quite warm – a 'hot spot'. He didn't remember anything else until he woke up - 'all groggy'. Locals assisted him and said: 'It must have been the UFOs in the area, we all saw them.' He admitted to dreaming of 'strange things' after that. I was rather disturbed when he told me that he thought my mother had also been abducted, but felt the beings were telling him to tell her not to worry.

"In 1998, we moved near Port Macquarie, where my father had a new manager position. One night there were unusual lights and noises. The next day we found cattle with their anus surgically cut out as well as flesh from their faces. What upset Dad the most was his favourite horse Toby, was similarly mutilated. It was horrible!"

Jackie reflected on her own childhood. When she was young, she would have dreams of flying, but also 'precognitive' dreams which were always accurate. On these occasions, she would always wake with a start at 5 a.m.

"In about 1978 we had a Christmas Eve get-together, and looked out to see lots of coloured lights in the sky. My aunty told me they were 'Santa Claus with his sleigh and reindeer'. A couple of years later, around midnight, I saw an object hovering over the neighbour's homestead. It was bigger than the house, round on the bottom, with a dome on the top and red, blue and yellow lights all around. It was totally silent when it moved away, and I tried to tell myself it must have been a dream."

Jackie then discussed her adult life. She married her first husband in 1988, when she was 18. Just after having her first baby, she woke to see tall figures at the end of her bed. She admits it may have just been a dream, but she was very frightened at the time. They were like ghosts, and had 'grim reaper' type hoods.

Everything was fine until 2001. She was 31, had divorced and remarried. (Her age at the time interested me, as I know several female childhood experiencers to have follow-up visitations in their early thirties.) In July/August she saw an unusual blue light in the sky on a few nights. It would hover for quite a long period then suddenly depart – leaving an 'aura' around the house. The neighbours also noticed this.

"Around about the same time I went to sleep in a sarong one night, and woke up to find blood on the front and back. I was really scared, couldn't think of a logical explanation, and got my mother to come over and stay. In September I heard an explosion and saw a light overhead in the sky. Suddenly my one year old son was floating in the air next to my shoulder! I grabbed him – terrified – and held him tight. What was happening – and who would believe me?"

In 2003, more abnormal events started affecting the whole family. Early in the year, her sister and her husband, who lived at Peakhurst in Sydney, woke to find their bedroom bathed with red light. At first, they thought there was a fire outside, but when they looked, there was what could only be described as a 'fireball' hovering nearby. Her sister recalled a similar incident in Picton two years before.

By March, Jackie was feeling so much discomfort in one ear she went to the doctor. The specialist couldn't see anything blocking it, but a catscan showed, deep down, a five-centimetre object. It was split in two halves, like a miniature 'brain'. She has a terror of needles, and didn't get it removed.

"In June, my father and his girlfriend heard a 'beeping' and a noise like a revving truck. By 3 a.m. they opened the window to look. The noise was still there, but nothing to see except a blue light some distance away."

While this is consistent with many other reports, it may have a logical explanation. Jackie, however, had further unusual happenings to contend with.

"My fourteen-year-old daughter told me recently that when she was eleven, she had a dream that a little man, with black eyes 'like an owl', had put a 'thing' in her. She said that later she picked the roof of her mouth, and something came out. Now, at 14, she is getting nose bleeds and had a similar dream. The man was there, with the stars behind him, and he told her not to be afraid."

Jackie fears for her children. She and her sister discussed their shared feeling that perhaps they were sexually interfered with as children. There no known culprit within the family, and neither has any memory of any abuse. They concluded it must have happened in their sleep, but both knew, in their hearts, that it was the strange, elusive beings who had haunted them.

(As a researcher, Jackie's case interested me. She was not aware that I heard of a similar situation, in the 1960s, from in Bunyip, Victoria. In *Contact Down Under*, Kasey Cook's family had several UFO sightings and the landing of a strange craft in their back paddock. There had been unusual blonde haired people in the area. She and her siblings had ongoing experiences and 'hidden memories,' and her father had gone missing for three weeks and could only remember one.)

Alien Healing

Another humanoid contact occurred nearly 90 years ago in the upper Blue Mountains, west of Sydney, and like most similar contacts was never reported. Belinda was a member of a large animal rescue organisation, and her entire home, in a southern suburb of Sydney, had been turned into an animal shelter. I used to volunteer there, two or three times a week, to help with the care of her little 'waifs'. It was a peaceful suburb, relatively crime free at the time. I noticed she would never go out at night without her large watch dog, and I asked her, who or what was she afraid of?

She hesitated for a moment: "I think you'll believe me – many wouldn't. In 1929, when I was twelve, I lived at Blackheath in the Blue Mountains. I had terminal cancer. My father had been a medic in the First World War, and all the doctors he had served with became top specialists in the Sydney hospitals. They all examined me, trying to cure 'their little mate's daughter'. All confirmed the diagnosis – there was nothing they could do."

Belinda was silent for a while: "I didn't have to go to school anymore. I was quite happy about that, and every day I would accompany my father to his piggery near the Jenolan Caves. When I was fifteen the doctors suddenly realised that not only was I 'alive and kicking' – my cancer was gone!"

She hesitated for a few seconds: "They said I was in remission, it must have been all the fresh air and sunshine. It wasn't that. One night I was walking home alone from a Girl Guides meeting. This flying saucer type thing came overhead and the next I knew I was inside. They were nice people, just like you and me. I don't remember much except lying on some kind of table. Before I found myself back on the street they told me they had cured me of the cancer, but if I told anyone about it, my illness would come back." (There have been other cases documented where a contactee was healed of a life-threatening illness – but warned not to talk about it.)

Despite having little formal education, Belinda became very gifted and intelligent, contributing to society as a volunteer, qualified veterinary nurse. She married an engineer, raised three children, and was quite healthy until just after she confided in me. Shortly afterwards she was diagnosed with bowel cancer, which modern surgery rectified. I wondered about her disobeying the 'do not tell' condition, and vowed to keep her secret for the remaining twenty years of her life.

Upon reflection, I wondered if there was more to Belinda's story. If her healing by the nice strangers was all there was to it, why was she afraid to go out alone at night? I did not know her ancestry, but her father had been in the military at the time of her conception. Her husband was an engineer, involved in 'classified' projects, and also interested in my UFO research without ever articulating a point of view.

She bore an uncanny resemblance to the 'other women', and had spent much of her life trying to assist animals and the ecology. Further, her brother was also exceptionally intelligent, and a member of Mensa. Was there more to her family – her father's military history, the exceptional intelligence of both Belinda and her brother, and her experience with humanoids? I suppose I will never know the full story.

The vast majority of the generational cases I work with had their families' origins in Western Europe, which sometimes presented a problem with more in-depth investigations.

Natalie

I have known Natalie for several years, and it took her some time to confide her experiences. Natalie herself is highly intelligent and artistic, and she positively didn't want any publicity.

She was born and lived near Turin, northern Italy in 1962. (Turin itself has a history of UFO sightings and rumours of secret interactions with aliens.) Her grandfather had been in the Navy in World War 1, and her father, who had been a young lad in World War 2, once confided a strange experience from that time;

It was in Northern Italy, when he remembers being in his bedroom, and seeing a very funny looking man. He was rather skinny and seemed to be wearing, a 'top hat'.

Her heritage included French/Italian descent, and she could trace her ancestry back to the Knights Templar. While much has been said about the Knights Templar, who have existed for centuries, it is not their hidden valuables that they will die to protect. The real treasures they are said to protect is an important revelation, a secret knowledge.

Natalie had always shown a compulsive interest in, and in some strange way, felt an inexplicable connection to the rumoured long-term underground base and presence of extraterrestrials around Turin. After she had given me all the details of the events which had affected her life, I asked if she had ever heard of the 'Amicizia'. She hesitated at first, then confirmed that she had heard of them.

Her mother was psychic to the extent that Natalie was always wary of upsetting her. In about 1972 she told Natalie she had seen a typical UFO through the window, and thought she must have been dreaming, until she saw a report in the paper the next day regarding the same sighting in America.

Natalie herself is unable to recall any of her childhood before the age of six, when she was involved in a car accident and rendered unconscious for a short period of time.

When she was fifteen, Natalie was out in the garden at about 5.30 p.m. when she saw two strange objects hovering over the clothesline: "They were both a grey metallic colour, shaped like dumb-bells. We could only see the undersides, but each side of the dumb-bell had what looked like a door, and was about 20 metres long, with the joining piece in-between, about eight metres long. My mother and two sisters ran out of the house, and we all watched for about ten to fifteen minutes.

"The two objects then flew away, speeding up as they left. We didn't think anyone would believe us, but the next day at school everybody was talking about it. One of the kids said his father worked for the military, and they had tracked it on radar.

Natalie's next encounter, two years later, was not so pleasant: "I had gone for a holiday with my grandmother into the Italian countryside. I had a separate bedroom, and woke up suddenly one night. I have these vague memories – don't know if it was a nightmare or not. There were two short men, with 'capes' over their heads, at the end of my bed. They were pulling the blankets off me from below, I was terrified." After that Natalie had a lot of problems with her menstruation, and was diagnosed with a polycystic right ovary –so common in my other female contactees.

By 1990 the family moved to Australia, and she was living in Liverpool in Sydney with her husband. Her doctor had announced that she was pregnant, but although everything seemed quite normal, he did a routine ultrasound at about three months. At no time had she suffered any blood loss, but the baby was 'gone', leaving a torn umbilical cord still attached to her womb. "I don't know if this is even significant, but at about the same time I saw a ten metre white light above the park in front of our house. My husband was too scared to even look!"

Natalie's marriage ended, and she has never had any children. She later moved to the Central Coast, north of Sydney, where she found a new boyfriend, David, who had more spiritual, New Age tendencies. She and David were together for a year: "It was strange, the first time we met, we looked at each other across the room, and there was an instant bond and attraction.

"He and his mates used to play music, especially the drums. They would go to the 'Egyptian Glyphs' at Kariong to play; they said it was a spiritual, psychic place. One night we were cuddling-up on top of the Skillion at Terrigal when I could feel the railings vibrating under my hand. I thought the vibrations were coming from under the headland, but could feel a breeze on my head.

"I looked up and noticed a grey see-through shape in the sky overhead. It was really close, and made a whirring engine-type sound then suddenly, with a loud clang went up and away really quickly. David freaked out and said 'he could see it, but not see it."

Like many others, Natalie had also seen the black cloud, with lightning coming out from all sides, over Forresters Beach at Bateau Bay, and noted the same black helicopters circling, as had been reported by other witnesses. (See *Contact Down Under*.)

She had also seen UFOs from a distance a couple of times. Once in 2005 when a large orange ball went up and down over the houses in Bateau Bay. It was there for 10-15 minutes, and the neighbours called the police. In early 2015 a small grey metallic domed disc was in the sky over Newcastle, about midday. It shot off when a fighter plane appeared and gave pursuit. Another summer morning, she was staying with a friend, and had got up early at six to do some ironing: "I suddenly got a strange feeling, and then her kids who'd been surfing, came racing in the door. They were really freaking out and said there was a massive UFO over the sea, which had taken off as they were running away."

I was intrigued with Natalie's experiences as she, and her family, had a great deal in common with the other women, and she had commented on her mother's secret interest in UFOs. If this was generational, had it started with her mother or even earlier? Further, Natalie had felt compelled to research the secret history of Turin, as it related to covert UFO groups and rumours of underground alien contacts.

She also reported strange dreams in both 1995 and 2000. In both she was running and hiding from a war-type scenario, and included the same beings dressed in black with high-tech guns. In the first dream, she detected lights and a humming at the side of her head. In the second, she was with her sister, and had a bad feeling in her head. This time when she woke up all the power in the house had gone.

Natalie's case, and some of the details also affecting her mother and sister, was quite intriguing. She does not to wish to be hypnotically regressed, but is on her own quest to gain a better understanding of herself and the world in general.

There are many other cases of strange craft, with humanoid occupants, which have been investigated, but we are unable to follow-up on any subsequent events or effects.

Italy – the 'Amicizia'

Natalie's case is only one of several similar incidents in Italy in late 1962 early 1963. She did know about the 'Amicizia', (Friendship), which was the name used for a very secretive 40-year interaction between normal citizens and humanoid aliens. To the best of investigators' knowledge, it began in 1956, however it might have been occurring much earlier. There is evidence of similar groups in Switzerland and other neighbouring areas, where the same terminology was used; 'Amitie' in France and 'Freundschaft' in Germany and Austria. (Given the still centralised area of these particular groups I have wondered how long they were actually there, and about any possible connection, good or bad, with the Third Reich who were the occupying force, during World War 2.) It was suggested that after the US rejected their offer for help in 1954, these aliens, (who were in opposition to another more hostile race visiting Earth) decided to convey their message of peace and morality to the general public.

Umberto Visani documented this situation, saying it did not just involve a small group of individuals, but people of varying walks in life from professionals to students and housewives. Further, there was ample evidence at the time, including recordings, photos and videos. In 2009 Professor Stefano Breccia, was apparently involved, and wrote a book *Mass Contacts* which details the accounts of Bruno Sammaciccia, the leader of the Italian group. Sammaciccia was a prominent Italian theologian and psychologist, and he entrusted his notes to Breccia, to be published after his death in 2003. Other books and articles have also surfaced, but usually after the supposed 'departure' of the visitors and the demise of the witnesses.

One observation which sounded familiar to me was that Breccia claimed that one of the Visitors told him, in 1967, that there was another star, as yet undiscovered, fairly close to our Solar System. (It reminded me of what the 'Khan' had told Ruth, and the multiple reports over the last few years, that there was a large body near the Solar System which some considered may be a brown dwarf binary companion to our Sun.)

Breccia said that while some of these beings were much shorter or taller than their human counterparts, others were essentially the same as us, integrating and living incognito in society. It seems that they have been here for a long time, and some are still among us. He claimed that they are so closely related to us genetically that they can, and probably have interbred.

In his book *Alien Base* Timothy Good discusses a case reported by the Italian Magazine *Domenica della Sera,* (translated by Gordon Creighton), where Italian engineer, Luciano Galli, said that in the late 1950s he met extraterrestrials who took him for a ride in their craft.

He was walking back to work from lunch, when a car pulled up, and a tall, dark man, with normal features, a moustache and very dark eyes, got out and offered him a lift. He had seen this man, who wore a business suit and spoke perfect Italian, several times around the town, and once, when he tried to speak to him he suddenly disappeared. Galli described him as having 'a face like an angel in plain clothes'.

There was another man in the car, and after Galli got in, they travelled 57 kilometres from Bolgna to the Croara Ridge, where there was a shining grey flying saucer hovering about six feet off the ground, and they all entered via a metal cylinder which 'came out'. Once aboard he could see what he described as a pilot's cabin with instruments and panels all around.

They seemed to be flying through space until they arrived at what Galli described as a giant dirigible, (I assume to be a mother ship.) At one end were six openings – each opening divided into six smaller 'cubicles' – out of which small flying discs were seen coming and going. Once inside the large craft, Galli could see about four to five hundred men and women, all very friendly and good-looking, walking around or standing in the hangers.

After being given a tour of the spaceship his companion took him back to the same spot on Croara Ridge.

Italian researchers Fiorino and Cabassi reported on another case in Bologna, a few years later, at 8.45 p.m. on 30 December 1962. The witness did not want any publicity, and had only come forward due to another experiencer being ridiculed.

He was 27 at the time, and walking down an isolated street, when he heard a hissing sound. To his left, over a park, he noticed a nine-meter, inverted saucer-shape object hovering about eight meters above the ground. It was metallic grey, with no visible portholes, and had a dome, around which several coloured lights were rotating.

He hid behind a tree, and the craft descended about ten meters away. A door opened, a stairway came down, and two 'human-looking' beings came down the stairs onto the ground. They were about 1.7 meters tall, with dark complexions, shining eyes and short dark hair. They were wearing close fitting yellow overalls, with a dark belt and a small rectangular box at the side.

The witness moved, and they noticed him. One of the beings pointed at him, with outstretched arm and forefinger, and spoke to him in an unknown language. The pair looked at each other, then returned to, and entered the craft, which took off with a hiss as soon as the door closed. Once it reached an altitude of about 75 meters, it moved horizontally to the south west and disappeared.

Unfortunately, this occurred over 50 years ago, and we have little chance of obtaining further details.

New Zealand *Xenolog* Number 107 details a 1952 report from near Mt. Etna, Italy. The witness, Eugenio Siragusa, was waiting for a bus, early one morning in Martyr's Square, Catania, when a white, mercury-coloured, luminous object appeared in the sky. As it zig-zagged and rapidly descended towards him, he could see it resembled a spinning-top.

When it hovered overhead, a brilliant ray left the object, and "completely pierced me!" At that moment, his fears turned to 'indescribable serenity'. The ray shrank back into the craft, which then moved left and right in an arc across the sky before disappearing. For the next ten years, his personality changed and he developed extrasensory perceptions, and telepathy.

One night in 1962 he felt compelled to go to nearby Mount Etna. As he was driving up towards Mount Manfre, it felt as if his car was being guided up the mountain by some superior force. He stopped his car at the side of the road, and as he walked along the path he saw two silhouettes on top of the isolated hill. They were two tall, well-built men, with long blonde hair and 'soft' features. They wore silver space-suits, with gold armlets around their wrists and ankles, a luminous belt and a strange metallic chest-plate.

At first, he was terrified, but one directed a green beam at him, from an object he had in his hand. Immediately he felt a sense of calm, and the men spoke to him in Italian, saying: "We have been waiting for you, record in your memory what we are going to tell you."

He was given a message to pass on to our leaders, similar to what other contactees of the day had been told: We must stop our warlike tendencies, especially nuclear weapons, and practice justice, freedom, love and fraternity to all. They mentioned being part of an 'Intergalactic Confederation', and said the 'Cosmic Counsel' condemns the people of Earth for their inhuman behaviour. Eugene heeded the message and dedicated the rest of his life to furthering their aims.

He had several other meetings with his mentors, who reiterated their messages, alluding to us ignoring previous missionaries being sent from highly evolved humanoids several light years away.

France – Freda Hollis

Freda was born in France, just after World War 2, and in 1973 was a ballet dancer of some prominence. She saw a daylight disc near the Bastille in Paris, but didn't recall anything strange about the event at the time. Later that year her dance company was in Cannes. One Sunday night she woke up at 6 p.m. thinking it was Saturday. She had 'lost' 24 hours but had vague memories of 'incredible men'.

This in itself does not indicate a UFO experience, and could easily have a much more mundane earthly explanation, except it was about the same time she unexpectedly conceived her daughter Jenna.

In 1979, she was experiencing problems with her ovaries, and was flabbergasted when the doctors told her she had obviously undergone prior surgery on her ovaries. This wasn't possible. Then she thought of that 'missing time' episode.

"While an inner voice kept telling me 'don't remember', like some kind of subliminal suggestion, I had flashbacks of doctors or spirits experimenting on me. They were telling me what they were doing, and spoke of putting in 'soul stitches' and said I had good hips and ribs. In 1980, my young daughter woke in fright and claimed I was hovering mid-air above her bed. I have little memory of this except for seeing Greys with big eyes telling me to go with them."

Both Freda and Jenna have developed heightened psychic abilities, and in later years both sighted a daylight disc with pulsating lights. Without hypnosis, which Freda had rejected, she can recall no more about how her blossoming career was cut short by the unwelcome visitation and subsequent pregnancy.

Spain – 'Julio'

In addition to Italy and France, Spain was also reporting unusual humanoid contacts. Antonio Ribera documented extensive research into the experience of 'Julio'. Early on the morning of 5 February 1978, Julio had set off to Soria Province for a little hunting, and was accompanied by his dog 'Mus'.

For about six minutes, near Boadilla del Monte, Julio's car was followed by an unidentified light, after which a voice seemed to direct him to stop at a roadside restaurant. He did this, but after half an hour nobody else entered. The waiter, however, seemed 'odd', and during their conversation recommended a good spot for hunting near Medinaceli.

After he left he drove for a while, but turned onto a small country road, about 15 kilometres from his intended destination. His car came to a halt, the engine, radio and lights all stopped working. It was 6.40 a.m. by then, and as he grabbed his Winchester and got out of the car, Mus started barking.

Two humanoid figures appeared on the road, and Julio felt surprisingly relaxed. They seemed to be communicating telepathically, and invited him to accompany them. He realised they were not from Earth. He didn't recall anything else until he and Mus were returned to his car, which now worked perfectly. It was bright sunlight, two hours later. Two of his shotgun shells were missing, and the dog had syringe marks.

Later, hypnosis was conducted by a psychiatrist in the presence of other doctors, psychologists, and researchers, who all considered his experience to be genuine.

The beings were just under six feet tall, and of general human appearance except they had no hair on their bodies. (Unusual for Spain, but not for other races in the world.) They wore one-piece bright green coveralls, with a buckle at the waist, and a hood covering their heads.

Julio and his dog walked with them for a couple of minutes to a mushroom-shaped object, which was hovering, motionless above a field. They entered a cylinder which had descended, and rose into the craft, as if on an elevator. The room inside had a metallic floor, tables, chairs, lights, panels, and screens. Julio's diagram strongly resembles descriptions and drawings of other experiencers I have interviewed.

Communicating telepathically, they asked permission to take a blood sample from Mus and then moved a black crystal over him, which he thought might be some kind of X-ray device. They then repeated the same procedure with Julio. He heard a loud sharp hissing noise, and his captors immediately sat down, and started talking in a harsh, monosyllabic language to an older character who had appeared on a screen.

Until that time, Julio had engaged in friendly telepathic communication with his captors, but after the conversation with their leader the previous friendly interaction ceased, and he felt he was being treated like a laboratory subject. He was taken to another room, where, after being paralysed, a metallic golden ball moved over his body. Coloured threads came out and 'penetrated all his natural orifices.' Many other unpleasant tests were performed, and he was told they were taking samples of liquid and tissue from his body.

It still wasn't over. Julio and Mus were strapped into special seats, where they were subjected to some form of gravitational test, where initially they could hardly breathe or see. They then began to float. Julio could see a vision of the earth, moon and stars through the window. They seemed to orbit the Earth, and after the aliens tied them back to their seats, experienced the same gravitational forces as they came back to land.

When asked their reason for coming, they told him a similar message about our destroying our own environment, commenting that the same thing had happened, centuries before, in their own world.

Russia – close contacts?

In the 1990s Rosemary Decker met Russian researcher Bhulautsen, and a couple of his colleagues, who told her that most Russian and Siberian contact claims were of a friendly or neutral nature, and abductions very rare. (I personally doubt if they were speaking the truth. Both Russia and China have kept this information under tight wraps, only detailing much more innocuous events.)

I am also friends with an older Russian, from Siberia, who alluded to a similar group to the 'Amicizia'. Alien interaction, sometimes extended high into the government, but was kept clandestine, and couldn't be divulged to anyone outside of those involved. In early 2017, as I was writing this book, she was very excited as a relative had seen another very large, spectacular craft in Novosibirsk.

In the mid-1970s, despite a ban on publications discussing UFOs, Professor Ziegel of the Moscow Aviation Institute released a copy of a lecture which claimed that over the previous 25 years 300 sightings had been recorded in Russia. Of course, this was only the tip of the iceberg.

At the end of the 20th century, when Russia became less totalitarian, some citizens and researchers were able to discuss these issues to a limited extent. They believed that there had also been UFO crashes in the Soviet Union, and there were secret facilities back-engineering them, as was the case in other countries.

Gorbachev said little on the matter, but did confirm UFOs were a serious matter, and had to be studied. Lieutenant-Colonel Marina Popovich, a former test-pilot with a doctorate in flight technology, later confirmed many thousands of UFO sightings had been reported in Russia.

Gordon Creighton, editor of the *Flying Saucer Review* (1990, Vol 35-3), published his translation of a report which appeared in a Russian industrial journal *Lesnaya Promyshlennost*: In June 1966, Gennadiy was fishing in the Kolyvanskiy Lakes near Novosibirsk in Siberia. He suddenly realised all of nature's sounds around him had gone silent, and a field mouse had crept between his knees, as if trying to hide. He noticed a light, and looking around, could see a machine hovering two to three metres above the ground, no more than ten metres away.

He said it was about six to eight meters long and two meters high, shaped like a 'flattened droplet' and made of a shining, silvery-coloured material. It emitted a faint, dull luminescence. As soon as he spotted it, part of the machine silently 'moved back', (I assume he may have meant a type of sliding door opened), and he could see three seats and a dark control panel divided into squares. There were three men standing in the opening.

He said they were "just like us, everything about them seemed just as it is with us." They were wearing smart casual dress, and of 'fine physique'. One, who appeared to be the eldest, was standing to the front, and two slighter taller men stood just behind. They had short, fair hair, normal straight noses, and tranquil, 'benevolent-looking' faces. Gennadiy noted they had an air of "quality – superiority."

They said: "You won't get away from us so easily ... Don't be afraid." When he heard them speak, it seemed like a mixture of sound and telepathy. He had the impression they were 'looking at him through his cranium'. They assured him he wasn't asleep or hallucinating, and invited him to ask them questions. The contact lasted about 30 minutes and all three communicated, but the answers were not always specific, and at times they even argued.

They claimed they were the 'Knowers' who are investigating the world, and are with 'you' always and it was not necessary to seek them out. If mankind had a very strong desire to do so, it would be possible to alter the biological program for the life-span. They also advised he should not worry about mankind perishing as it was their job to make sure it didn't happen.

Gennaldiy realised they were skilfully avoiding direct answers to some questions, and when he asked about the future, one said: "You are tired. You need to rest." He closed his eyes for a moment, and then opened them again. The craft was gone!

Gennaldiy did not speak about this for over 20 years, fearing people would think he was a 'madman.' The incident did not change his life, but Gennaldiy had always felt that one day his secret would be of use. (It is also of interest that this occurred in Siberia, which is an ideal location for concealed bases.)

United States – Robert Baez

There are countless reports of contact from all parts of both North and South America, many of which come from the USA.

Robert, lived in St. Louis Illinois, was born in 1948, and had served in the US Coast Guard 1970/71. His case was investigated by Leo Wicklinski from MUFON.

At about 10 p.m. on 14 November 1973, Robert was home alone, when he got an inexplicable urge to go outside. It was a cold night, but he walked to the end of the street and saw a huge, brilliant ball of yellow light approaching from the south. As he stepped into the middle of the road, to get a better look, yellow light enveloped him, creating a warm sensation.

He was slightly fearful when, still inside the ball of light, he suddenly found himself seated in a comfortable arm chair, in a large, dome-shaped room. He experienced a sense of weightlessness, and also felt that he was being watched.

Suddenly a male voice came out of nowhere: "Robert, do not be afraid, we are your brothers. We do not wish to harm you. Please feel calm." He asked who this was, what did they want? In circumstances similar to the Dan Fry case, the disembodied voice went on to explain they knew all about Robert and his family. It was through him, and many others like him, they wished to make contact.

He asked where he was, and the voice replied, "You are with us in this vast spaceship. We are now travelling through space, and we will return you as soon as we complete our findings. Afterwards you may tell others of this experience, and you will be contacted again at a later time. What has happened to you has happened to others, and will continue to happen until we are sure that our brothers will receive you, and others like you, as we receive them. We mean no harm, and want to save them from their own epitaph so we could be reunited again."

Robert was returned back to the empty street, feeling very weak. The light had gone, and upon his return home he rang the local Air Force Base, who referred him to the police, who took his report.

About a month later, on 13 December, he was sitting alone, listening to music at about 9.30 p.m. when his doorbell rang. There was a man outside, about 30 years old, six feet two inches, Caucasian, wearing a conservative blue suit and tie, with a dark felt 'snap-brim' hat and a black attaché case. He thought he was an insurance man or similar, and invited him in.

After telling him he should quit smoking the stranger said, "I am your second contact, Robert, did you tell anyone of your experience?"

Robert explained that no-one seemed to believe him, and the man said that regardless they were here to help him and others like him when the need arose. "We are walking along and among people of this Earth, trying to pick up the fallen ones. We want you to know there is an eternal energy and you people are all part of it." He continued by telling Robert to go on contacting others regardless of the sceptics.

Baez reported another encounter with the alleged UFO occupants at 9 a.m. in February 1974, during an unscheduled stay at a motel in Missouri. When Wicklinski tried to contact Robert the following September, he had disappeared without a trace, moved out of his home, disconnected the phone, and left his job. Nobody knew where he was.

United States – Betty and Barney Hill

This case is probably one of the best-known and researched cases in UFO history. Betty and Barney, who appeared to be genuine, intelligent and credible witnesses, have been subjected to so much unwarranted ridicule and disbelief, despite a great amount of evidence substantiating their claims.

Betty and Barney Hill were driving home through the White Mountains in New Hampshire at 10 p.m. on 9 September 1961. They had noticed an unusual light for some time during their journey, when they had stopped a couple of times for their dog, Delsey. The last time they pulled up it was much closer, a large 80-feet, glowing white disc hovering very low over a nearby field. Barney, taking his binoculars with him, walked a short way towards it. Betty lost sight of him in the dark, and was trying to call him back.

As Barney ventured closer, he could see about six figures, wearing black uniforms, through the windows, which were curved around the disc. He realised he had been seen, but found himself unable to move. The craft slowly descended, extending its 'fins' and a ladder-like structure from underneath. Barney forced himself to race back to the car, and they sped off down the road.

They then noticed an irregular beeping noise and vibration from the boot, and both felt dazed, with a tingling sensation. Barney was still driving, didn't know why he made a left-hand turn, and was eventually lost. After a while their 'awareness' returned, and they could still hear the beeping noise, but it was regular. They were now some 35 or more miles away, and didn't reach home until 5 a.m., two hours later than expected.

There were several anomalies on the car, Barney had some odd physical marks, and Betty suffered ongoing nightmares. They notified the police about the unusual craft and occupants, and were later interviewed by an Air Force officer who noted all details, and told them there had been similar reports. They were interviewed at length by a NICAP investigator, who although sceptical of any reports which included beings, concluded they were telling the truth.

By mid-1962 Barney had problems around his groin. His health had deteriorated to the extent he was referred to an eminent psychiatrist who used hypnosis to treat psychological disorders. The doctor was sceptical, but individual sessions with both Barney and Betty indicated they were taken from the car by several men, all dressed alike, and carried into the craft.

Barney had been taken into what looked like a pale blue hospital operating room, put on a table, and a 'cup' put over his groin. He got off the table, feeling happy and relieved, and was guided back to the car.

Betty recalled being taken from the car and calling out to Barney, who didn't pay any attention. One of the men spoke to her, in what seemed like a foreign accent, saying: "Don't be afraid, we are not going to hurt you." She recalled walking to the craft and two of the men taking her by the arms when she didn't want to go in. They were taken up a corridor, and then separated, the man explaining: "No, we only have equipment enough in one room to do one person at a time. If we took you both in the same room it would take too long."

Another man came up, pushed up the sleeve of her dress, and using what looked like a big microscope and 'letter opener' scraped flakes of skin off her arm, and put them on a piece of plastic. He also took a sample from inside her ear, plus a sliver of her fingernail and a couple of strands of hair. (This suggests either a health or DNA check, or both).

The 'doctor' then examined her eyes, teeth, throat and ear, then touched her all over with needles attached to wires. Afterwards they got her to remove her dress and lie on a table. She became concerned when they inserted a long needle into her navel, which was quite painful. She didn't believe them when they told her it was a pregnancy test. It seems that at all times they conversed in English, and as in many other cases, the leader put his hands over her eyes when she became distressed at the needle. The pain went away, but she was sore later. Betty disputed that it was a pregnancy test, but he didn't respond.

She was told she had to wait for Barney before returning to the car, and in the meantime asked if she could take something to prove the event. After finding a large book, with strange text which ran up and down, rather than across the page, the leader said she could have it, only to change his mind before she left, as the others objected. They felt it best if Betty didn't remember anything, but added that the Hills could find them again if they wanted to.

Betty was taken to another room where she was shown a map of the cosmos, and talked with the other beings who showed her various trade routes, but avoided pinpointing their own home planet. The map had been rolled-up, and was an oblong 2-dimensional depiction of star systems. After hypnosis Betty recalled a 3-dimensional hologram, which she was able to draw. It contained 16 precisely drawn dots of varying size, connected by solid, dotted or dashed lines.

The Hills were taken back to the car separately. It is unclear who was returned first but they found their dog, Delsey, frightened but unharmed.

In 1966 an Ohio school teacher, Marjorie Fish, was fascinated with the idea of the star map and wanted to see if she could match it with known cosmology. She persisted, making a total of 26 3-dimensional models of nearby star systems before she found an exact match to Betty's map. This only became possible after a new Catalogue of Nearby Stars was published in 1969, when she concluded the map used Zeta Reticuli as the base-star start point. Her findings were verified by the astronomy department of Ohio State University. Betty's map had been drawn years before these additional stars had been documented! Recently, others have disputed Marjorie's findings; they still believe the validity of Betty's map, but due to later discoveries in astronomy, consider it relates to a different part of the galaxy.

Brad Steiger wrote about an interesting case from a small Arkansas community, where Jo Ann had a boarding house. Ernie had rented a room, he was a nice man, but he seemed a little strange, and never divulged any personal details. After getting himself a truck and a job, he moved out.

One night Jo Ann saw him at the foot of her bed, and when he motioned to her, she followed him without waking her husband or son. He apologised, but insisted on blindfolding her before they drove for miles. They got out, and he led her a short way and up some steps before removing the blindfold.

She found herself in some sort of laboratory aboard a spaceship, with entities in long, dark hooded cloaks around her. They put her on a long table, placed wires on various parts of her body, and appeared to be examining her. One of the entities asked Ernie how come he didn't know Jo Ann couldn't have any more children due to previous surgery?

Ernie answered: "No, I came to know her and her son. I thought she had the potential to be a good specimen for artificial insemination. I thought she would be an excellent mother for our child."

Jo Ann was released, and taken back home blindfolded. The next morning she wondered if it had been a vivid dream. A few days later government officials investigated a circular burned area on the other side of the local airfield. The night of her 'dream' a car had been taken from a rental agency, driven 25 miles, and then left on the tarmac. The ignition key had been removed from the still locked rental-car building. That same night Ernie vanished; his truck was left abandoned on a city street, and three years later had not been claimed from local police who had towed it away.

Chapter Fifteen

Leesa

I first met Leesa and her family, who lived on the coast, south of Sydney, in the late 1980s. She was unsure who she could turn to, and over the years, as we began to unravel her strange experiences and hidden memories, we became firm friends.

I was privileged to get to know her parents, and in addition to learning of the experiences and events, I started to investigate Leesa's family history to determine any common denominators with other witnesses. The crest of one of her forbears has the words *Sic Itur Ad Astra* – 'This is the Way to the Stars.'

I had to trace back a couple more generations to find three different ancestors who were *fleur-de-lis* bloodline, one descended from Norman roots. This made me think perhaps I was wrong as to this being the only common denominator among the witnesses, although one branch of their family also came from near The Wrekin in Britain's West Midlands.

Grandfather

Leesa's grandfather, James was born in 1905 and became a shipwright. He spent time, between World Wars, in the Delta Division of Papua, where he and his brother worked building boats for the missions. They returned after several months when they found themselves in the middle of massacres between the coastal natives and the Guku tribes from the interior.

During World War 2 he served in 3-Squadron Australian Flying Corp and later flew out of Bankstown Aerodrome on aerial surveys. He was a member of the local Masonic Lodge. One of his aunts disappeared without trace, at a very young age, sometime in the mid-1800s.

Grandmother

Leesa was very close to her grandmother, but she was never told of Leesa or her mother Linda's unusual experiences: "As an adult my grandmother used to joke with me (well at least I thought she was joking), about spacemen coming to visit her in the night. We both used to chuckle light-heartedly and I was hesitant to ask if she *really* meant it. I began to wonder if she was testing the waters to see how I would react.

"We were very close, and similar in nature. She died in 1997, so I shall never have the opportunity to ask her if she was also an experiencer."

Father

Just like Elizabeth, Lydia, Vera and the other women, Leesa's father and all his family were aviators. He also took her out, as a small child, to look at the stars.

"He carried me out and pointed to the myriads of tiny pinpoints that made up the Milky Way", she reminisced. "The stunning beauty of the night sky just took my breath away, I loved them even then. When I was only a toddler, I remember lying on my tummy on the floor in front of the television, watching very intently as Neil Armstrong walked on the moon. Despite my young age I was fascinated, knowing there were other worlds out there, within our reach."

Leesa also wondered if there was any connection to an unusual amulet – a family heirloom. "While I was reading some literature on ancient cultures I saw a drawing of an emblem, a Winged Serpent and thought 'Where have I seen this before?' Then I remembered an item, which had been in my father's side of the family for over 100 years, long before my grandfather brought a few artefacts back from New Guinea. I don't know its origin, but when I discovered it in Dad's dressing table drawer it was black with age, so caked with grime you couldn't make out any pictures on it.

"I don't know exactly what it is, but it is in segments, made of something similar to bronze, joined together in links. I worked on it, scrubbing and soaking it in vinegar, and then from under all the dirt came these beautiful Egyptian images, on both sides of each link, and also the Winged Serpent. It was like a type of déjà-vu."

Mother and birth

Leesa's mother, Linda, had devoted much of her life to her family and grandchildren. She was always a gifted and intelligent child, and her abilities continued throughout her life. In her younger days, she had acted in Gilbert and Sullivan operettas in Sydney. She wrote short stories and poetry, and won many literary awards. She always fought against injustice and in addition to many pets of her own, actively supported Animal Welfare organisations.

Leesa's birth was a miracle in itself, as her mother Linda had a womb 'ripped to shreds' with what they thought to be fibroids, but they really never knew what was responsible. (We can only speculate as to the cause of this unusual damage.) While doctors considered she would never be able to carry a baby, she gave birth to Leesa, nearly five weeks late in 1966.

She had displayed psychic abilities since childhood and was passionate about spiritual pursuits and the environment. I was privileged to know Linda for several years before her recent death, and she confided some clairvoyant instances when she saw the spirits of departed family and pets.

One instance however, was much different, and left her quite shaken. She had just slipped into bed, beside her sleeping husband. Their elderly cat Samantha was at their feet, and Benji the dog near the door.

She was startled and fascinated to see a tall column of glowing light, which lit up the room: "I had a feeling all the time that there was a being within the column of light, although I only saw a slowly moving light. I watched as it slowly moved from the edge of the curtain and along the foot of the bed. As it passed the dressing table, there was no reflection in the mirror.

"I was not dreaming or hallucinating. Samantha was staring and following it with her gaze, then rose to her feet, fur bristling on end, hissed and growled as if faced by a dangerous enemy. As the light passed through our bedroom door Benji ran down the hall yelping in terror. I raced after him, to find him cowering wide-eyed and shaking in his favourite place of retreat.

"After I switched on the hall light I could no longer see the 'illuminated column', but from then on Benji refused to sleep in our bedroom, and always went to his safe place."

Along with Leesa in later years, Linda researched the long-lost ancient truths of civilisation and humanity.

Leesa

Those around Leesa referred to her as a gifted child, and the offspring of a gifted mother. She was advanced for children of her age, preferred adult company, and displayed a keen interest in astronomy, physics and science in general.

Due to health problems in her teens she left school early, and developed her literary and artistic talents, winning many awards and eventually securing a job as a photographer with a government department.

Leesa is not sure if she had any experiences as a small child, but wonders about a long-forgotten incident between the ages of 7-9 in 1974/75: "We were living in Penrith at the time, and I vaguely recalled hearing about a UFO landing somewhere near Warragamba Dam. We were driving through the area, past the turn-off to the dam, and as I saw a hilly area, with thick bush extending behind it, I thought: 'That's where the UFO landed, up the back, in that bush!' It was as if I could 'feel' where it had been, but didn't understand the significance as I didn't know what a UFO was at the time."

31 January 1976

Leesa and her family sighted an unusual object at about 4.30 p.m. while driving home through Kangaroo Valley on the NSW South Coast. (I didn't ask the family if they checked what time they arrived home, however this was interesting to me. It was five days after Elizabeth's abduction in the Blue Mountains, and a short distance inland across the several cliffs and valleys.)

"I had just had my tenth birthday, and we had a day out in the Valley," Leesa recalled. "I was sitting in the back seat, looking at the beautiful tree ferns at the side of the road; they created a primeval-looking half canopy over the road and the top of our car. Where the canopy parted I saw this object above us, clearly outlined in the blue sky. I opened the window for a better look.

"It was higher than Mt Cambewarra, a thin cigar-shape, dull silver aluminium colour, not exceptionally large, but definitely not a plane. It had no wings and could have been a disc side-on. It was at an odd angle – fairly close, about 500 meters away, and was moving in a straight steady trajectory at a fairly slow speed. At times, it almost appeared stationary – just floating. I don't know if it was pacing us as our car was also moving in the same direction.

"I couldn't hear any noise other than our car's engine," she recalled. "As I watched out at the craft it suddenly accelerated, moved very fast and veered away. I lost sight of it as it passed over and to the side of the mountain." (In those days, Mt Cambewarra didn't have all the mobile phone antennae which have since been installed.)

"There were no other cars on the road, so when we got home Mum and Dad rang radio station 2ST. They had received other reports at the same time. The local newspapers also mentioned other witnesses in their next edition."

12 October 1978

Leesa looked hesitant, and took a quick gulp of her coffee. "When I was twelve, nearly two years later, more disturbing, insidious things started to happen. It was only a few days before the disappearance of pilot Frederick Valentich over the Bass Strait, although there's probably no connection.

"It was Thursday night, when the shops stayed open late. Dad had headed off to the supermarket, and Mum and I were going to the newsagent. As we entered the arcade in the main street of Nowra I found my eyes locking onto three strange fellows who looked like they were out of a B-grade spy movie. They were all dressed the same, black suits, white shirts and black ties, hats and shoes. They looked like triplets, and their suits appeared to be brand new as if straight off the shop's hangers. Each had dark black sunglasses, which was odd considering it was nearly dusk. They were medium build, about five feet seven inches and seemed to be in their mid-thirties to forty. I got the impression they might be oriental as their skin colour was slightly darker than mine, a kind of pale yellowish colour."

These strangers made Leesa and her mother become a little nervous: "They were standing near the entrance to the Darrell Lea chocolate shop, and as Mum and I entered the arcade it appeared that they were looking straight at us – never let us out of their sight. It was very unsettling to both of us, and while we said nothing at the time, we both agreed later that we 'felt' those penetrating stares. As we walked on I could sense their eyes piercing the back of my head, and the hair on the back of my neck was standing on end. I don't know what prompted me, but I got this knee-jerk reaction to make my mind blank, and imagined a blank sheet of white paper to block out all other thoughts and images.

"They looked so out of place in our country town, almost like the Blues Brothers (not screened until two years later)" she reflected, "yet no other shoppers seemed to notice them. As we walked faster they started following us. We quickly got to the other end of the arcade, and joined a mob of people crossing the road. As soon as we reached the other side we nervously turned and looked back – it was as if they had disappeared into thin air within seconds.

"When we finished shopping and were driving home, I got the strangest feeling we were being followed, although there was nothing to validate this."

As Leesa was telling me about the unusual men, Linda came into the room and joined the conversation: "Yes – I'll never forget it! Leesa and I were going into the arcade from the Woolworth's car-park when we spotted these very thin chaps, who looked sort of eastern-oriental in appearance and all dressed the same. They stood near the entry to the lane where we were about to go, and were staring very intently at us.

"They were just inside the doorway of the Darrell Lea shop, and I didn't like the look of them at all, or the way they were concentrating all their attention completely on us. We both felt this strong fear, and Leesa and I couldn't get out of there quick enough. We both had a strong feeling of danger, and nothing would have made us go past those sinister looking men. They just stared and stared at us! I was getting goose-bumps and got that creepy feeling in my spine that always warns one of impending danger."

She stopped and looked at me, "I know you may be thinking we're two imaginative women, fantasizing that three strange fellows were 'men-in-black'. It was what happened later that evening that got us thinking."

Leesa joined in: "I was in the garden at about 7.30 p.m. We had unpacked the shopping, and Mum was cooking dinner while Dad was in the shower. I was still feeling uneasy, with this weird feeling something was about to happen. After a while I noticed three steady red lights, in triangular formation, heading north to south and coming directly towards me. At first, I thought it was a plane on night manoeuvres from the nearby naval base at Jervis Bay, but this was no aircraft or helicopter.

"Leesa came racing in the door," Linda said. "I was trying to prepare tea and here was my twelve-year-old child, with a space-age mind yelling 'Mummy! Mummy! Come and see the funny lights in the sky! They're heading right this way! Hurry!' I was in no fit state, health-wise, to hurry and slowly followed her into the balmy night air.

"Leesa was still carrying on: 'Quickly Mummy, we'll miss it!' In the privacy of my own mind I was thinking that she had *Close Encounters of the Third Kind* fever – just another aircraft and a vision of a world 'where no man has gone.' I saw the three lights and waited for the sound of the plane engine, but there was none. The sound of crickets and frogs in our immediate area had ceased, the dogs stopped barking and there was just an eerie silence. Leesa was jumping up and down in excitement: 'I told you Mum – it's different.'

Leesa recalled, "You could have knocked Mum over with a feather! As it drew closer we were both frozen to the spot in awe. It was so low and slow –and was travelling at about walking pace. So low and silent, this dark solid form that blotted out the stars behind it. We felt we could almost reach up and touch it as it moved over the top of our gum tree without disturbing the leaves or branches. We stood staring, for at least ten minutes, as if in a trance."

Mother and daughter watched as the craft passed overhead, skimming the treetops without touching or moving them. It was black, about 50 feet long by 20 feet wide, with a dull red glow along the boat-like hull. There was no movement of air around it and they couldn't see any wings, propellers, landing gear or tail. They could make out huge, smokey-tinted wrap-around windows in the front, with sharp lines in the centre of the nose. They both tried to rationalise the sighting. Linda felt it definitely wasn't any known craft or the later publicised Stealth prototype. She could make out some light – a reddish glow, coming through the front window, but it wasn't very bright.

They watched until it suddenly disappeared over a park two houses from where they stood. They raced back inside and babbled the story to Mr Donaghue, who had since come out of the shower and wondered what had become of his family and dinner. He was unsure how long his wife and Leesa were outside, and said it could have been much longer than the ten minutes they had estimated.

Linda was not going to let Leesa know just how amazed she was, and got her husband to ring HMAS *Albatross* who said there were no aircraft of any kind in the vicinity. Linda's family were associated with the military, and she wondered if they had seen some kind of secret aircraft being tested. She was perplexed, but said no more, not just out of fear of public ridicule, but also not wanting to reveal what might be some kind of defence secret.

"After the incidents involving Quentin Fogarty and Frederick Valentich at about the same time, I did confide in a close friend, and he said there were some odd things happening at the time in the area. Others had seen strange lights moving in the sky and over a local park later that night. He told me how he and his son had recently seen a craft rise vertically out of the water at Jervis Bay. It came straight up out of the ocean and had flown off into the sky."

I was gathering up my notes from the interview and Leesa followed me outside to the car. "There was something else," she confided, "but I didn't want to mention it until I felt I could trust you. I have this vivid memory, or was it a dream? It happened that night, I think. I remember being on that craft, but no recollection of boarding or leaving it.

"I was escorted down the centre by a tallish 'being', and had a feeling he was male. He looked human but I'm just not sure." She hesitated, "from what I can remember this seemed to be for my education or something. I was not being exploited. Rather being taken into their trust and care, almost like a teacher-child relationship. He seemed to know about my craving for knowledge about the universe and everything astronomical.

"In the middle of this craft was a 'thing' sticking up with lights and switches on it. What caught my eye was a monitor with a black screen and green diagrams. Sensing my curiosity he took me over to it. He told me about how the whole of space is divided into sections of planetary bodies and solar systems, with nothing between. I remember his communication seemed more telepathic than vocal.

Under hypnosis Leesa felt no fear, just kindness, as if they were teaching her. She remembered being told there was a lot of life in space, and there are various dimensions to both the space we can and cannot see. She also recalled there were other aliens present, who were smaller and did all the work.

"Another thing about the craft was at one stage the windows were dark, and you couldn't see through them, like they were tinted, and it was dark outside. The next thing the windows were crystal clear and it was as if we were in orbit. From windows up front I could see a corner of our planet Earth. It was vivid blue, with white swirling cotton-ball clouds, and the space behind us was black.

"There were other people around under the windows, who wore different clothing, maybe of a lower rank. Something frustrates me terribly. When I have been in very close proximity to these beings, often only a foot or so away, I cannot for the life of me recall what their faces look like. They are all faceless people, as if someone just wiped them completely from my mind, and I can't remember with any clarity significant details about their appearance. It's the same with those three strange men dressed in black – I cannot clearly recall their faces now."

At this stage I had no way of knowing what, if anything, had happened to Leesa's mother Linda, either now or in the past. She was present when they encountered the 'men-in-black' and also the strange craft over their backyard. She seemed to be so matter-of-fact when confirming the two incidents, as if she was not totally surprised by it all. The next morning, when Leesa told her parents of her experience they did not seem overly concerned, and I began to wonder about the generational contact and manipulation which was becoming evident in other cases.

1979

The next year was not kind to Leesa, although there is no way of knowing whether her problems were in any way connected to events in October, 1978. Throughout 1979 Leesa became progressively sicker and weaker. She often got pain around the area of the right ovary, and in November she had an extremely painful period which lasted 19 days. She was getting giddy from blood loss, which included passing clots. The specialists were becoming desperate, and said they had never had to treat someone so young for this problem.

Leesa remembered how sick and weak she had been, her skin so pale from apparent anaemia; "The doctor sent me for a blood count. The pathologist who took the blood samples returned with the results. She was puzzled, and stated there was a problem, around half my white blood cells had been killed by exposure to radiation.

"She wanted to know how I could have possibly come in contact with so much radiation, and Mum and I both just shrugged our shoulders. We were both thinking of that night in October 1978 when we saw that strange craft. But Mum's blood was not affected, indicating there was something else in relation to me. The doctors worked with intensive diet and medication to restore my health."

Another interesting anomaly was discovered during the pathology tests. Leesa's blood type is RH negative, however her mother is B-positive and her father A-positive. (Some researchers have suggested that a lot of experiencers have inexplicable negative blood types.)

13 June 1981

Leesa described another unusual event a couple of years later: "Throughout the day I had this eerie feeling I was not alone. Something else was in the room with me – ever present, and following me around. A couple of times I heard a small sneeze, but there was nothing and no-one to see.

"At about 1 p.m. I suddenly became extremely tired, and fell into a deep, dreamless sleep until about 5 p.m. It was like I was heavily sedated. I got up long enough to have some tea and watch the news on television with Mum and Dad, but was back in bed by 7 p.m., unusual for me.

"I had thought about changing into my nightclothes, but something stopped me. I could still feel this strange presence. I have never felt anything so intense before. When I sat on the side of my bed I had this strong sense 'it' was sitting beside me. At one stage I felt something touching my hair, as if someone was running their hand lightly through it.

"After I fell asleep I saw the image of a dark, long, winding square tunnel – joined together in sections with a 'ribbed' look. At first, I was just floating, and then suddenly speeding through it – really fast around the bends. I don't remember reaching the end."

We eventually arranged for several hypnosis sessions for Leesa with a qualified medical practitioner where some of her memories returned. (While it helped her recall some of the events, they were discontinued as she was always left in tears and with subsequent migraines.)

"My next recollection is being led down a corridor into a room. It was white, very bright, with something like an X-ray table and a ceiling light overhead. I don't remember getting undressed, but next thing I was lying naked on the table, with four 'beings', two standing either side looking at me. The room temperature was normal, but the table felt cold.

"The beings started at my feet, and systematically worked their way up my body. Further down they were 'doing things between my legs'. It was more uncomfortable than painful – they were either putting something in or taking something out."

She wavered a little: "I desperately wanted to move a little, talk and ask questions. I could do none of those things. I felt completely paralysed and except for my mouth being open, I could only move my eyes. One being, who appeared to be in charge, produced some kind of instrument which he went to put down my throat. There was an unusual smell, like plastic and I got really nervous. I know he telepathically said something reassuring before covering my eyes with his black gloved hand.

"That is the last thing I remember until I woke in the morning. As I lay there and tried to swallow, the pain in my throat was intense. For the next five days, it was sore and swollen, as if someone had scraped it raw inside. My naval seemed to be inflamed inside, and wept a pungent-smelling clear body fluid for the next week. There was a faint red ring on the top of my breast, and another on my right temple, just under the hairline. These rings would vanish, only to re-occur from time to time in the following months. I also developed Labyrinthitis deep in my inner ear."

She stopped, and looked a little puzzled: "After that I had a real problem with the television. Every time I pushed the ON button, I got an almighty shock as the current surged through the set. You could actually see a blue spark jump between my finger and the television. It would turn my whole arm numb, but did not affect Mum or Dad that way."

1983 – the Dreams

During 1983 when she was 16, Leesa had several vivid dreams which still remain clear to her today.

"In the first I was looking at what I thought was the full moon. However, it was an opaque bubble-like spaceship. It moved over the mountain range and came over our yard in front of me. The occupants, who didn't look quite human, were all pressed up against the misty looking walls, looking out at me."

Two days later there was a similar event which she is unsure was a dream or actual experience. This time she was in the house watching television. "A voice, I thought came from the television, told me to go outside where there is a full moon just to the left of the mountain. A ship will come from there."

She went outside and saw what looked like two full moons. One was the same opaque bubble craft, which moved along the mountain tops and down over her backyard in front of her as before.

"It seemed to land, and an alien version of my family came out. They did look kind of human. There was a mother, father and a daughter about my age. Instead of names they had numbers 2., 4, and 8, which I am sure were symbolic for something else."

The most disturbing dream Leesa encountered was longer and more complex: "I was in a clearing in a heavily-wooded forest. A bright glow in the night sky was engulfing the trees, creating long finger-like, dark shadows between them. I stumbled into the light and found an apparently abandoned spacecraft. I went inside and felt an indescribable sensation. As I walked around the maze of corridors, it all seemed familiar somehow."

She was fascinated with all the advanced equipment, and got the impression the occupants had mastered time as well as space.

"I found three 'cassettes', blue, red, and yellow, numbered 5, 10, and 15, and wondered if they were 'keys to time'. I put two of them, the yellow and blue, into a 'console' and the ship seemed to be transported into the future. It was still in the same place where I had boarded it, but when I looked out the window I saw a desert wasteland of red dirt and rocks. The lovely green forest was no more, just a dark red sky and cyclonic dust storms whipping up the remaining surface of the planet into space.

"Was this the beautiful planet I knew in the past ... oceans, blue sky, fluffy white clouds, land with lush green plants, where every corner just oozed life? Now it was an inhospitable lifeless desert, devoid of atmosphere and ravaged by solar winds. I thought to myself how could mankind be so ignorant and stupid as to let himself and his greed come before the well-being of our world, our only home?"

Leesa felt something was terribly wrong, and sensed an invisible evil presence on the ship. Where were all the occupants, what had happened to them? She managed to get back to her own time and went back into her home to tell her father.

"I heard noises at the front door, and what came in I can only describe as spirits or inter-dimensional energies. One had an evil yellow hue and the other one a more benign blue – had I released something when I used the time cassettes? The yellow one was constantly shape-shifting and trying to kill my father – was it because I had told him of my discovery? The 'blue' was just staying out of the way."

Some inner knowledge, perhaps imparted by the Visitors, came to Leesa: "These entities can only exist in their own dimension, where they are very real with very real powers. Perhaps the occupants of the spacecraft were of the same dimension and not so lucky. While in our dimension they are virtually non-existent, they can somehow manifest themselves through our thoughts or some ability we do not understand."

She concentrated and the entities were gone, and then went back to bed. She woke to hear a report on her radio that "This is the first time the sun has shown us this type of radiation in particular, which is a highly dangerous nuclear radiation." She opened the curtain to see the sky was red, and on the power lines birds were twisting and writhing in a very disturbing way.

"I thought it was all over ... In my dream, I thought I was dreaming, but actually in my dream it was really happening! When I actually woke up I had to pinch myself to be sure I was awake, and look out the window to make sure the sky wasn't red."

(As an investigator, I asked myself was this a real experience – a dream – or an out-of-body episode? Had the Visitors placed all this into her mind earlier or via the implant we later found? I did not know the answers, and wondered if it were a warning of future things to come – or was it to inform us of the dangers mankind was inviting if we continued with experiments into other dimensions and similar uncharted territories? The later research Leesa and her mother felt compelled to undertake may also hold some of the answers.)

What Leesa had described created many new questions in my mind. Many investigators are aware of inter-dimensional occurrences. Were some of the Visitors from another dimension, and using human hosts as a conduit into our time and space?

Following these events Leesa, herself, sought out qualified psychological help. I have the transcript of intensive communications and question-answer sessions with one doctor, who pronounced she was quite sane and normal. At one stage she had made an interesting observation: "Sometimes I feel like I have someone else's knowledge in my mind. It's like I have been told things, forgotten them, and then they surface again later as a logical idea or theory."

This had some consistency with Elizabeth's remark that sometimes she just 'knew things' – as if she had a slow release 'time capsule' in her mind.

17 November 1994

Leesa met her husband in 1984 when they were both working at a military base. She said that the first time she saw him, she knew this was the man she was going to marry. Even after she settled down to family life, the previous events still haunted her. By 1994, whenever her husband was away, Leesa could not sleep alone without the light and television, or radio on. (I reassured her that this was also the case with Elizabeth, Lydia and other experiencers.)

Leesa had taken my advice, and had just been in the process of arranging her first hypnotherapy session with a practitioner I had highly recommended. She went to bed at about 11 p.m., rather tired. The previous night she had felt restless and nauseous, with very little sleep. "No sooner than I had settled down I heard a noise downstairs. It was weird, my first thought was 'What if it's 'them'? I'd better put my nightdress on.' Before I was able to do that I must have fallen asleep.

"At about 1.30 a.m. I woke, and got an extremely vague impression of three dark figures, just inside the bedroom door, near the wardrobe. I had a sudden flashback to those men in black, and felt nauseous. I jumped out of bed, thinking I was going to throw-up, and now fully awake could see there was no-one there.

"It may have been co-incidental but the hypnotherapist suddenly cancelled our appointment. I sometimes feel that I am trying so hard to find the answers and I just keep coming up against road blocks. I don't know what to do, it's rather frustrating. I suppose I'll just have to be patient."

1995

In early 1995 Leesa's labyrinthitis returned. At one stage, she suffered nausea and vomiting, headaches, extreme vertigo, and total loss of balance and co-ordination, to the extent she could not walk for two weeks.

"I was referred to an ENT specialist for hearing and balance tests, plus CT scans and skull X-rays to rule out the possibility of a brain tumour. During the tests both radiologists came hurrying out of the booth and one asked me if I had any previous procedures performed on my head. I thought this rather odd. When I said 'no', he gave his colleague a quizzical look, as if he doubted my answer.

"They finished the tests and confirmed there was no tumour or anything visible causing the problem. Their initial conclusion was that something undiagnosed was disturbing the balance mechanism in the part of my ear where sound is converted into electrical impulses connecting to the brain.

"When I brought my X-rays and CT scans home I took a good look at them. The scans didn't show much but the X-rays were different. There, beneath my jaw bone and just near the front of my neck, was a solid L-shaped object. I tried to rationalise the object by telling myself there was a glitch in the film, but all three X-rays clearly showed the anomaly from different angles.

"Even though I consciously remembered the pointy probe coming towards my open mouth that night in 1981, I just assumed they were taking a swab, and everything went black after the being put his hand over my eyes. I had an awful sore throat, and could barely swallow for a week afterwards. Implants weren't widely known about then, and I just didn't want to acknowledge that the artefact on the X-ray was anything but a fault on the plate."

We managed to arrange hypnosis for Leesa with another very qualified professional in July 1995. It became clear that she was scared to find out the truth, even though she really wanted to know. If what had happened to her was a reality, she could no longer hide from the vagueness and push it from her mind as just being a bad dream. Furthermore, if she re-lived the incident would the illnesses also return? At one stage, she said: "It seems like two different realities. One is real with physical persons and environment. The other is just like a dream, but it is as real as being awake." She did recall some additional memories she would rather have forgotten.

"Something is going on between my legs – I can't see, it's out of my line of sight, but it's uncomfortable. It's like an exploration ... maybe taking something out ... I don't know ... They're doing something in my right ear ... My mouth's open – I don't know how it's open – I can't move. An instrument is going deep down my throat ... Before I can feel any pain, his hand comes towards me and rests on my eyes. He's telling me not to be afraid, it won't hurt."

Some aspects of Leesa's experience had a very familiar ring to them – so similar to very many of the other women. Not only did she suffer severe menstrual problems following the encounter, after she had her first child her second pregnancy ended in what the doctors termed 'an incomplete miscarriage' – the baby was gone but the placenta had remained!

This regression occurred in 1995, and explained Leesa's health problems and side-effects following the earlier experience during 1981. She decided not to have any more hypnotherapy because it always left her weak and disorientated, her eyes sore and puffy from crying. Very little specific information was forthcoming to supplement her conscious recall.

"The psychologist and I agreed there were strong emotional blocks, which were more than likely to be hiding something traumatic. The general consensus between us was that my subconscious was blocking some of my memories. After counselling I came to terms with the fact that most people would not believe me, but someone out there knew the truth."

In 1996 Leesa met a couple from Brazil, who had moved to Australia and become neighbours. Leesa found it difficult to communicate with the husband – as if there was 'some kind of barrier there'. His wife started to notice both he and Leesa would be strange and moody, and get migraines and other ailments at the same time. Once they both simultaneously got a large bruise on the same arm which lasted for the same length of time.

"Neither of us knew its origin," she said, "but I discovered he was also an experiencer, and there were many other instances, even parallels of our UFO experiences from childhood, that are just too coincidental. Sometimes it really scares me just how in sync we are. It was kind of quirky at first, but now it bothers me terribly. That's why I think I avoid him, because it reminds me of all those things, and I find it hard to cope."

Children

After her marriage in 1984, Leesa had five children over the following years, however she never told them of the experiences of either herself or their grandparents. "I didn't want anything to trigger the same thing in my kids – that is if 'They' hadn't started on them already.

"Before my son had turned three he was scribbling something which looked rather triangular with other angular protrudences. I asked him what he was drawing and was startled when he answered: "It's one of those scary things that flicks in your eyes." Motioning with his small hands he made a flicking movement with his fingers, as if a light was flashing near his eyes.

"My body tingled and my heart sank. What he said in his baby way rang a bell and sort of made sense. 'Oh God, here we go again,' I thought.

"About a year later when I was heavily pregnant with Tahlia, eleven months after my 'incomplete miscarriage', I again sensed a strong presence in the house. Even though there was nothing visible I went around cautiously ensuring all windows were shut and locked. That night I had an unusual dream of a weird cat which had a huge head, ears and eyes, which was out of proportion to its body. I wondered how the poor thing could support such a large head on such a small body.

"But was it a dream? At 4 a.m. Kevin, aged three and a half, woke up screaming and extremely distressed. I rushed to his side and calmed him down. He recounted a nightmare about something that had a face that 'looked like a power point, and green 'pointy' things were going into Mummy's eyes or face."

The last of Leesa's five children, was born in October 1998. As a youngster, she had felt very little fear of the Visitors, but as an adult, and a mother herself, was a lot more apprehensive.

March 1995

She woke one morning to find spots of blood on the clean sheets on her side of the bed, and then noticed a tender needle-like spot, with bruising around it, on her upper left arm. It remained for two months, although she had no recollection of how it got there.

Visitation

Leesa had spent five years trying to pretend the unusual object showing up in the X-rays of her jaw was just a glitch, but in July, 2000, after seeing an article with a photograph of a defence worker's jaw with an identical object, she took another look at her own tests.

I went over to see her, examined the film, and had to agree it did indeed resemble an implant. She admitted it was very disturbing to her. "I wonder about the reasons for it being put under my jaw bone, via my throat. Surely it would have been easier to just pop it in under the skin in my neck or somewhere else for that matter. I guess if it were done that way, it would be easier for curious prying humans to remove.

"What is the reason for it being there at all?" she queried. "Is it to chart my movements so they can find me at any time? Is it close to my vocal chords to listen in on my conversations – or near my thyroid to monitor secretions? I have no idea."

I asked her if she wanted to get it removed – after all it would be a great windfall if we could get our hands on one to forensically analyse! "I guess if it went in via my throat it needs to come out the same way. At this stage I don't see me having it taken out by anyone, no matter how skilled the surgeon. I really don't want to go through that pain again, after having something shoved down my throat.

"And I don't fancy the attention it would attract to 'Them' if they realise that a piece of their technological handiwork has been removed. What if they come looking for me, or worse still, decide to replace it?"

It wasn't long before she rang me again. "Remember when I saw you a couple of weeks ago about the doctor finding the implant on my X-Ray? A very odd thing happened only four days later. Mum and I went into Nowra, but weren't together all of the time. I had the two little ones in a tandem stroller, and went into the newsagent before heading for the chemist.

"It was a tight squeeze trying to get through the people with the stroller, and right in front of me was this rather uncouth looking fellow, looking at, of all things, a UFO magazine. Would you believe the front cover showed an article about the removal of implants!! Before I could politely ask him to let me through he had already turned around and stared at me, as if my arrival was anticipated. He moved aside, and his eyes followed me as I walked behind then next to him to look at the magazines.

"He continued to smile and quietly said something verbally which I couldn't understand. His eyes never left me for a second, with a look as if he were recognising an old friend. This was even more intense, like he could see right into me. I felt uncomfortable, and felt a chill go through me. He was craning his neck, trying to look into my eyes, not something a normal person would do.

"It was as if he needed to make that initial eye contact, which I was avoiding, in order to establish some form of communication that he had failed to make verbally. I just *knew* deep down who he was and as he was standing next to me I recalled all the past experiences I had managed to comfortably confine to a little slot in the back of my mind. I experienced the same reaction I had as a child to those 'men-in-black' – to make my mind blank and avoid eye contact, otherwise they could lock onto my particular brainwave, like tuning into a radio frequency. If that happened they could locate and communicate with me anytime, and I did not want to open the floodgates to this all happening again.

"His appearance rather threw me. He was middle-aged, Caucasian, of solid build, about five feet eight inches tall, with sandy, slightly greying hair pulled back in a short ponytail. Whilst my conscious mind warned me this might be some 'psycho' my subconscious instantly recognised the strong electric-type vibes that emanate from these beings. He was not one of us, and yet here he was in broad daylight in the middle of the shopping centre's newsagent. I thought perhaps they come to our normal environment so as not to frighten us.

"As he stood by my side a silent dialogue commenced between our minds. 'Are you?' I queried. 'Yes, I am who you think. It's been a long time, I said we would return.' I was freaked out - in a state of shock, confusion, and panic, but tried not to show it. This guy was talking to me telepathically.

"My legs felt shaky, I had the sensation of static electricity, and I couldn't handle my feelings or the truth. I just had to get out of there, and pushed the stroller out of the back door towards the chemist. Out of the corner of my eye I noticed he was following, in a strange purposeful manner. His movements were odd, as if his gait was in slow motion.

Leesa continued "I met up with Mum for lunch, and as I was sitting in the coffee lounge he walked past the window and over to the car park, coming to a halt right beside my car at the end of the row. My hands became clammy and I just froze with a half-eaten piece of quiche in my mouth. Why next to MY car? I was thinking to myself 'I hope I locked the doors properly – I don't want some 'Grey' dude, or something equally weird sitting in the backseat on my ride home!

"I didn't tell Mum, and sighed with relief when he seemed to wander off. We continued with our shopping, and later I was waiting outside while she was in the sewing shop. I was bending over the stroller when the silent stranger sauntered around the corner. I pretended I didn't notice him, but that wasn't possible as he brushed past me and leant against the wall behind. He folded his arms, and had one foot on the ground and the other against the wall.

"He was smiling and blatantly staring, trying to make eye contact again. There was the same sensation of the air around me being electrified. By this time, I was in total panic, and another conversation from him seemed to be happening in my mind.

"He was asking me; 'Why are you behaving like this? You wanted proof. You wanted to see me, here I am! Why are you running away?' The thoughts were conveyed in a very calm manner, and even though I knew what he was thinking, I realised he had never said a word in the four hours he'd been following me, except for the first mumble I didn't understand in the newsagent.

"He seemed interested in my babies as well as me, and I realised the last time he saw me I was in my early teens. I was now 33 with children of my own.

(I was concerned that the Visitor had shown an interest in her kiddies, the next generation, but kept my thoughts to myself.) I asked Leesa could she explain the telepathic communication. "It wasn't so much like hearing words in my head, as feeling what he was feeling. The thing is they don't really need to talk to you to communicate. Everything they do, the way they appear when trying to get your attention, has meaning. Once you are aware of what they are doing, it is a very subtle form of communication, and they can speak volumes without even opening their mouths.

"Mum was still in the sewing shop, so I sought the safety of the crowds in Woolworths. He started to follow, and I put on a burst of speed and raced in and down one of the aisles. He came through the turnstiles, following my path. I thought, 'This guy must have GPS.' While I thought of ringing the police what could I say? My conscious mind was trying to tell me he was just some 'psycho.' Deep down I was recognising the same mannerisms from all those years ago. I was torn between my feelings, partly recognising him, but at the same time wanting to reject the notion. Maybe it was just pure denial.

"I was looking out for Mum from behind the bread rack, and while I kept my eye on the turnstiles, suddenly realised that he hadn't left, but the 'dude' was nowhere in any of the shop aisles. He'd just disappeared into thin air, the same as those men in black suits had done in the arcade all those years ago.

"I kept looking over my shoulder all the way back to the car, and Mum and I picked up my three other children from school. All the time this man's image was burned in my mind, and I recognised and accepted who he was, suddenly remembering being told they would come back to see me when I was about 33. I felt as though the telepathic link was still there, and all of a sudden some answers to questions, I had been asking myself for years, came flooding into my mind."

Leesa's experience in 2000, reminded me of an incident British researcher and author Timothy Good, wrote about. In February, 1967 he was sitting in the lobby of the Park-Sheraton Hotel in New York. He decided to try some telepathy, to test his theory of alien contact, and concentrated on any 'entity' in the area to come and sit beside him, 'and prove who you are.'

After a while a man walked up, sat down beside him, and superficially scanned a copy of the *New York Times*. He was about 35 years old, of tanned Scandinavian appearance, five feet ten inches tall, well-proportioned and immaculately dressed. No words were spoken, so Good said in his mind; 'If you are who I think you might be, raise your right index finger and place it to the right side of your nose.' The man immediately did just that, and Good regrets not saying anything. He tried a bit more telepathy, but the man stood up, looked at him very seriously, and walked away.

A 'Vanishing' Act

What Leesa did not know was that I had investigated several other reports, from different parts of Australia, where seemingly normal fair-haired humans, present around the time of sightings or abductions, had either imparted a meaningful message or suddenly disappeared into thin air.

Another case of a strange fair-haired human was reported by British researcher Timothy Wyllie. In 1962, he was hurrying down a London street, mentally stressing about the possibility of nuclear war. He bumped into a casually dressed man, about mid-thirties with a pleasant face, short, light-coloured hair, and unusually blue eyes. Facing each other, with their eyes locked, they both simultaneously moved the same way, from side to side to let each other pass.
After the third time, he looked straight into Timothy's eyes and said: "Don't worry. We can pick the rockets out of the sky ... just like *that*!" He clicked his fingers with a loud snap in front of Timothy's face, and slipped past into the wet afternoon.

Leesa and Linda's 'strange men in black' also reminded me of a similar case, investigated by a colleague, and published by *Rapport* in 1996:
In 1967, the 14-year-old witness had been at home and she and her parents had watched a large metallic saucer hovering over their house for over 20 minutes in Hertsfordsire, United Kingdom. (Her father took a photo showing the object, and the same company which routinely 'loses' Australian UFO photos, lost this one as well!)

Three weeks earlier, she and her mother had been in London one hot April day: "We both noticed a man standing in the doorway next to Boots chemist. Although it was rather warm, he was dressed in dark clothes, raincoat, gloves and standing rather stiffly, just staring ahead. He was about five feet ten inches, with blue/black hair, rather Hispanic, dark eyes and yellowish skin. He was strangely handsome, but dispassionate.

"My mother commented on him, as he was looking at us as we passed by. We continued along Bond Street, and some way down, stopped to look in a shoe shop window. My mother suddenly grabbed my arm and said, "he is behind you!" I started, and looked all around. "I can't see anyone, what do you mean?" She was upset and frightened. She had seen that strange man appear behind me and then disappear; I had not.

"Three weeks later, we had that experience of a saucer over our home. My mother said to me: "Do you think it is anything to do with that strange man we saw?" We both psychically connected him with the event. Why, I do not know.

"After that my mother had strange, personal things happen to her, involving an invisible entity, seemingly present over the bed, and a humming noise both she and my father could hear." The witness went on to have several experiences, and her latent psychic abilities have improved.

United States researcher Lee Walsh reports a similar incident near Maybrook, New York in 1975. Several police officers had stopped at a red light, and when a strange man passed their patrol car all power stopped for a moment. They could feel the hair on their bodies 'stand on end'. Then the man seemed to vanish before them.

A waitress at a nearby restaurant advised this same man had come in for several days. He would order breakfast, but not eat it. Everyone remarked that his eyes were strange; "like he was looking right through you". She commented on some form of telepathy, as she knew what he wanted before he even made his order.

The ability of these Visitors to disappear is a mystery. Many cases of this nature mention the Visitors have a small box or device at their waist, which seems to activate this occurrence. Some researchers into the phenomenon liken it more to Harry Potter's 'cloak of invisibility', and suggest that it could be from the formation of a light-absorbing, free electron cloud around the 'disappeared'. Since light waves will not pass through the person within the cloud they suggest that a mist of free electrons will absorb all light entering it, neither refracting nor reflecting light waves.

Since light is necessary for our retina to see something, there is no light contact with the vanished person who is still there, but becomes invisible to the observer who see nothing. In one case investigated by Amy Herbert, multiple witnesses, who were filming something at a distance, did not actually see the being who appeared only six feet away on the photographs. She suggested the use of electromagnetic frequencies to mask visibility may be used by UFO occupants while outside their craft.

The After-effects

Leesa reflected, "I even wondered if the strange character who followed me around is partly responsible for my change in thought. I have begun to understand some of the psychology he has used on me. It has helped my mind to evolve slightly. They have led me to believe they don't think in the same chaotic manner we do. We have to figure some things out for ourselves, and take-on a sideways logic when we consider things. The big picture is a result of this different way of thinking."

Leesa developed an understandable concern about the world. Her husband studied geology at university, and she interests herself in global fault lines, and their potential to create a domino effect resulting in massive earthquakes and upheavals.

"When he was six, my son Kevin started drawing the Kabbalistic 'Tree of Life', without ever seeing it. He usually gave his pictures a name, and when I asked about that one he said it was 'Mummy's people'. Along with other instances, this made me realise my children were also involved, and there was little I could do about it."

Rationalisation

Leesa is now a grandmother, and has reflected on her unusual experiences for many years: "I wonder about the true purpose of it all. There seems to be a tremendous amount of something going on behind the scenes. It seems to be of great importance to Them, and although some may seem a little emotionless whilst performing their tasks, I don't feel it is entirely intentional. Rather they lack some of the feelings we seem to take for granted. Maybe they are just doing a job and have to switch off as we do.

"They seem so different, and I wonder if they have the same fears and uncertainties as we do? I'm sure they would find it terrifying if they hadn't experienced such raw emotion before. Then again, they may be well acquainted with our emotions and psychology; they may even be human!

"I believe everything gives off vibrations – a resonance, and when we come face to face with them we sense their different vibes and automatically construe them as negative. This has led me to question myself, and my varying reactions. Am I dealing with the same entities in all these encounters, or are there more than one with differing underlying agendas?

"Even when they are physically gone there seems to be a residual effect that takes a day or so to wear off. I think it may be something to do with an energy field that comes from, or surrounds them. Perhaps it's the vibrational difference, a psychic link, or even a combination of both. They are expert at using psychology and subliminal communication, sometimes I felt a second consciousness within, like the melding of minds. This had the effect of my feeling he was looking at us through my eyes, and I was perceiving things through his.

"Sometimes I sense a wise and great consciousness, and while we exist in this material life, we have to understand our connectedness to everything around us."

The Bloodlines and Children's Abilities
I realised I was looking at four generations of Leesa's family with possible alien interaction. Her family tree traces back to France and the royal bloodlines. Interestingly, Leesa's blood group is A- and her husband AB+. Her children are all A or AB+, two have married, and both their partners are A-.

Her five children are all very intelligent, could read at a very early age, and have varying psychic abilities. Her three grandchildren are also very advanced. None are aware of Linda and Leesa's experiences.

Leesa and Linda's Research
Both Leesa and her mother felt 'guided' by all the various co-incidences and experiences to seek out the truth in many ways, including along a personal spiritual path. They researched their family history, which led them back in time.

Their ancestral Basque connection led to a crop formation which was translated on the basis of the Basque alphabet, but was actually a form of ancient Hebrew. Their subsequent research into crop circles (which she believes contain an imbedded three-dimensional image), led to further research into symbolism, ancient cultures and finally back to the Mystery Schools of Ancient Egypt, the Sumerians and the Anunnaki.

"We eventually realised that many of our mysterious monuments, ancient wisdom, crop circles and religion, from around the world, all came from the same source. My mother and I knew nothing of the Anunnaki or Sumerian, Babylonian or Mesopotamian history. Although I had never read any of Zechariah Sitchin's books, I constantly felt drawn towards the ancient Sumerians.

"Between us we have gathered, or I should say have been led to, an extraordinary amount of data linking humanity to a group of ETs from long ago in our ancient history. Often, they were regarded as Gods, due to our species' infancy. Other researchers have already followed this train of thought in the past, and have met with harsh criticism by academia.

"Our research led us to the same conclusions as many others. Primitive man was genetically altered with some Anunnaki genes in order to assist them with an urgent mining project on Earth." (This directed my thoughts to the belief that the little Greys may be biological robots – engineered as workers. If so, why weren't they used? Perhaps the Anannaki didn't have the expertise all those thousands of years ago. Maybe they just hadn't brought the manufacturing materials and equipment with them.)

Leesa continued explaining their research: "We were created in the image of our flesh-and-blood alien forbears, by an extraterrestrial geneticist, hence the beginnings of misrepresentation in some religious scripts. This certainly does not negate the supreme Creator, our real God. The Anunnaki acknowledge quite readily that they too come from the same Creator of All.

"We were never meant to be anything other than workers, and were not supposed to have the knowledge and powers of our masters. However, some received extra genes, and also other Anunnaki bred with human women, and their descendants continue until this day. Is this such a foreign concept, given our own scientific genetic experimentations in recent times?

The research Linda and Leesa have done is extensive, and would comprise another book. What was astounding to me was that they had gone down the same path as Rosemary Decker, and arrived at similar conclusions, including the three-dimensional qualities of the crop circles. They did not know her, and were, to the best of my knowledge, unaware of her work or writing. They had followed the trail, often from sudden compulsions, ideas or thoughts which had suddenly come to mind. Were they all being telepathically influenced by the same alien intelligences?

Given my current area of research, I did ask her what she had discovered about DNA, and the alleged interference with the human genome. She indicated that in the beginning 'They' had removed some original DNA to stop us using powers we and they may not be able to control. Are some people now being enhanced with some of the missing genes?

Linda and Leesa's research also led them to the Twelfth Planet, Nibiru 'The Planet of the Gods.' Cuneiform pictographs depict it as the 'Planet of the Crossing'.

"Even some time ago, I felt a sense of urgency coming from the synchronicities drawing me ultimately to the Anunnaki (Sumerian Gods) supposedly from the planet Nibiru, which some people are relating to Planet X. Planet X does seem to exist, according to the scientific information I have read, although there does seem to be a lot of back stepping around what some scientists have already admitted.

"Maybe there is something, a planetary object, approaching us and affecting things like gravitational pull and solar flares. Maybe it has the possibility of causing a pole shift, like Earth has experienced in the past, which caused much catastrophe. I feel a strong link drawing me back to the past. When I hear of natural disasters I just cringe; I feel like I am waiting for something much bigger to happen.

"I have always had unusual predictive visions, usually before earthquakes or volcanoes around the world. Lately my worries come from recurrent dreams of rising water and a huge tidal wave. I see it looming on the horizon, and I'm on the roof of my house, trying to drag my children and the cat up to safety. I have always wanted to live on the top of a mountain, or high in the mountain ranges. As fate would have it, I live on the coast, only a few miles from the sea!"

I wondered about the synchronicity and telepathy evident among this category of experiencer. Are they on the same frequency, so to speak? Did this explain their strange compulsions to move away from the coast or earthquake prone areas, and the stocking-up of provisions and extra bedding? I was certainly aware of the possibility of unknown planetary bodies orbiting around the edge of our solar system. It was recently stated that a large planet, some call 'Planet X', passes by about once every 27 million years. While the accompanying debris is blamed for mass extinctions, it is not due for another 16 million years!

Nibiru is another matter. There is much speculation and conflicting reports about an unknown body or system present near us, in space. It is also said that the ancient Sumerians knew the accurate size, and distances between, the planetary bodies in our Solar System, indicating a knowledge which was not their own.

Leesa concluded, "What we believe to be our history is the real myth. All ancient cultures contain similar myths and legends, which are, to a certain extent, our true history from their perspective. Perhaps, if any of these myths contain truth, it could put a whole different perspective on our situation as contactees and abductees. It may relate somehow back to our deep, distant past, the possibility that we are part Anunnaki, we are part Extraterrestrial!

"Perhaps it is something to do with our bloodlines, but the information imparted to all of us on the same frequency seems very important for some reason. Unless mankind realises we are one, with the same origins, and if we continue on the path we have been following, it will undoubtedly destroy us."

I thought about the connection many experiencers felt towards the ancient Sumerians, and the information they claimed was given to them by the Nefilim scientists. Some of their astronomical records and knowledge have only been discovered by our own scientists in the last 50 to 100 years. They had information just not possible at the time, and since the source cannot be found on Earth, we must consider they were in contact with intelligent beings from elsewhere.

Much later in their project, Leesa and Linda stumbled upon an internet site called the *The Wingmakers*, which is vastly different to most blogs. Some information complements and confirms their research. It contains pictures of glyphs, crop circles, art work, poetry, music, philosophy and scientific papers translated from tunnels and chambers found hidden under New Mexico. Some people claim that certain music, and glyphs on the site affects their consciousness to the extent they almost feel they enter into another dimension. Another suggestion is that it is a time capsule and the whole scenario involves time travel. Due to a possible extraterrestrial connection, the project is said to have been originally undertaken by the *NSA*, and archived under the code name *Ancient Arrow*. Two scientists, using pseudonyms, claimed to be continuing the work. Some of their findings were released via the organisation *The Wingmakers*.

There is much quiet controversy about this organisation and who or what was really behind its promotion. It has been associated with a 'time-shifted human faction or sect.' Others claim it involves the secret government and Illuminati and more say it is some form of subliminal or other programming. Regardless, it seemed a lot of people, especially the authorities were *not happy*. When two crop circle researchers, purportedly affiliated with *The Wingmakers* died within days of each other, Leesa and Linda decided not to visit the site any longer, sensing there was some form of danger associated with connecting to it.

Chapter Sixteen

Alien Bases

If humanoid aliens were visiting Earth, one might ask where were they based? Some may be integrated into society, but with our own modern surveillance systems and technology, they could not risk some mother ship hovering up-high without being discovered. Perhaps this explains, to some extent, their partial withdrawal in the 1960s.

Many of the women had intimated at alien-human involvement and co-operation before and during the World War 2. It was the concept of these clandestine projects which interested me, how and where were they conducted, (apparently by both sides), safe from detection of both their own people and the enemy. If in fact our own governments were already back-engineering alien craft, how did they keep the operation so secretive?

Many contactees have mentioned being told of alien bases in both the Himalaya and Andes mountain ranges. United States researcher Ted Phillips undertook extensive research and trips to the High Tatra mountain range in Slovakia, where there is an underground area called 'The Cave of the Half Moon', which it is said Hitler's SS began searching for in 1939.

Mankind has sought refuge underground since the beginning of recorded history, be it caves, dungeons, cellars or purpose built installations. It is well known that covert facilities do exist under buildings, cities, countryside, mountains and remote areas, and yes, most probably even under the sea.

I realised that most advanced nations today would have subterranean bases, essential for military purposes, secret technological projects and experiments, and for the survival of government. Maybe, just maybe, there is provision for some of the normal population. Threats to a nation's infrastructure may come not only from civil unrest and all facets of war, but also natural disasters. Certainly, in the US there are many documented Federal Emergency (FEMA) underground locations designated as 'Continuity of Government Facilities'. Would living under the surface of our planet provide some protection from enemy attack, and the harmful energies and anomalies emanating from space and our own Sun and Solar System? Perhaps so, but maybe not earthquake and volcanic activity from the Earth itself!

I wondered about the existence of similar facilities between 1930 and 1945. Germany had large underground factories, and tunnelled into mountains, such as Nordhausen, where V2 rockets were produced. Hermann Goering had an underground base in Wildpark, Potsdam. In Sweden, the Musko Naval Base, a huge facility with water access, was built deep into the side of a mountain. In neighbouring Norway, there are many rumoured enormous bases which various whistleblowers have disclosed.

Many capital cities have underground railway systems. Cellars and basements were reinforced to provide shelter and also protected command and control centres. Natural cave and cavern systems, mining tunnels and complexes had been in existence for much longer.

As early as 1955 a Rand Corporation- sponsored symposium, attended by all the major defence industry corporations, discussed Deep Underground Construction. Also in attendance were the Colorado School of Mines and major construction firm Bechtel Corporation. Some years later in the 1970s, it was revealed that a huge nuclear powered tunnelling machine was already quietly in use. Basically it heats and reduces rock to liquid magma, creating a lined tunnel when it cools after the machine has passed through. Over 30 years later, several large corporations were developing and employing sophisticated machinery, and the size and capabilities of contemporary tunnelling and excavation technology is mind-boggling.

For over 100 years mining projects have extended for miles from the coast under the sea. With our sophisticated machinery, huge military type land bases could be constructed without the use of any large, obvious infrastructure support. Although underwater bases would ideally have land and deep sea access, modern methods may well confine a secretive base to submerged entrances only. Large covert installations of our own may well, and probably do, exist under both land and sea. Dr. Richard Sauder discusses this in detail in his books, including *Underwater and Underground Bases*, and his articles can be found in *Nexus* Magazines Aug/Sept 2001 and Oct/Nov 2004.

If aliens were already present on Earth, then there would be no way to know of their hidden locations or possible secret bases. Timothy Good wrote about one witness, Joelle, whom he knew well. She claimed contact with two Visitors, Mark and Val, who she had met in 1963, when their craft landed in the Derbyshire Peak District. For well over a year she maintained contact with them at several places in England, and entertained them in her flat on at least two occasions.

Joelle claimed they were physical beings who looked totally human and fair-skinned, with perfect teeth, although she noticed that there was a dark-skinned man who was part of the group. They spoke their own language together, but could also use mental communication between minds, and advised they usually employed telepathy to influence people, and on odd occasions interfered directly. They told her they came from a similar planet in another Solar System, and admitted that on two occasions in the past, their people had genetically interfered with us. While they did not discuss their reasons for coming, they did suggest that we need to evolve psychologically and spiritually, and remarked: "What a beautiful planet. Such a pity you're destroying it." They also referred to other extraterrestrials also coming here, who were 'not so well disposed towards us'.

They had told her that their 'people' had facilities in several countries including South America, Australia and the Soviet Union. She also claimed they said they had been liaising in secret with a team of scientists from several nations, and some of them had worked at their bases. In 1967, three years after her last contact with Mark and Val, Joelle received a visit from two people from the Home Office in London. They were enquiring about the disappearance of some scientists who were mutual acquaintances. They seemed reasonably knowledgeable about everything, but actually seemed pleased when she refused to answer certain questions.

During their discussions, Mark had mentioned that to Joelle they had bases on two unspecified moons around Jupiter. (Upon reflection, this made me consider there may be other similar bases 'out there'. Since we are on an outer arm of the Milky Way, perhaps our Solar System has some significance – a military outpost in the Galaxy? Is there more than one extraterrestrial race anxious to have a presence? No wonder the aliens were getting fidgety about our own ventures into space!)

Given their obvious superior technology, it is certainly possible, and indeed logical that the most undetectable place would also be under our oceans. This would certainly account for the multiple reports of unidentified objects flying out of the water, especially in the South Pacific. There have also been reports of craft shooting out of the Arctic waters before taking to the sky.

South America

German Admiral Karl Donitz stated, in 1943; "The German submarine fleet is proud of having built for the Fuhrer, in another part of the world, a Shangri-La on land, an impregnable fortress." Later, in 1944, he stated; "The German Navy knows all hiding places in the oceans, and therefore it will be very easy to bring the Fuhrer to a safe place." Many have interpreted this as referring to the Antarctic, but I personally consider South America, where many U-boats were intercepted, to be much more likely. By the end of the 19th century there was an estimated half a million South Americans of German descent and affiliation, and a sizable German economic presence in South American countries, such as Argentina and Chile.

There have been many rumours of Hitler escaping Germany and fleeing to South America. I have unsubstantiated but plausible witness reports that before escaping Germany in 1943-44, Hitler underwent plastic surgery, leaving a doppelganger in his place. He died, in his 90s, in a monastery in El Salvador.

Covert alien underground bases are also much more conceivable in both the jungles and the mountainous regions of the Andes in South America. There have been multiple reports over the years to indicate that this may be the case. Dr Irena Scott and William Jones were told by a US Navy flier that he often took investigators to South America via very unusual routes around the world.

Gordon Creighton discussed a case on 5 June 1964, when a doctor and his passenger's car engine failed, and they found the road blocked by a large machine in Cordoba, Argentina. There were three beings, all dressed in grey, and one came over. The stranger then suggested he try starting the engine again, and after it started, he said in Spanish; "Don't be afraid. I am a terrestrial. I am carrying out a mission on Earth. My name is RD. Tell mankind about it in your own way." He slowly walked away, and all three entered the craft, which rapidly rose and vanished from sight, leaving a violet coloured trail.

The APRO organisation reported an incident near Americana in Brazil on 26 November 1967. A highway patrolman suffered a headache when he heard a strange humming, and the lights and engine failed in his police car. He could see a huge, bright metallic object, with enormous rivets, hovering 50 feet above the ground. Once the object left, his vehicle returned to normal. Two days later he encountered the craft again, and he felt paralysed. Two men, in close-fitting clothes with glowing belts, came out of a cylinder underneath, and spoke to him in Portuguese. Before flying away, they told him to put away his gun, and not be afraid. They would return.

The Arctic

Up until a few decades ago, the most shielded, and unobtrusive locations for alien strongholds would have been at the frozen extremities of the globe. While there is no land mass at the North Pole itself, there are the vast uninhabited surrounding areas of Tundra in Siberia. Since 1853 there has been the occasional mention of mysterious domed structures known to exist in Yakutia, a remote part of north-east Siberia, near the Olguidakh, and upper reaches of the Viliuy, rivers. They were also reported by a geologist in 1936. These structures resemble gigantic metal/copper cauldrons – *olguis,* buried in the ground, with only the rims visible. Some streams in the area bear the name 'Olguidakh', which translates to 'Cauldron Stream'.

In the early 1950s very large craft were reported in the area, which were unlikely to be of earthly origin. On 9 February 1951, a Navy transport plane was flying to Newfoundland after a refuelling stop in Iceland. The entire crew, including over twenty passengers (all military pilots, navigators and flight engineers), saw huge circular white lights below them, and were startled when they dimmed and one started climbing rapidly towards their plane.

It drew level, and began moving alongside. They could see that this unknown craft was metallic, shaped like a saucer, and about two hundred feet in diameter. After about two minutes, it moved away and out of sight within a few seconds.

They all estimated its speed as being above fifteen hundred miles per hour, and radar operators in Newfoundland confirmed they had been tracking an unidentified target at 1800 miles per hour.

The Russian *Zhurnalist* magazine reported that in November 1967, on a Ilyushin IL-14 flight to Irkutsk in Siberia, the navigator in the blister top of the plane spotted a bright light which suddenly appeared over the top of them, illuminating their craft with various colours and hues. While he described the object as being as big as a two-storey building, it was not detected on ground control radar. The object seemed to be exerting some control and a downward pressure on their plane, and they eventually lowered their altitude to 1500 metres in an attempt to escape.

One British colleague advised of a couple of reports which indicated alien-Russian contact in the 1980s, and that a top Russian astrophysicist claimed a 700-page blueprint was retrieved from a 'star-ship' that crashed in a remote part of Siberia in the summer of 1988. Valery Uvarov of Russia's National Security Academy has been reported as saying that on 24-25 September 2002, a meteorite was shot down over Siberia by an unknown installation.

Parts of Siberia, Canada, Alaska, Greenland and Scandinavia are also within the Arctic Circle, and we mustn't forget Iceland, which has been the location of many mysterious reports and rumours. Since World War 2 the Arctic has been dotted with radar installations to detect intruders, and often over the years, there have been sightings and radar contacts, causing scares and premature alerts.

UFO Encounter Queensland Journal, February-March 1995 reported on several incidents in 1992, when Russian divers in the Gulf of Finland encountered an enormous craft shooting out of the sea. In December that year, there were reports from Iceland of fishermen seeing rapidly-moving underwater craft with flashing lights, and also of three UFOs descending and entering the sea off Langness.

While in Australia, shortly before his death, Graham Birdsall told me about a military encounter, involving several countries, with UFOs, some underwater, which occurred over the Christmas-New Year period 1992-93.

British colleague Tony Dodd followed up with further details. He reported that at least four UFOs had been seen descending and entering the sea in that area. The incident involved the Icelandic, British and American military, including submarines, warships, gunboats and Coast Guard vessels. Despite a great deal of secrecy, it was said they were searching for a surface vessel which had reportedly gone missing.

In February 1993, after an American contingent of three destroyers had told all ships to keep a distance of three nautical miles, 16 airborne objects were seen hovering over the US flotilla. Tony then reported that on 15 April 1993, only two US warships could be seen. The Russian Navy joined the operation, which was purportedly to search for the missing American destroyer. One radio operator advised overhearing a communication between the Russian ships to the effect that they were 'engaging unknown underwater craft'. The press reported it as 'joint military exercises', which later moved on land to Tiksi in Siberia.

In 1997 Graham Birdsall wrote in his *UFO Magazine* of further reports received from terrified Icelandic fisherman, about numerous UFOs in the sky, some of which entered or exited the sea. The most amazing was a telephone call he received on 23 April 1996. The fisherman claimed they were working fairly close to a group of

American warships, when there was a sudden blinding flash of light, and 'one of the warships just disappeared in front of our eyes!' The Americans ordered all fishing boats out of the area, and the caller's captain 'retired to his cabin with a bottle of whiskey'.

US Admiral Byrd apparently had an experience in the Arctic, which he was forbidden to discuss. Many years later there were some publications which released what are purported to be copies of Admiral Byrd's personal diary, in which he detailed a flight over the North Pole in February 1947. (I do have a problem with this date, given his better documented excursion to the Antarctica at the about same time.) I must stress there is no way of confirming if this information is genuine and accurate, but it is worth considering. My other problem with the credibility of the entire sequence of events is the location of this miraculous city, unless it was much further south than he reported. Perhaps today we might venture into that icy wilderness, but in 1947 few sane people would attempt to fly a small plane over the most northern part of the Arctic in the middle of winter.

Byrd records flying over a small range of mountains he had never seen before, and finding forests and a green valley, with animals and a small river, which astounded him. His controls, radio and instruments were either going haywire or not operating. This may indicate that he was way off-course, but doesn't negate the lack of authenticity due to the dates given.

A bit further on he saw what looked like a city, and then encountered strange craft closing rapidly on his port and starboard wings. He described them as 'radiant disc-shaped craft' with a type of Swastika marking on them.

He lost control of his plane, and a voice over the radio told him they would land him in a few minutes. His plane was brought gently down, by some unseen control, and several tall, blond-haired men approached and told him to open the cargo door, which he did.

He reported a cordial welcome, and he was boarded onto a small platform, which moved without wheels, and transported him and his radio operator to a 'shimmering crystal city'. Upon arrival, they were escorted into a building, and later into an underground area where he met with 'the Master', who appeared as a slightly aging human. He regretted that we had not heeded repeated warnings about our use of atomic energy, and sent Byrd away with a message of a disastrous fate for all mankind. (This, in fact, is consistent with the reports of the appearance and message of the 'human' aliens, described by many of the witnesses in this book.)

They were escorted back to their plane, guided back to familiar territory, and returned to base. Admittedly some of these people used German phrases, and there were what appeared to be Swastikas on the craft, but the message was not hostile or threatening at that time. (It appears more logical that Nazis would flee north to remote Arctic areas with their technology. Further, the German Thule Society had liked and respected Richard Byrd.) Byrd then recorded a meeting with the Pentagon, where after advising of all that had happened and been said, he was ordered to remain silent.

While many people subscribe to a Hollow Earth theory, (with entrances at both Poles), and countless fables and accounts by the Eskimos and other indigenous people, I don't think there has been any modern evidence to substantiate this. However, it is possible that previously there were alien bases in the far north, which would explain the indigenous stories of the 'Sky-Land' where these visitors lived, often breeding with, and having children by earthly women.

It is not really possible to determine the authenticity of Byrd's report, or his reputed last diary entry on 31 December 1956 – 'that we are all in danger, it is evil itself.' This quote has been attributed to others at a much later date. If, and it's a big 'IF', the report is genuine, it seems Byrd was not speaking of the unusual occurrences and people that day at the North Pole, or the events in the Antarctic, but rather the 'monstrous military industrial complex', to which he had 'done his duty, completely against his values of moral right'.

Antarctica

Most underground bases would be quite undetectable, and except for the odd conspiracy theory, very few people have considered the best location of all, beneath the ice and snow of the continent of Antarctica, the fifth largest continent, with a land mass of 14 million square kilometres, larger even than Australia. While the surface of Antarctica is totally inhospitable for most of the year, this would not necessarily apply to subterranean areas. In 1995 Russian scientists found a 'warm' 250-kilometre-long lake under their Antarctic base.

Until recent times, and the advent of widespread satellite surveillance technology, this part of the world was safe from spying eyes. Even now, satellites do not cover the entire globe, although one which can do so is being proposed in 2017. Perhaps earlier claims of alien activity on this mostly-forgotten continent were not so far-fetched after all!

The Piri-Reis map was made before modern Europeans discovered Antarctica, yet details the sub-glacial geography of the continent. How and when this information was first obtained remains a mystery. In 1513, Ottoman Admiral Piri Reis had the map compiled from 20 different documents, many very old (some dating back to 400BC or earlier), and sourced from several countries. It has, in some respects been verified, but details show it does not reflect a complete knowledge of modern Antarctica.

The continent is placed hundreds of kilometres to the north, with a warm climate. However, modern science indicates this situation hasn't existed for many millions of years. The detailed topography suggests that either some source maps were well over 6,000 years old (the last time this continent was free of ice), or else it had been charted from above, using technology only available to our current society.

Some early researchers into ancient civilisations believe that Antarctica was once located further north towards the equator, and had moved to its current location at the South Pole by 'crustal displacement'. Charles Hapgood expands on this theory in his book *Earth's Shifting Crust*, and apparently had the support of Albert Einstein. He maintained that a very advanced civilisation existed there, although other experts strongly disagree with his theory. Modern photographs show what looks like a pyramidal structure near the Princess Elisabeth Station (Belgium), but it may well be only a natural formation.

I sometimes like to employ a 'what if?' mode of thinking. Therefore, one can hypothesise that an extensive self-sustaining underground base could have been constructed by aliens, or long ago by an ancient unknown civilisation, maybe both. Further, if the alien claims are correct, and they have been here for a very long time, the Antarctic might very well have been their base camp!

The first-known modern expedition to Antarctica was in 1821, when Mikhail Lazarev and Fabian Gottlieb von Bellinghausen landed there with Russian explorers. During the nineteenth century other missions were undertaken, including two by Germany in 1910 and 1925. After an initial voyage by Captain Ruser-Larsen, in the early 1930s, the Norwegians began exploring Queen Maud Land, between the Stancomb Wills and Shinnan Glaciers, which they 'annexed' in 1939. From December 1938 to February 1939, during the summer months, under Admiral Ritscher, Nazi Germany began expeditions and plans for a base in Antarctica. Their stated reason for this was to make formal claims on a little-known part of the continent (the same Queen Maud Land, claimed by the Norwegians), and they renamed the area Neuschwabenland. They claimed their defeat of Norway, early in World War 2, legitimised this claim in the name of the Third Reich.

In 1938, the German Thule Society invited Richard Byrd, the first man to fly over the South Pole, to lecture their personnel before they departed for Antarctica. (It is said that Byrd had also flown over the South Pole, but others claim he merely reported on the flight of a Lt Conrad Shinn. Shinn said he had flown over a 'strange, great ice-free valley, twenty miles long and eight miles wide, with a large number of black 'hillocks' about 15-30 feet high.)

A converted German aircraft carrier, the *Neuschwabenland*, left Hamburg in December 1938, arriving at the Antarctic in January 1939. Two planes onboard made numerous aerial mapping flights, dropping swastika flag/markers. The official reason for the 'German Society of Polar Research – New Schwabia' expedition was to establish a whaling station, as they needed whale oil, and did not want to continue to depend upon the Norwegians for their supplies. They also reported discovering a 300-square-mile, geothermally heated, ice-free region containing several lakes with a connection to the sea.

There have been many unsubstantiated reports about German machinery and technology being taken to the area over the next few years. Certainly, the Nazis had the requisite expertise and fleet of U-boats. It beggars belief that they also had a large enough Navy and sufficient man-power, manufacturing ability and raw materials to establish an enormous self-sufficient base while conducting a war across Europe and the north of Africa.

The British military and security agencies closely monitored this activity during and after World War 2, with secret military bases of their own established on the Antarctic continent, as well as the nearby Deception and Wiencke Islands. The codename for their covert presence was *Operation Taberlan*, and in 1946, using their 'sovereignty' of the Falkland Island Dependency, declared themselves legitimate owners of territory in the Antarctic, including parts which Chile and Argentina could also claim.

The British had sufficient intelligence reports to indicate that many Nazis may have fled there in submarines, and had a large underground base with advanced technology. We can only speculate that they already suspected they were more alien than human facilities. They wanted to retrieve this ahead of both the US and Russia. The British already had a well-established base at Maudheim, 200 miles away from the suspected Nazi or alien position, and it was from there they launched an expedition in 1945. The entire team perished, but not before they sent radio messages about Nazis, strange men and tunnels.

The next summer Britain sent another expedition, which purportedly found a self-sufficient base, with a massive network of tunnels and caverns, which they partially demolished after considerable loss of life.

Later, in 1946-47 during the following Antarctic summer, US Admiral Byrd, conducted *Operation High-Jump*, to supposedly investigate possible sites for bases, as huge mineral deposits had been found in this vast unexplored continent. The four participating military groups were collectively referred to as *Task Force 68* participating in 'The United States Navy Antarctic Developments Program'. (It has long been believed this was actually to eradicate the remaining Nazis or aliens. And if the reports are accurate, Admiral Byrd spoke of well-documented German activity there before, during, and after, the War. I consider this was a 'cover story' and that he already suspected an alien presence.)

At the time it was commented, that from the several thousand US military personnel and the ships and air-power involved, it looked more like an assault team than a survey mission. The expedition included flagship aircraft carrier *USS Philippine Sea*, with many planes, destroyers *USS Brownson* and *USS Henderson*, submarine *Sennet*, two tankers (the *Canisteo* and *Capacon*), and the supply ships *Merrick* and *Yancey*. There were two icebreakers, the *Burton Island* and *Northwind,* plus seaplanes and helicopters. (Hardly necessary for a few penguins, seals, and large fish!)

They 'expedition' built a headquarters and made numerous reconnaissance flights, recording over ten mountain ranges. *Operation High-Jump*, planned to last several months, ended prematurely after 40 days in a strategic retreat. The US contingent met stiff resistance, and engaged in several battles, suffering many casualties. There were reports of 'ray-type' weapons and Byrd described 'flying objects that could go from pole to pole at incredible speeds.' A Chilean newspaper reported, at the time, that Admiral Byrd had advised the US to initiate immediate defence measures against hostile forces threatening from the Arctic or Antarctic! He is also quoted as saying this resulted from his personal knowledge gathered at both the north and south poles! Of course, once he returned to the US, the matter was conveniently covered-up.

Personally, I believe this was indicative of a covert, advanced alien presence. What type of alien, and if they were connected to the Third Reich, would be a matter of conjecture. The Nazis did not have the ability or technology, at the time, to construct a substantial, meaningful, permanent, underground base in such a hostile environment. If they had possessed the craft documented by Admiral Byrd, Germany would have won World War 2.

The British did not return to the Antarctic until 1948-49. It is rumoured that 'hostile forces' were later eliminated by several 'large explosions'! The truth of what happened will probably never be known.

In the 1950s, the post-war powers agreed to co-operate in their activities on this icy continent. In 1957, the Americans and scientific representatives from 67 countries, officially returned to the Antarctic as part of the International Geophysical Year. Many stations were established on the continent.

On 3 July 1965, a giant lens-shaped solid flying object was seen, tracked and photographed over the Argentine Scientific Naval Base on Deception Island off the Antarctic coast. Lieutenant Daniel Perisse watched as it alternatively hovered for up to 20 minutes at a time, then accelerated and manoeuvred at tremendous speeds. Its colour changed from red-yellow to green and orange and caused strong interference with the variometers they used to measure the Earth's magnetic field. The object interfered with electromagnetic instruments and magnetograph tapes showed unusual registrations.

Similar reports came from the British base and a Chilean naval transport ship, the *Punta Mendanos*, whose compass needles pointed directly to the object, over a mile away, indicating it emitted an unusually strong force. Altogether, the craft was sighted by 31 people and none of these many witnesses believed the object was of terrestrial manufacture. (Recently, Russian scientists have theorised that electro-magnetically operated extraterrestrial vehicles would take advantage of the streams of magnetic energy, which is at its greatest at the North and South Poles.) Admiral Byrd was apparently tasked with recording such forces.

In 1976, it was reported that years previously, Brazilian scientist, Dr. Rubens Villela, saw a strange object which looked like a 'silver bullet', while on an icebreaker in Admiralty Bay. It came shooting out of 40-foot-thick sea ice. It flew off, high into the air, and huge chunks of ice 'came hurtling down'. In the large hole left in the ice, the water seemed to be boiling, with steam all around.

From time to time there have been more reports of ice-free regions and lakes. In 1977 scientists from the Scott Polar Research Institute discovered 17 lakes under the Antarctic Ice.

In 2002 British investigator, the late Graham Birdsall, attempted to research current scientific activity in the Antarctic, and was met with a fear to speak by some who knew the details. Graham and Dr Richard Sauder wrote about this in *UFO Magazine*, and it certainly appeared there was far more happening in the Antarctic than we were being told.

In *Contact Down Under*, I discussed the 1979 case of a New Zealand airliner, which crashed into Mt. Erebus in the Antarctic. Some ham radio operators claimed they had picked up transmissions from the doomed aircraft, saying it was being 'buzzed by a UFO'. As I pointed out in the book, it may have been trying to warn them they were on the wrong course – we will never know.

(There have been cases of unidentified objects saving our pilots from crashing. Keith Flitcroft advised of a close encounter in 1942, when he crossed the Normandy coast while flying a Wellington bomber. Due to cloud cover, they were at an extremely low altitude, and had to veer off course because of continual harassment by a small ball of green fire. It was only when he returned to base that he learned that his sudden forced deviation had prevented him from flying straight into a mountain dead ahead in the low cloud.)

What of the Antarctic today? In 2015 Linda Moulton Howe published information from a retired US Flight Engineer stationed in Antarctica during the summer season, in 1995-56. On several occasions he saw silver aerial discs darting around over the Transantarctic Mountains. One area was designated a 'no-fly' zone, which he was told was an 'air sampling' area. Once, when traversing it for a medical emergency, they saw a very large hole, like an entrance, going down into the ice. The debriefing they received indicated a lot more than an 'air sampling area'.

They were told 'they had never seen it', and never to talk about it. After their flights they would have a few beers at the bar, where they heard scientists talking about 'guys at the South Pole working with strange-looking men', and confirming a future trip to the 'air sampling area' (ie. big hole in the ice!) 'to meet-up with the ETs that were there.'

We have to ask where did the unusual craft, seen over the last 60 years originate? Were they ours or Theirs? More recently, there have been reports of secret visits to the Antarctic by some of the world's influential leaders. Why?

Chapter Seventeen

New Zealand

In 2000 I met Becky who worked in a local shop. As we became friends and she learnt of my UFO research work, she decided to confide in me about the odd events her family had experienced in New Zealand, and the reason they had moved to Australia and settled in the Blue Mountains. She was concerned about recent incidents which involved her daughter, Patricia.

She couldn't say very much with customers around, and suggested we meet with 'Patty', who could fill us in on some of the details. Fellow researcher Bryan Dickeson and I met her in Katoomba, and I visited Patty later at her house in Lawson. Her lifelong friend Gillian and Patty's boyfriend, Mark, were also there, and over the months and years of friendship that followed, it became apparent that an amazing series of encounters had affected not just Becky's family, but many others as well.

What made this case so interesting, from an investigator's viewpoint, was that most of the witnesses had not read UFO literature, or attended any meetings or conferences on the subject. Becky was in denial, and if she had experienced anything she refused to discuss it, and eventually moved to a property in Western New South Wales. (This was interesting, given that many experiencers felt the urge to move away from the coast and become self-sufficient.)

Becky's ex-husband James (Patty's father), was certainly deeply involved in 'aliens', but not influenced by outside information or the media. They were all very concerned about recent contacts in Australia, but I managed to get them to start from the beginning.

Patty and Gillian were in their late twenties and early thirties. They met and became good friends as children on Waiheke Island, in the Hauraki Gulf some miles east of Auckland, New Zealand. Patty was born in London in 1972, and migrated to New Zealand as a child with her parents, to join family on the island .in 1974.

Gillian was born in Naples, Italy in 1962, and her father, who was in the Italian Navy during the War, was from a seafaring family, with an added mixture of Scottish and gypsy heritage from her British mother. (Much later, when I researched their family history that I thought to myself, 'here we go again'!)

Gillian started to explain. "We migrated to New Zealand in 1965, when I was three, and lived first in an isolated cottage in the central North Island – an area they call the King Country. It's funny, I can't remember many details of my life before the age of nine, except that there were strange events and energies, which affected my mother. I used to sense that 'energy' and often felt frightened in the house. I have this sense of 'feelings' and knowing that more happened, but just cannot recall it no matter how hard I try. I have been told that there are very powerful energies in the area, which is apparently prone to UFO activity.

"We moved to Waiheke Island when I was about eleven. We lived in a semi-rural area again. About two kilometres away was this huge property, which took up all of one headland. It was supposed to be a farm, a sort of 'New Age' place owned by two wealthy Americans, LP and MW. They were overseas some of the time, and their farm manager, Jack MacKay, was specially brought out from Scotland to manage the property. In fact, LP chose all staff," she reflected.

"LP lived in the main house, and MW in the homestead just below. It was difficult to access the house; one side was on the edge of a cliff going down to the sea, and the other had lots of dips and hollows. A third cottage nearby was also connected with LP and MW. This was always closed up with darkened windows; the locals said it must hold something secret, or be some kind of gathering place."

Gillian explained her own connection to the farm: "My mother got some casual employment there, and when she babysat for the LP family, we usually stayed overnight, sometimes for a few days. Occasionally Patty stayed with us as well. There were three children – an eighteen-month baby, Paul, a girl of four or five, and son Max, who was incredibly intelligent. It was whispered he was being groomed for something, but I don't know what.

"The place was sometimes referred to as a 'farm stay', but the locals were always suspicious and whispered it was a cover for something else. A lot of extra stuff had been specially added. They built an odd, large landing pad, supposedly for helicopters, but no-one ever once saw or heard a chopper coming!"

(Becky, Patty's mother told me there had been strange comings and goings to the farm as far back as the 1950s. She named some well-known people from overseas: "Originally LP had claimed he was going to build a community, but of course, this never happened.")

Gillian continued, "There was an office which I wasn't allowed to go into, and it was all very secretive. Sometimes I would see the door open and strange, non-local, scientific looking people would come in and out, usually with LP or MW. Through the door I caught glimpses of banks of electronic equipment which seemed to have cables going out the window.

"There was a locked basement downstairs, which LP said contained 'his stuff', and I wasn't allowed to go there either." She paused, "I can still remember. The stairwell was dark and foreboding, but one night I noticed the door at the bottom was open, and nobody around. I ignored my fears and snuck down. Once inside I was amazed. I saw square boards of machines with dials, knobs, indicator lights and cables. There were technology screens, like something out of *Star Trek*. I was nervous about breaking the rules and going in, when I suddenly saw what I can only describe as a shadow of something or someone, which seemed to be fleeing for cover. I got out of there very quickly, and from then on was always scared of going downstairs near that basement.

"I was even a little afraid of sleeping in the guest room, and would sometimes hear a continual steady, background humming noise. One night we heard a noise, like a loud detonation. It was not a gunshot, more like a deep resonating boom above the house. It shook the whole place. There seemed to be strange vibes all around the back part of the house.

"It was what happened a short time later that really freaked me out," she faltered. "Max came running into my mother, saying 'Paul is weird. He's laughing and talking in a deep voice.' Mum told me to stay in bed, and she spent the rest of the night in Paul's room."

Gillian left Waiheke in 1979-80 and didn't return for 20 years. She and Patty, who had a very strong 'psychic' bond, remained in contact the entire time.

Patty told me about her life on the Island, which even today she still thinks of as 'home'. "As a child, looking back now, my life seems to be a blur. There seems to be pieces of my childhood missing somehow. At the age of about two or three I did spend some time living on the farm when my parents were away. Gillian and her mother were also there looking after the children.

"I have fond memories of the Island, and remember spending most of my time with my grandparents. I loved being with them, it seemed routine to live half my time with my parents, and the other half with my grandparents, who lived in the rural area. In fact, my grandmother also came to Australia and the Blue Mountains with us."

Patty recounted events during her childhood: "I have always been curious about the unknown, even when very young, and often looked up at the stars and dreamt of faraway places. When I was four, I was staying with my grandparents, and probably asleep in bed at the time (my grandmother told me about this many years later). She and my uncle were watching television when all power in the house went dead. They were sitting in complete darkness, and thought a fuse might have blown. When they looked out, they realised it was a blackout as they could not see any normal street and house lights shining in the distance.

"They went outside. They could hear an unusual humming, and smelt a strange fume-like odour of some kind. Down in the valley Gran could see a circular object with lights all around it. She said it couldn't have been a house because there were no homes in that area. To this day, Gran is sure it was an unidentified flying object."

'Gran', who now lives in the Blue Mountains confirmed this for me, and insists that a flying saucer had landed in the valley below. "That was not all," Gran said, "A few days later a strange woman came to my door, and asked if she could come in. I think she was European, she looked and sounded as if she was Swedish or similar. She wanted me to join a meditation group at the farm, and when I told her 'No', she played me a tape. It was the strangest music, a mixture of squeaking and humming. She said it was a communication from another world.

Under hypnosis Patty recalled an event from Waiheke Island at about the same young age. She woke up in bed on night when a blue light was coming through the closed window. She had 'seen this light before', and got up to look through the curtains. The whole house was surrounded in a brilliant blue light. She couldn't believe it, but was not worried as her 'Friend' was coming with several of his small companions.

She saw him appear within the blue light, and then he came through her window into the room, which was flooded in blue. He was accompanied by six or seven 'little people' – small, with medium-sized, oval-shaped heads, creamy-brown skin and big black eyes 'like dark mirrors.' They were not much taller than Patty, and had long, skinny arms with four fingers, but no thumb, on each hand. Her Friend was much, much taller. They were all wearing a similar, neck high full-body suit, which was a blue-grey shiny material, like a wet suit, with a red triangular motif on the right-hand side.

Once in the room, her Friend bent down to her and put out both his hands. He looked down and she placed her hands just above his, without actually touching. "He spoke to me, but his mouth didn't move. I felt good, and wasn't worried, when he explained we would always be friends, and not to be afraid.

"I knew that sometimes they took me up into the space ship above the house, and this time I was going there to play with the little people. The small ones stepped into the blue light, which covered the roof of the whole house, followed by me and my Friend. I felt good and relaxed, and it shrank, like a spotlight, as we went up."

Patty's next memory was of being on board the craft. "The little people were around me, running around and chasing each other, playing tag or something like that. I had seen them before, they were always there. I was more interested in a strange lady who had just walked in.

"She looked different to my Friend, more human-like. Her face was like the aliens, with a small mouth, two dots for a nose, and no lips, but she had very blue human eyes and long, white straggly hair. She was wearing a long, white loose robe, and had browny-cream coloured skin with normal human-type hands.

"She was scary, and seemed angry, looking at me as if I shouldn't be there. I had never seen her before, and as she walked away I think my Friend was having an argument with her. I kept playing with the little people, and after a while she went off down a corridor. My Friend came back, and calmed me down with 'feelings'. (He could communicate feelings without actually saying anything.)"

As with other experiencers, Patty had described entering the craft through a 'porthole' in the floor. "There were a series of very big octagonal rooms, on the same level, joined together by a series of corridors. After the nasty lady left, my Friend took me into one. There were four blank walls behind us, and we were facing the other four which had big screens.

"He had brought the little ones with us, perhaps to take our minds off the big argument. My Friend turned the screens on and showed me so many pictures; lots and lots of stars and galaxies. It was so much to take in all at once, different planets, somewhere else, not here! At first, I thought they were taking me away, it seemed I was being 'drawn in', moving through space, with stars going by. Really strange!

"We arrived at an unusual place, which I think was his home planet. The landscape was mostly red dirt, with a prehistoric look about it. Everything was big, with lots of strange desert plants, big multicoloured leaves, which apparently ate insects. There were lots of concrete buildings, which looked like huts, but they had connecting tunnels. My Friend told me that it was too hot for them to live outside.

"Inside, everything was round and bright white. The windows were triangular, but although tinted, still had light streaming through. I saw a see-through glass or plastic table with stools all around, and I was shown metallic capsules, which shut when they go inside to sleep. I was told they don't sleep much and only eat infrequently."

Patty said the experience was weird. She was there, she could see and feel everything, but not actually touch anything.

"He took me to his house, and I met his family. His wife was a bit shorter than him, no hair, but softer skin and normal body with two small breasts noticeable beneath her clothes. She seemed nice, not like that other nasty lady. He had two children, a little boy and a little girl, who looked identical but had different characteristics. They all wore the same blue-grey outfit with the red triangle motif.

"We played different games, some on the screen, some running around, and one with different coloured balls which floated. There were solid balls and others that were more ethereal. After saying goodbye my Friend took me by the hand and led me away."

As she was undergoing regressive hypnosis, Patty's description of the next experience was a little childish. He told her it was time to go home and they then went back through the tunnels and entered "a big, big, big, big room where there are lots of ships. The ships are round and they've got – they're huge. This one – it's round like a saucer and shiny, metallic, very reflective. It's like a place where you keep planes. It's huge, like a big cave."

Patty's Friend then took her back home – through the blue light and her bedroom window. Once he put her back into bed he left. The next morning, she did have some memory of the event, which faded soon afterwards.

I was interested to know more about Patty's Friend, and how long he had been a part of her life. Later, under hypnosis, Patty recalled an event from Waiheke Island when she was about three and a half years old:

"We were at the 'homestead' having breakfast. We always had breakfast there every weekend and there were lots of children and adults present. My Dad was there but my Mum didn't like these occasions.

"I can see all the people – the group we were in. MW was there, other parents, and a visiting artist – a painter. My Dad was sitting out on the porch and I was in the garden making daisy chains. The chooks were all around me – it was a wonderful time.

"All my little friends, my friends, four other children, went running into the neighbouring bushland because there's a path up to the house on the top of the hill. We were running along this path, playing hide-and-seek. I could see a strange figure standing behind a tree. I was on the pathway, looking out into the bush and he's peeking, poking his head around the corner.

"I've never seen a head like that before. It's got big black eyes, like a mirror black; he's very tall and he's talking to me – in my mind. He's telling me not to be afraid; we've been doing this a long time: 'I'm your friend, can I play?' I feel that I have met him, that I know him.

"He started playing with all of us, just joined in with all the children. They all know him too. We're walking, making our way up to the other house on the top of the hill. He's with us, leading up to the house. It's still morning.

"I can see something. It's like a strange saucer-shaped thing on the ground nearby, next to the house, on the ground. It's got, like 'spikes', coming out from underneath it and these hold it up from the ground. Its roundish, mainly, a bit under 20 feet across, to the right of the house and slightly down the hill, near the flying fox. I think I've seen something like that before – it doesn't look 'alien' to me for some reason. It doesn't worry me at all, and our tall 'leader' is very nice.

"The kids are all playing on the flying fox up near the craft. Then these little people come out of the disc-like object. They're shorter than my Friend. Taller than me, but very small compared to him. They're very little – they look like little children. I think I've seen people like them before, and I don't feel worried at all.

"The four other children – and about six of the little people. Gillian is there too. She's up at the big house, keeping an eye on us from time to time – she looks after us; she looks out for us. She's the only one there; all the other adults are down at the homestead, after breakfast.

"We're laughing a lot and running around and they're taking us into the little disc. There's a little, flat ramp that comes from underneath and an open door into the centre of the disc from the bottom. The four spikes that keep the disc off the ground are quite solid, metallic.

"The craft is completely metallic and there's oval windows – windows all round. It's like a disc, and then there's a rounder lump, or dome, on top which has the little oval windows all round that. It's like two deep saucers one on top of the other, but quite small. The little people are in there already. Then my Friend is leading the way, followed by me and then my friends. It's quite cramped so the little people are moving aside to give us room.

"Inside it's like – it's very small and round. There's one seat in the middle of the room, a black seat, with no controls. There's one screen in front of the seat. And there's a window in front of that. The screen thing has lights inside it, but it doesn't have any controls.

"We're all standing inside the craft and I'm looking at the seat and screen. There are small bench seats behind the central black seat. We're all inside, looking around. It's got an open grating-type floor too. You can see through that to something that's underneath – it's probably the 'engine room' area. We're so small that it seems big, but it's not very big at all.

"We had all wanted to see inside the craft, to 'have a look', because it seemed interesting. The chair, which has a leather-type of feel, is just like an office chair, but there are screens on the arms, where you put your hands. I sat in the chair for a while, but they don't really want the children to play with the screens at all – they say it could be dangerous, 'We're only little.'

"We were all looking around and playing – not asking questions at all, we're just interested and want to play with things, but we're not really allowed to. There's nothing on the screen; it's all 'shut black.' The oval windows have shutters down on them or something, so you can't see through them. They say that when you fly, you can see through them.

"They're explaining that they come from a very, very long way away. (Patty's new Friend is explaining all this.) 'They've been doing this for a very long time. They've been visiting us for a long time. Don't be afraid. They are friends with my Dad's friends.'

"We are not worried, just laughing and playing and looking around. They must know my father's friends, because They're at the house – They've got their spaceship parked there.

When the children got bored, they went back down the ramp to the flying fox to play. The Friend and his small people just watched them from near the craft.

Occasionally, Patty looks over towards the space craft, but she is mostly playing on the flying fox: "It's still there – they just watch us and some of the little people go back inside the disc."

Later, Patty can see all the other adults coming up the track from the homestead – the spaceship was still there. They come up the path and seem to know her new Friend. They talk to him. The children are still playing on the flying fox and the adults stand around in a circle, near the Friend and talk. Patti's father, MW, LP, and the parents are all there – just talking.

Then all the adults go into the house, with the Friend. They're in the house for a long time; "The kids are on the flying fox – there's so much to do!

"There are a couple of little people inside the disc, working on something. There are four in the house, but none near the flying fox. Two 'little people' are under the spaceship – they've gone inside it, underneath, doing something. There's a hatch, near the main access door – they climb in there and they're not coming out."

After a good while Patty's father came out of the house, down the path towards the flying fox and said that they had to go home now. The space craft was still there with the little people inside the hatch. Patty's new Friend came out of the house to say 'Goodbye' and Patty and her father headed down the track, back towards the homestead. Occasionally Patty looked back to see her Friend standing there, watching them leave. There were no little people visible, but Patty said MW also came out of the house to wave goodbye.

Patty and her father went back down to the homestead where her father's car was parked outside in the driveway. They could see the house on top of the hill but not the spacecraft at all – it was parked slightly down the hill in 'a bit of a dip', well-obscured from the road.

Patty and her father drove home, but didn't tell her mother anything about it.

After describing the recovered memories, Patty continued; "When I was about eight there was an occasion when I flew down my street towards my family home. I don't recall who or what was in control of my 'taking to the air', and when I told my mother she laughed and said 'it was only my imagination.' I felt cheated by this comment, and was frustrated because I seemed to be the only one who could grasp this experience as reality. I felt alone.

Patty contacted her father 'James', still living on Waiheke, who rang me, quite anxious to talk to someone, away from the Island, whom he could trust and confide in. He also put me in contact with MW (since moved to Australia) who admitted to being the 'area manager' and confirmed much of what James said. It was invaluable to my research to get first-hand verification of the 'project' from one of the senior scientists and facilitators.

James was able to tell me much more about the 'farm'. MW was rather lonely and found it hard to fraternise with the locals on the Island. He had become firm friends with James over a 25-year period, and in fact they saw each other most days. James would have a communal, weekly breakfast with him and a couple of the 'group', until MW's wife 'put a stop to it.'

"She, in fact, was the real one 'in charge', but MW told me a lot of what had really been going on up there over the years. Apparently after World War 2 a group of ex-German Nazis lived on the Island. One of them was a 'Swedish' scientist, a woman who experimented on 'rats', but we suspected it was humans. She often went to LP's place and was part of his group. A friend of mine, said she had spoken to someone in German, expressing guilt over the Nazi experiments.

"The entire group was originally made up of US military people and scientists, working with advanced electronics to make contact with aliens. I think there was even more to this, there was a definite agenda which I was not told about," James confided. "I don't know how successful they were, but certainly the Waiheke residents reported a lot of sightings in the 1970s. One UFO entered the water near a small island on Church Bay. I also saw lights over that area.

"Once I saw a scientist coming down from where the Experiment was being conducted, and I will never forget his face – it was ashen! The children who lived on this property (now adults) still talk about this and Patty could tell you about what they said, as she is their age. At that time, I was living here, but not yet part of the experiments."

After a while a second project was begun using meditation or the power of the mind. This secondary project claimed that they succeeded in several UFO landings. In the late 1970s LP (connected to the US military) who was more involved in the electronic experiments, moved to Australia, rather than back to the US. In the 1980s MW moved to the village, and it seems a secondary project continued for many years. MW's Mexican wife was involved with the Gurdjieff movement, which although only playing just one part of the experiments, incorporated a form of meditation which 'made all quiet inside' and 'blocked out the past and future'.

Both James and MW were very cagey about some details, but admitted they had contacted UFOs all the time on the island. The initial project was a secret US Government (Electronic) Experiment to contact their 'friends'. It was much more complex than anyone realised, and sometimes done simultaneously with the US.

Both scientists commented that there is so much we don't understand as to how the universe works, and that often our perception of the physical world depends on our state of mind and spirit. Not only did they use Earth-energy Ley Lines, they also encompassed sounds, vibrations and levels of mental and spiritual perception.

The night the UFO had landed below Patty's grandmother's house they had been broadcasting a tape of 'alien vibrations.' They also divulged that data from famous New Zealand researcher, Bruce Cathie, who had specialised in Harmonics, had also been involved, but he was later silenced and ridiculed.

(This brought to mind the experiments documented by Dr Steven Greer – also essentially CE5s – where in 1973 he discussed a method of 'not only sounds and light, but also non-local consciousness and directed coherent thought, to communicate with extraterrestrial beings and their electronic devices'. He also described methods including not just telepathy, but also technology. A technological interface device, with specialised physics and electromagnetism, was also used, and later formed a basic part of psychotronic weapons systems.)

Thinking about Elizabeth, Vera, Lydia and other subjects, I checked Patty's bloodlines. Sure enough James himself, and therefore Patty and her paternal grandfather, were full *fleur-de-lis* on his British side. I was going back three generations, and I was experiencing some difficulties tracing back the military history, although one person had been in the Dutch underground during the War. In a slight reversal of the combination, it was Becky's father who served in both the British Army and the Irish Guards during the War, just before Becky was conceived.

I was also not surprised to find that Gillian's ancestors were also *fleur-de-lis*, but I was taken aback when I discovered that LP, who was ex-senior military, was also the same bloodline.

James and I corresponded and spoke on the phone for some years before his death. He asked me not to contact him by electronic mail, as he didn't want any 'sensitive' information to be examined by the 'Government Surveillance Echelon Computer'. He tutored me in some of the alien contact methods, and wanted me to go to the Island for further knowledge. Unfortunately, family circumstances stopped me going.

James explained, "I should also detail how, as a westerner, I come to know these methods so well. My father was in China when the Japanese invaded and he rescued a Chinese Master and brought him to England. As a result of this, I have practised Shuichuan since early childhood and know all three styles of the subject very well."

James continued, "These beings are so far ahead of us and have a different state of consciousness. They communicate in a state of peace and mindlessness, and often can be reached through, dance, music and song, which can produce an amazing aura of intensity and energy."

(Australian aboriginal elders have explained to me that some of their sacred knowledge was, in part, that the 'vibrations' in their song, dance and instruments enabled contact with entities. Elizabeth had also commented that she had always been able to heighten her psychic vibrations and abilities through certain music.)

While James admitted he had friends who had been abducted, he was reticent about his own possible experiences. "Now, I can't say if I was abducted, but probably was. Since coming to New Zealand I seem to be compelled to live on Waiheke Island, which is an important place for Alien activity. I do curious intuitive things which have no explanation; perhaps I was 'programmed'. They appeared once at my house, and seemed to be examining it with some weird equipment. I was not afraid, and I don't recall them affecting me. I used my Qigong and was in a peaceful state. I think that is what they require to make contact with us, peace and mindlessness, for this is the way they are."

He admitted to using a form of Qigong and an Indonesian meditative exercise called 'Latihan', which had also been part of the second project. I began to realise, even though James denied it, he not only must have played a significant role in the second project, he in all probability helped initiate it. It was most probable that second project comprised not only elements of Gurdjieff practices – (which originated with the Russian Ivanovich; 1866-1949) – and James' input of ancient Eastern knowledge, but some components of the scientific electronic experiments.

(A lot of new questions and possible insights had arisen. There is so much about the Universe that we don't understand. Our perception of the physical world depends on both our state of mind and spirit. Why do some people see UFOs and not others? When they got them to land or appear, were they being attracted or manifested?)

James admitted to knowing of a future Earth cataclysm, and the reason for the visitation of the aliens. This had in part been confirmed by MW, to both him and me, and it was more natural disaster he was articulating, rather than warfare. One of the objectives of these particular aliens was to assist us through difficult times. "Alien abductions are the result of a beneficial need on their part to preserve colonies of human beings (of good spiritual quality), so that our race continues to survive and move forward." I have thought long and hard and decided it would be irresponsible to divulge any further details.

It is not known how much the events and experiences were affecting Patty's mother, but she was 'falling apart'. James and Becky were divorced, in fact she was frantic to get off the Island. With James's encouragement, Patty, Becky and her mother had all left New Zealand and moved to Australia. He was happier when they relocated to the Blue Mountains west of Sydney. He felt if the predictions were correct, they would be safer there.

At my next meeting with the women, Patty and Gillian continued telling me what had happened in the last couple of years. To a great extent, they thought they had put Waiheke and the past behind them, but recent events were a little disconcerting.

Patty spoke first: "I met Mark about a year ago. We seem to have a special bond and are really in tune with each other. He is also curious about the unknown, just like me.

"I have always been afraid of the dark, ever since I was a child. In July 1998, it was getting worse. For no valid reason, I was becoming paranoid about the security in our apartment, and would check the locks on the doors and windows several times. I was restless most nights. On this particular evening, I drifted off into a slumber soon after.

"I found myself in another world. It wasn't like a dream, it seemed too real. A woman wearing a white gown came to me, in some ways she was similar in appearance to my mother. She took me by the hand and led me through a garden, down some stone steps to a grass lawn with a white tent.

"Inside was another woman, lying on a bed. She looked just like my grandmother. She looked very peaceful, and I got the impression I was being shown the death experience. I watched for some time, and then the being who had led me in began to speak to me telepathically about my health.

"She said that I must give up smoking and live a healthy existence. It was a very strong message, but one that cannot, for some reason, be described in words. It was more a feeling that she seemed able to plant into my inner self.

"We then moved on to another place which looked like a barn. I saw my step-grandfather (who had died three years earlier) and others who were standing around him. They all spoke to me telepathically about life, my health and love. The funny thing is that I can't put into context what they actually said to me, but I 'felt' it.

"I woke up, and as I opened my eyes found myself gasping for breath and tears rolling down my cheeks. I became quite hysterical, and Mark woke up. I told him of the experience, and he made us both a cup of tea and calmed me down before we both went back to sleep."

Patty paused, "Everything was fine until about three weeks later. Mark and I went to bed, and I dropped off to sleep soon after. I woke at about 3 a.m., turned over to Mark and he was staring right back at me. He asked me what I had dreamed, but I could not answer. I felt scared, almost stunned, but my reply was simply 'Nothing, I don't want to talk about it.' We then both went straight back to sleep.

"The next morning, I could remember everything that happened in my experience the previous night. Today it is still vividly etched in my mind. I was in bed asleep when a blue light came through the window, and took both Mark and me through a hole in the bottom of a huge craft. I found myself in an octagonal, Spartan room. Its floor, ceiling and walls were all a shiny metallic black. A tall grey being was standing in front of me, his black eyes staring into mine, like he was penetrating my soul.

"Our arms were stretched out in front of us, and our hands were on top of each other. They weren't touching, it was an energy thing. I knew Mark was there somewhere, but not exactly where because I was so mesmerised by the being that stood before me. It seemed to be feeding me some kind of energy. No words were spoken, just feelings.

"After a few minutes, he spoke to me telepathically, saying: 'Don't worry, we've been doing this for a long time, everything is going to be OK.' I somehow felt relieved by this message, and felt completely safe and secure. Next thing I recall I woke-up in bed. I felt there was a lot more to this experience, but for some inexplicable reason I could or would not remember for some time.

I turned to Mark who had been sitting quietly while Patty told me her story; "My experience that night was somewhat different," he said. "I recall lying on a solid table and was surrounded by beings. There were two or three steps, at the foot of the table, heading into a corridor where I felt Patty was. I was trying to scream, but something was blocking me from talking or shouting.

"I remember this telepathic thought, a sort of communication; "We've been doing this for a long time and everything is going to be all right." I woke up in bed screaming out, and turned to look at Patty. She was wide awake, but never heard me calling, which is quite amazing."

I arranged for Patty to have a session of light hypnotic regression with a qualified practitioner and she reported back to me afterwards. "I have had some flashbacks since. When we were inside some smaller creatures were hovering a few inches up. They took me by each arm and levitated me across the floor into the first room and the taller being. I also recalled a second room. The floor was also a black metallic colour, with almost a mirror finish. The walls were dark, with dim lights in the ceiling. This area was octagonal with a steel clinical chair in the middle. It was a bit like a dentist's chair, which swivelled when I sat in it. I was shown a different screen on each wall. I can't recall the vision, but it was something to do with the planet." (The hypnotist encountered a block when he asked what was on the screens.)

"Afterwards, the tall being (I somehow felt he had been my friend for years), took me to a small room, and Mark was on a table with other shorter beings doing something to him with lights. They took him off the table and then put both of us, feet first, into a porthole through a blue-purple light."

Mark and Patty had been living on the shores of Sydney Harbour, but after the experience moved inland to the Blue Mountains. "Our lives turned around dramatically after this experience. We left Sydney in a panic, a drive or force of some kind seemed to push us in this direction," Patty said. "We were frantic to leave Sydney, and I can't explain why."

"In April 1999, about five months after settling into our new home in the mountains, something else happened. I found myself at the back door one evening, but don't recall how I got there. I felt kind of groggy, but still alert and aware of what I was doing. As I walked down the hallway towards our bedroom, I noticed a strange taste in my mouth.

"I started to panic a little, but when I got into bed, couldn't wake Mark no matter how hard I tried. I heard noises in the house, like people walking around, but couldn't seem to move. Everything went silent for a few seconds, and after I heard a humming sound outside, somehow went back to sleep."

Mark confirmed that the same night he also had a dream: "But I was on a train. I could hear noises and sensed there were people around me, but couldn't see anything, not even when I woke up."

After this incident both Patty and her young son Charles suffered nosebleeds. Patty had lots of dried pus up her nostrils, and felt 'something is up there that won't come out'. She sometimes gets a high ringing in her left ear, often feeling 'removed' from everything, and also has a cyst in her right ovary.

Charles has told her that in the night-time 'Alf takes him in a basket' and the aliens come and play with him, which spooked Patty somewhat. I began to suspect, given the bloodline and generational aspects of these encounters, that Patty and Charles were the main target of these experiences, and perhaps Mark just there by circumstance. (I also recalled Jane, see Chapter 18, seeing her young son Bruce, playing on the space craft, and his comments about 'going for a ride with Peter Pan.)

Much later, when Patty felt more able to cope with any hidden memories, I arranged for a further hypnotic regression.

Under hypnosis Patty remembered that after hearing the noises in the house, she saw a man near her bed. He was of medium height and wearing a dark cloak. She thought he was her Friend's friend, and he told her he'd come to take her back to see him. He put his right hand into hers, and as he led her out of the bedroom, and into the lounge room, she could see Mark, still asleep.

Patty's four-year-old son Charles was in the lounge room, laughing and happy, playing with three little entities, just as she did as a child. As they neared the back door, she saw four more small beings. All were dressed in the same blue-grey bodysuits with the red triangle, which she recognised. Everyone left together, the four little ones first, followed by Patty and the taller 'man', with Charles and his three playmates coming up behind.

Once outside Patty could see a huge craft, very high above the back garden, with a blue light shining down from it. It was a flat metallic disc, with lots of red, yellow and green 'spotlights' underneath, and round windows all around the top. The blue light then flooded the garden as they moved towards it, and were taken up inside via the memorable porthole, which she noticed was slightly to one side of the base, and not in the centre as she previously thought.

Once in the larger octagonal room, Charles and his new companions were enjoying themselves playing with coloured airborne balls. The other four small beings disappeared down a corridor. Her cloaked escort had also gone, and she turned to her Friend who had been waiting for her. He took her back to the familiar smaller octagonal room with the screens. He put out his hands and the screens came to life.

He communicated with her telepathically, saying he was happy she had moved out of Sydney; he had wanted her to move away from the ocean, as there may be disasters in the future. He told her she had to be careful, as there was a long journey ahead for mankind. She saw images of disasters, cities desolate and destroyed, burned environments and people starving. He told her he was sad about the way humans are and what they have done. 'They' didn't want that.

He told her she needed to keep aware, and to work towards becoming self-sufficient, showing her various methods. He said she mustn't worry, They will always come back if there are problems. There will be some people who survive. They have a place on Earth – a sanctuary where people who want to, can escape. (It was a whole village – and although Patty didn't recall being taken there before –

she did get to see the area during later 2009 and 2011 experiences, some of which she consciously recalled.)

He showed her many things on the screens and told her some of their history. They came to Earth a long time ago and while living here, genetically engineered apes, who became cave-men and later, humans. Their own world was dying, but they are living the best way They can.

He explained we cannot live where they do; the temperature and atmosphere are not compatible, and we could only ever visit for a short time. He explained it was the same for Them, They cannot live on Earth permanently.

Patty could see Charles happily playing, and asked what was in a blue lighted room down the corridor. They went in to what looked like a laboratory, and she saw the 'horrible' lady with the bright blue eyes, who seemed to work there.

Patty said it was scary; cages with strange creatures; lots of weird aquatic-looking things. She got upset. Her Friend said they weren't doing any harm, just trying to help these creatures, who were from their world and other planets.

Patty and her Friend went back to the room with the screens, to continue their discussion. Patty was so overwhelmed she had to ask him to "please slow down". He apologised for pushing the visions and information so quickly, but they wanted her to be one of the few 'survivors'. People need to learn these survival skills.

All their communication had been telepathic, and Patty found it hard to absorb it all. Her Friend said it was time to go, and along with Charles they stood at the porthole looking down at the ground, far below. As the blue light shone down, she felt the familiar 'sucking' feeling; it seemed to take forever to descend into their back garden.

"The next thing Charles and I were at the back door. I was now fully conscious, and very confused, as I didn't know how I got there."

Gillian had been compelled to return to Waiheke Island in August 1999. She didn't know why, but felt she had some purpose there. Patty and Mark went back to visit James in November 1999, and they all met up in the local pub, where Mark and Patty were singing in their band.

Gillian reminisced; "It was so strange, a lot of others were there, people we had gone to school with. It was like something had simultaneously drawn us all to come back at the same time. Many of our contemporaries were very musical, it was something in the notes and rhythm, and we all felt this tremendous bond and connection with each other.

(From the beginning of time, acoustic phenomena – sound, pitch, rhythm, frequency, vibration, resonance – have all been known to produce an amazing effect and outcomes in unimaginable ways.)

"I met Patty and Mark the next day, and we discussed the farm, or the 'Large House' as we called it, and what had happened in the past. We went up there, however new roads and subdivisions were on some parts of the property. As we drove around, we were stunned by the strong physical and emotional responses we felt in some areas. The old energy grids were still there."

Patty gave a sigh: "When we were in-line with my grandmother's old house weird things and strong physical effects started to happen. The radio turned on by itself, and I felt a tingling in my arms and hands. There was a tight pressure above my eyes and nose, like a force-field was blanketing my head. I started to get woozy and lightheaded."

Gillian continued; "We went around the road to a lower spot, further down – a hollow where we used to play as children. It was odd, LP used to let me play with his kids down there, but was paranoid about letting any adults into the area. Then I realised that the remains of what I had thought was a woolshed, was in fact more like a military barracks or bunker.

"I felt drawn to the area, but by this time both Mark and Patty were feeling very nervous, drained and exhausted."

Gillian confided that since the trip with Patty and Mark she had gone back to that spot to sit and meditate, usually feeling the same side-effects. She had several friends on Waiheke of Maori origin, who had recounted alien abductions. (Gillian never discussed her presence on the farm when the aliens visited, but she asked if I could arrange a hypnotic regression for her, later on.)

Gillian took one couple who were psychic and sensitive – familiar with indigenous knowledge and understanding. They went individually and separately to the spot to see if they could discern or recall any information. Dawn and Jean both felt nauseous in the area, as did Noel, who was more scientifically minded. Jean was quite sick for several days afterwards. The consensus was that the anomaly was not an object, transportation device or portal area. Instead there was a 4-dimensional 'energy field' located under the area, which was to help humanity, and would activate during a particular transition phase, due to occur in the next few years.

Any further questions they had were blocked as the timing was not right. Gillian later decided it was important to return to and remain on the island. She felt compelled to stay on Waiheke as she had a 'purpose', but didn't know what it was. Later, she just disappeared; nobody knows where she is! Dawn thought Gillian was 'not completely human and had a specific task in relation to this'.

Noel said that during the intervening period some people, who had roles to play in relation to the site, would come to the Island. He also warned it was vital that none of this became public knowledge for some years, and I promised Gillian I would not release any information about Waiheke for at least ten years. Although Gillian has since 'disappeared', I have waited 15 years, until James died. (Much too young, though I don't know if this was connected with his activities.)

I looked into the history of Waiheke, and soon realised it is an ideal location for clandestine experiments – as a remote, sub-tropical island, only a short ferry ride to Auckland. It is hilly (Mount Maunganui is 231 metres high), is 19 kilometres long, and varies from 0.64 to 9.65 kilometres wide. Originally occupied by the Maori, it has a long history of bloody tribal battles. The first Europeans set foot there in 1801, but white settlers only arrived in 1830.

The population was sparse, only numbering 835 at the end of World War 2. A few years earlier a network of tunnels and gun emplacements was constructed to defend the eastern side of Auckland Harbour; it is possibly that at this time its potential was recognised. Residents remain few – 2,144 in 1955, 3,500 in 1978, 4,554 in 1986 – by which time the main facility had shut down.

There are few local government structures or services, and building constructions have been unregulated and unsupervised. There was no full local government until 1970, and very little oversight until amalgamated with Auckland in 1989. It would have been easy for any quasi-government or military agency to bring equipment, supplies and provisions in, without attracting much attention from authorities or the locals.

Islands are an ideal location for these types of secret facilities – hidden away from public scrutiny and difficult to access!

Patty remained in the Blue Mountains, and enjoyed a few years of 'normal' life. There was one incident in 2002 when she lived in a cottage in Katoomba overlooking Catalina Park – a traditional, aboriginal, tribal area. It was about 2 a.m. and a wind had sprung up – for some reason she was always frightened of the wind. Patty looked out and saw a huge square, grey, craft with a mixture of what looked like letters and numbers on it.

"In some ways, it resembled a flying shipping container – bolts, but no lights and 'funny' legs. It moved very slowly over the top of my house and appeared to land in the park. I was so terrified I just grabbed my seven-year-old son, jumped in the car, and raced over to my mother's place for the night."

About 2009 Patty's contacts resumed; "It was another really windy night; I had gone to bed, but something drew me outside in my pyjamas. Next thing I was on a little craft with windows all around. I was taken to a place with a lake, pine trees and snow-capped mountains behind. There was a group of about ten of us, all in our pyjamas. We got out and it was like stepping into an old cowboy movie. It was a deserted community settlement, like an old mining town, deep in a pine forest. It was an old town, and we were being shown a shop and log cabins with handmade benches and kitchens. There were even fires burning in the fireplaces, as if it was ready to move into."

She continued; "There was a woman at a counter. She looked like a normal human with brown eyes, I had seen before on the spaceship. I went up to her and asked why we were here? I was stunned when she screeched at me – I got the impression I wasn't supposed to approach her, and she didn't like me! There were other aliens present, but they communicated telepathically. I got the impression they were showing us some kind of 'refuge' for times to come. I still feel physically shaken when I talk about this."

There was another night when the unusual wind suddenly sprang up. I could sense Their presence, and I ran outside and begged 'please not tonight'. The wind seemed to die down and no more happened that I can remember."

It seemed Patty's Friend felt the necessity to impress upon her the existence and location of the 'safe haven'. Although her previous trip was consciously recalled, some of this next experience was retrieved using hypnosis.

"In late summer 2011 I was camping with my then boyfriend David. We were near Whyalla in South Australia, close to a beach. It was an eerie sort of place. I think there was an Army Base nearby.

"I was walking around the remote campsite, just admiring the night sky, which, in Australia, can be magnificent away from the major cities. The moon was just so bright, almost like daylight. As I looked inland, I could see six craft hovering and moving over a mountain.

"I was terrified, and raced back to the tent, waking my dog and David. I told him I didn't feel safe, and we had to leave **now**! He wanted to pack up our camping gear, but I told him something was wrong, and to just leave it. The Australian outback can be a dangerous place to be alone, so he didn't argue. We threw some bedding in the back of my ute, and drove for about 25 minutes back along the main road towards Whyalla. We stopped a few kilometres out of town, and slept at the side of the road, the dog in the front seat, while we squeezed into the back seat."

The next thing Patty knew was waking to find the vehicle surrounded in blue light. She felt scared, but got out of the ute to investigate. As she stood there, the blue light shrank around her, and she found herself being lifted up to the familiar 'porthole' beneath a craft.

"It seemed to be the same ship as before, and I was all alone in the large, octagonal room with black shiny walls. I felt more relaxed when I saw my Friend coming towards me, and he put out his hand and told me we were going somewhere special. A few other men and women joined us, and I'll never forget an older man who looked really scared.

"The 'little ones' arrived, and each took one of us by the hand and led us back to the entry 'porthole'. My 'Friend' didn't appear to be coming at first, but soon joined us. The porthole in the floor was open, and below I could see a smaller ship.

It was round, and although bigger than a car or truck, not very large. Much, much further down I could see my own ute on the roadside."

The little disc moved up and underneath them, and connected to their porthole via a hole in its top. Each of the humans, with their little companion, had to go backwards down a ladder into the smaller craft.

"There was a red, shiny horseshoe-shaped bench-seat around the curved wall of the small craft. We were all seated. I didn't recognise any of the other people. The elderly man was there, still looking very scared. There were windows, like portholes, all around the top of the cabin, but we could see little through these, except the black night sky.

"There was a door at the break in the horseshoe bench, and slightly offside, facing us, was a female alien behind a box-like podium structure. She was similar to the 'nasty' one I encountered on that trip in 2009, a bit taller than me, with very large human-like brown eyes. She looked basically human, but had smaller ears. Her shortish hair – sort of grey/black/blonde and streaky – was standing on end as if she'd used gel. She was thin, wearing a suit, a black skirt and jacket with a collar, buttons and pockets either side – her collared shirt was white."

The porthole in the roof closed and little craft took off. They could not see anything but dark sky through the windows. Patty approached her to ask where they were going, and got a similar response as she had the previous time.

"Her eyes went wide; she opened her mouth and loudly screeched at me! She sounded like an angry possum! I hurried back to my seat, and noticed the old man looked even more frightened."

After a short while they could see daylight streaming through the windows. The craft was flying on an angle, downwards, and she could see they were approaching a big lake with pine trees all around. They landed slowly and smoothly upon the water. After a side-door opened, her Friend exited first saying 'Come on everybody'. She followed, her 'little one' holding her hand, and they all walked up a small boardwalk or jetty towards the shore.

"Then we walked up a medium-width path. I could see the blue sky, and a few clouds. I could smell the fresh fragrance of old pine trees, and looked back down to the lake and our craft. There were no houses visible anywhere around the shore, but further up we came to a log cabin.

"The building was like new, with beautiful polished wood fittings, all built in an 'old-fashioned' way. It was quite big, two-storeys, with furniture, china, cutlery, and everything you could possibly want. My Friend told us there were more of these cabins; they would be a haven when the world got bad."

Patty commented that everybody was looking more relaxed, and started looking around and checking out the bathroom, and the rooms upstairs. The elderly man, who said his name was Bob, started talking to Patty. He was from America, and had been contacted for a long time also, but this was his first visit to her Friend's retreat.

"We were led outside, then further up the path, where I could see lots more cabins scattered around. This seemed to be the same, or a similar place, I'd been brought to before. We were given ten minutes to explore, and I walked up to what seemed to be a row of shops. It looked like they were older buildings, in the process of being renovated. Most shops were empty, but I could see what looked like cans and bags of rice through the window of one."

Bob walked over to join her. He seemed to feel more secure, chatting to Patty as they walked back to the first cabin. Other people were returning, asking so many questions at once. Patty found it all rather overwhelming, but her Friend seemed to be coping.

"They were different people from different countries, with different accents. There was a German lady, who didn't speak English, so my Friend was communicating with her separately by telepathy. She seemed to understand – perhaps he spoke German?"

Her Friend explained again that this was a sanctuary he wanted to share with them, and they would continue to visit it more than once. At that stage, Patty had forgotten her previous trip. This time more details were imparted. There were humans involved, and this community project had been set up by humans, most of whom had previously been in the Air Force or worked for the Government. There was a garden further up, to make them self-sufficient.

As they were all ushered in a line back down the path, they were joined by their little guides who took them back down to the jetty and the disc.

"I could still smell the pine trees, and didn't want to leave. As we got into the craft, that horrible woman was there again, and glowered at me. Bob and I sat together for the return trip, and as we rose from the surface, I could see the small village from a height. It was surrounded by forest, and I wondered if it was in the middle of a national park or something."

Patty felt 'movement', and saw the darkness return outside the windows. Soon they reached the larger ship and re-entered the same way they had left. Her Friend asked them all what they felt and thought, and since everyone was much more relaxed they were all 'talking over one another' at once.

She then felt tired, everything was going 'blurry'. She didn't really know what happened until she found herself back in the ute. David was snoring and the dog was asleep. She started questioning herself as to 'what the hell had happened', but was so tired and groggy, decided to try and get some sleep.

The next morning, they drove back to their original campsite, to find everything still intact.

Near the end of 2016 Patty had to live in Sydney for three months. "I don't know what happened, but something scared me. I couldn't get back to the mountains quick enough, and got the urge to go further west, to live off the land, where my mother has a property."

Patty has had gynaecological problems for many years. Doctors considered endometriosis until an ultrasound revealed an ovarian cyst, similar to many of the other women.

Patty's career is devoted to helping others. Outside working hours, she writes and plays music. It is a talent others from the island have acquired.

Her son, Charles, now in his 20s, is very intuitive, and aware of the world around him, but sometimes gets a little anxious. He told Patty that when he was small, and the aliens took him to play, she used to scream. (Patty cannot consciously recall this.) He is very talented and artistic, and besides writing is musical like Patty, and sings and plays the guitar.

While this was only one of the 'generational' scenarios, as an investigator I found it to be one of the most astounding cases I had ever researched. Many of the details were corroborated by multiple witnesses, including people involved in the original scientific project.

Chapter Eighteen

More Generational Cases

Jane and Christine

In *Contact Down Under*, I wrote about the case of Jane and Christine who lived in Dover Heights, across the water from a naval base, and one of the more affluent suburbs on Sydney Harbour. They were best friends, and lived a couple of streets apart. Jane's house was two-storeys, with wonderful views up and down the harbour.

This case is of some importance, because it involves possible contact by three generations of Jane's family, all similar to other contactees I had been working with in different countries.

On 23 August 1992 Jane saw a series of lights over Sydney Harbour, which moved around for well over an hour. She noticed one had come a lot closer, then it disappeared again.

"It reappeared a short time later, small at first, then getting bigger and brighter, like an explosion. It remained at this large size for about an hour. It made no noise, and definitely wasn't a helicopter – I see those all the time. I was feeling a little guilty, my young son had said in the past that he saw a 'thing' in the sky – 'they come sometimes'. I had not believed him. Why shouldn't I be surprised when I asked my father to bring my binoculars, he just ignored me. I found my video camera, only to discover the battery was flat.

"I noticed one of the objects had been moving around and was now over the Bondi Beach area, near the cliffs at the back of my house. I could see it a lot better. It was a dull grey colour, no lights except for a 'dull redness' in front. It was like there was 'something' I could not see surrounding it. I think it was a glass front, or something similar. There was a faint humming noise. I've never heard anything like it. My dog started to bark, then suddenly stopped, which was unusual."

Jane went inside, and when she came back out it had moved to the Rose Bay side and had a 'strange beam'. She rang her friend Christine and asked her to go out and verify what she was seeing.

Christine said: "In one way I was excited, as I had seen a similar object a few nights before, but no-one wanted to know, or believed me. I'm afraid this time I was a little sceptical, but to humour Jane I went down to the end of the street, taking my cordless phone with me. I saw this big, bright yellow light, at least four to five times bigger than a star. It disappeared for about five minutes than came back again. I was fascinated and confirmed that while it made a funny noise, it was definitely not an aircraft. It was below the clouds, would hover or remain stationary for five minutes, then suddenly get brighter and move."

Christine drove over to Jane's house and Jane got the video out again and tried using it with a 'battery charger on the wall'. One object came across the harbour towards her, and hovered over the top of some houses in Rose Bay. She started filming it, as it hovered for about three minutes, before expanding into a huge light, about half the size of the moon. The light itself was bright yellow, and a whitish-yellow beam came from underneath, like a reflection.

"It was really low," Jane said," and we watched as it did aerobatics. Suddenly, it made a swift move upwards and there was a huge beam, like a band of white light. What was strange was that the object vanished – disappeared – but the band of light stayed there for another five minutes. We kept watching and were sure we could see another object, much further down the harbour. It was hard to see the details, but we could make out a grey dome on top, and rotating lights around. It was moving slowly, at a tilted angle, going upwards, and was gone."

Jane and Christine rang the Department of Meteorology which was closed. The local police had gone home. Christine rang a Sydney television station. Their switchboard operator said a lot of reports had come in, and was very interested that they had taken a video. Jane said she did not want to give an interview, but shortly afterwards a journalist arrived on her doorstep. He said they had another report, but it was different and conflicted with theirs.

"Maybe it was a trick to get the video. I hadn't even seen it myself, and was having trouble getting the tape out of the camcorder. He virtually ripped it out, saying he would return it later. He subsequently claimed that after four hours of viewing it only showed 'flickers of light' and they had passed it on to another department. (I was later advised by friends that my footage had gone to air). I was furious; I couldn't get my tape back. Several weeks later it was returned, with a huge piece blanked out! By whom and why?"

At INUFOR I had received a couple of anonymous messages from motorists in the area, reporting strange lights in the sky and Bryan Dickeson had made enquiries. Some months later he spoke to a radio announcer from Gore Hill, who had been rostered on the overnight shift at the time. He had been inside the studio, but when he finished his shift at 5.30 a.m., security staff were still talking about the unusual lights circling above them the evening before.

Jane desperately wanted a conventional explanation, but we couldn't give her one. She was annoyed that the most important footage from her video had been 'cut out'. She and Christine had desperately wanted it to prove what they had seen.

A couple of months later, at 6.30 p.m. 21 October, I got a call from an elderly woman at Rose Bay who had seen two large white lights come down the harbour towards her, and over Dover Rd. She thought at first they were the headlights of a plane going in to land, but there was no noise, and they were hovering over the ocean behind her house.

I had been liaising with Jane and Christine since their report in August, and telephoned them to ask if they could take a look for us. They went to the end of Dover Rd and the cliffs overlooking the ocean.

"We could see it straight away – a bright white light which was circular at first, then changed to a 'hot dog' shape, with little white lights around the bottom. It wasn't actually over the ocean. It was hovering high overhead, above the cliffs."

This time they had both brought along normal and video cameras – there was no way they were going to let anyone take any footage they might get. Christine got into Jane's car, which was pointed towards the object, and they started flashing the car headlights, to signal it. The craft dimmed and flashed back; it seemed to be getting bigger and closer.

"I don't know what happened," said Jane. "Suddenly it was gone, no longer there! We drove around a couple of streets looking, but didn't see it again."

The time frames Jane and Christine gave me didn't 'add up', and in light of later events it is not known what happened after the object signalled back and came closer. They certainly had no photographic evidence on their equipment, which they had taken especially, to get some shots, given the 'loss' of their previous evidence.

There was another strange anomaly in the details given later to other investigators, who didn't realise that there had been two separate incidents involving the two women. Christine had originally spoken of only going to the end of her street before going to Jane's home on 23 August. She described that object as being a 'bright light, four to five times the size of a star', and then went home and drove over to Jane's home to watch the original objects.

During later interviews with other researchers, she talked of being at the top of a hill, consistent with the 21 October incident. The details she gave also indicated she was describing the craft they encountered on the top of the cliffs that night. She talked about a huge object, only a couple of hundred metres away. (Estimated at about 250 metres in diameter.)

"It had a translucent surface, a bit like creamy-yellowish lampshade parchment, or eggshell. It was lit from within, but did not cast any light or create any shadows around me. It had a distinct rim, with a flattened top and a wider/deeper bottom. It looked a bit like a 'hot-dog' shape in cross-section, but had an overall 'round', or disc-like appearance, and was tilted at about a 45-degree angle."

Soon after the two Dover Heights incidents, Jane began experiencing flashes of memory and vivid dreams. However, there were a lot of blank spots she wanted to clarify. She had trouble comprehending what had actually happened. She seemed to 'know some things', but didn't know how. There appeared to be more than one of these obscured incidents, apart from the extended experience when she and Christine were on the cliffs in October 1992.

"I remembered I was woken up one night and made to go downstairs. A brightly-lit white object hovered over my yard making a funny high-pitched noise in my head. The white light was coming from a dome-shaped top, and underneath the object was a sort of glass-partitioned base with bright red and green lights rotating very quickly.

"In the middle, above my head, was some sort of door opening. My dogs remained asleep, and the next thing I knew I was aboard the craft."

(In November 1992, before any chance of outside influence to affect her recall, Jane had two hypnotherapy sessions with an experienced practitioner. She provided me a transcribed overview of those sessions when I next visited her.)

Jane described the craft as being circular, in three or four layers: "The bottom was the landing area, with a metal door which opened and shut in a retractable manner. It seemed to be constructed in a spiral-type fashion leading from one level to another. The walls were a metallic grey colour, with brackets of some kind. The walls curved outwards then back to meet a low ceiling. The floors looked like a type of black glass material with dull lights underneath.

"Around the side of the craft there were grey metal doors, each had a different purpose and they slid into the wall and closed. It had observation domes in the front for close viewing. When travelling at high speed the domes have a protective metal covering. There are two lights inside the craft which are some form of 'defence laser' to attack anyone who threatens them.

"In the centre of the craft was a quite large, glass-like cylinder, which made a noise and was bolted to the floor and ceiling. There was a circular hole or opening around it. It seemed to have a thick liquid inside, which moved in different directions and radiated pink light.

"The air was heavy, like a sauna without steam, not as moist. I could breathe it, but it made me feel groggy. There were symbols on the wall, plus more dots and funny lines.

The symbols that Jane remembers correspond closely to characters Penny from Roma recalled, and the automatic writing by Trevor in the Northern Territory. (Both discussed in my book *Contact Down Under*.)

"The walkways were very busy, with humans and aliens walking in and out of rooms. I was shown some of the rooms. One was very different – a nursery of some sort, with balls and square-type objects for children to play with. I could see a human female playing with and nursing babies and a child. A lot of them did not look human and I didn't really like them. I got a shock when *I saw my own child* also playing inside.

"Two of the taller aliens took me into another room which had a screen and 3-D images. The screen had dots down the side and showed clusters of stars, with not much open space between. I think I was told it was 'Polaris', or something like that. There was also the letter 'Z' – it meant something, I'm not sure but I think it stood for a longer name."

"Their 'Polaris' has beautiful green vegetation, but the buildings are different to ours. The sun is reddish-orange and it has three moons. Then they showed me what an atom bomb could do to a planet. They told me their planet is dying and they have lost the ability to breed like us. They can't understand the fuss about what they are doing; they don't want to hurt us or cause any pain.

"They showed me an image of the earth, and said they are sick of trying to tell heads of government to stop what they are doing to our planet. What we do affects them and others in our galaxy. Unless we get our act together they will show themselves in force to the world, because people don't believe they exist.

> **What we know about 'Polaris'**
> *Polaris* is our name for the northern hemisphere's Pole Star – presently the closest star to Earth's celestial North Pole.
> It is the brightest star in the constellation Ursa Minor – the *Little She-Bear*, or *Little Dipper*.
> It is a *white-yellow supergiant*, a triple star, and *unusual* – known as the closest *Cepheid variable*-type star to us, only 375 light years away. At present, Polaris, and the six other stars in the same constellation are thought to be too young, and therefore very unlikely to harbour any life forms.

"I looked through another open door and saw a sort of dormitory with about fifty tables containing humans, some asleep and some awake, who looked like they were in a state of shock. I can't remember much more, because it was after my examination, and I was feeling sick in the stomach and head, and my eyes were red and sore."

The Aliens

Jane gave a very detailed description of three different types of alien she saw during her experience. When she entered the craft, one being was walking ahead of her: "He was about five foot two inches tall, and gold in colour, with a long neck and square shoulders. While his legs were short, with square-back funny heels, his body and arms were long. His arms didn't appear to have joints, and he had four long fingers on each hand which had pads on the ends. The spinal cord looked more like deep indents running down his back."

He later examined her, and was apparently 'the doctor.' She noticed he had a large, pear-shaped head with a lot of wrinkles and almond-shaped eyes.

"There were four little grey guys, about three feet tall, with big brown-black, cat-like eyes, which were mirror-like, almost glassy, with no white or pupils. There was an extra flap of skin over the eyes, and they had no ears, just dents. They had small noses and well-shaped mouths, and they walked very strangely, with small steps like rubber men. When I was lying on the table, one looked into my face and he had a very funny smell.

"One was thin, six feet tall, but human in appearance. He wore a tightly-fitting, greeny-gold coloured suit which also covered his feet. On his shoulders were metal badges with something like a bird or animal on the end of I t.

"He had white skin and small features," she said. "Although his ears looked a little different to ours. His face was perfectly shaped, long black hair to his shoulders, the most beautiful being I have ever seen. His eyes were slightly larger than mine, no whites, just unusually blue, almost violet. I liked him from the moment I saw him; the next best thing to seeing an angel. He seemed to be in charge. Throughout my examination he was there, standing behind me."

The Examination

"I was taken to a circular room with a door, and in the middle a low table with a light inside. It seemed to be made of the same material as the floor. I felt groggy, as if I was on some sort of medication. They put me on the table, with a hard, plastic-type head rest, because I felt a jolt. The table itself was not wide, it just fitted my body, and they put brackets on my arms and legs, so I couldn't move, and two metal squares either side of my head at my temples.

Four little greys were at my feet, and appeared to be talking to themselves. I could only hear funny noises, and never saw their lips move, but sometimes it seemed they were 'talking in my head'. I wasn't afraid. They said they wouldn't hurt me and I believed them. The good-looking 'human' was standing behind my head, and the 'doctor' bloke walked in. (Again, a similarity with other reports, where a 'humanoid-type' being stands near the head of the abductee – comforting them while procedures are performed.)

"I remember my left shoulder hurting, and the doctor placing a thin needle into my ovary on the left side. I could see liquid and an egg being extracted. Some form of light came down from the low ceiling. It was so bright I told them it was burning my eyes which I couldn't shut – Please Stop! A hand went over the front of my head and temples, something was put into my right ear with a 'pop' and I was told to sleep."

Two days later Jane had to go to the doctor with a very bad infection in both her inner and outer ear. There were several red dots burning under the skin on her leg, which later disappeared, leaving a small brown circle.

The 'Twinned Dreams'

While Christine did not have not have hypnotic regression, both she and Jane had reported 'twinned dreams,' some of which Jane detailed. One of these took place at 3 a.m. A being was in her lounge room, which was full of yellow-white light. He told her he had not come to hurt her or her family, but not to come too close as he was not yet 'detoxified'.

"I asked permission to call Christine and she arrived soon after I rang, wearing only her bedtime white sloppy-joe. We asked him questions and he answered telepathically. Basically, he was saying that the Earth and our human race were on course for destruction. There was some suggestion we could go away with Them, but we declined when it became obvious our husbands were not included in this offer."

Another memory Jane had was of being in the craft on an examination table, and the aliens asking her where she got two unusual scars from a spinal operation two years earlier. "While they were doing something to my back, I recall telling them not to hurt my friend's head as they were pushing her too hard." It certainly seems possible that Christine also had some interaction with the beings. However, unlike Jane she decided not to pursue the matter.

The experiences Jane recalled under hypnotic regression are typical of those provided under hypnosis by other abductees: The free mingling of aliens and humans on-board alien craft, medical examinations (albeit under a form of medicated control), the presence of children in an educational/assessment environment, a fascination with our nuclear weaponry, frustration with corrupt Earth authorities, a home planet a bit like ours but slightly exotic, their present inability to breed, and so on.

In recent years, my colleague Bryan Dickeson has undertaken an assessment of 60 years' worth of UFO reports from Australia and New Zealand. He has come to the view that there are dozens, possibly hundreds, of alien civilisations out there, all more advanced than ours, and more are on the way. Many Visitors just take a few samples and carry on to the next star system.

(It seems one group of aliens likes to visit earth every 17–18 years just to see if we're still here, and is usually surprised to see we haven't destroyed ourselves in the meantime. Apparently, the transition of a sole-species dominated planet such as ours, into a star-travelling civilisation is not easy. Failure is common, and while we are quite interesting, it's best for aliens not to get too involved.)

Some months went by, and I received a call from Jane. Over the previous months 'strange things had been happening'. She and Christine were having unusual, identical dreams, in which both participated and interacted, and remembered the next day. "This is weird" Jane said. "It's almost like 'twin dreams.

"My main worry is Bruce, my four-year-old son. You remember how I didn't take any notice when he told me 'they come sometimes', recently he's been telling me that 'Peter Pan comes to see him every night and takes him for a ride in his train.' He's never heard of 'Peter Pan and Wendy' – it's not a book we've ever got for him."

Were the Visitors subverting fairy tales to interact with our young – not realising modern kids watch very different content on media? This was not the only case I'd come across where the same ploy is used by Visitors – one witness was told, as a child, she was going on a trip to 'Never Never Land'. I was also concerned about Jane's reference to 'twin dreams' and a similar connection between a small number of experiencers.

My friend and colleague, researcher Rosemary Decker was visiting from the USA, and expert at dealing with troubled children. When we arrived at the house, Jane whispered to us; "Be careful, Bruce's grandmother, Sylvia, is here. She doesn't even want us to mention unidentified flying objects – says it's all nonsense!"

We all sat down to afternoon tea, and discussed Jane and Christine's 'twin dreams' and a few other phenomena. I had a large question mark in my mind. Were the identical dreams more of a 'flashback memory' than something inter-dimensional? Their most vivid dream was of seeing each other being carried down some stairs by unusual beings with greyish skin and large, dark midnight blue eyes.

Sylvia was hunched up with a grim, disapproving scowl on her face. As we started talking to Bruce, I noticed there were tears streaming down her cheeks, and her wall of denial came tumbling down. Amid sobs, Sylvia told of how, when she had been a girl in Eastern Europe, she had gone to play with other children in the park one morning. The next thing she knew, she was still in the same place, but it was dark.

"All the villagers and my family came running up; 'Where have you been? We've been searching all day!' All I could say was that a lovely, tall blond 'angel' had been looking after me." Sylvia then clammed up, and would say no more.

Rosemary and I looked at each other, both realising this case involved the grandmother, her daughter, and grandson — three generations of the same family, and couldn't help thinking about the generational experiences we and others had already researched. We agreed that some families have a long history and a complicated link to this phenomenon — possibly an ongoing relationship with alien life forms that deserves closer attention.

Jane later moved to another State, and became much more spiritual with an interest in crystals and 'alternative' therapies. The opportunity to delve deeper into this family was lost.

Flora Lewis

Flora first rang me to report an unusual phenomenon she witnessed on 17 November 2016 from 9 p.m. onwards. She had been with her twelve-year-old daughter, Janet, shopping in North Hobart, when they saw a solid bright white light stationary in the sky. It looked about the size of a pea at arm's length, much bigger than the surrounding stars and planets. It was definitely not a satellite or the Space Station.

"We caught a taxi home," Flora said, "and as we crossed town we could still see the object. I noticed a solid red light at the bottom, and opened the cab window to be sure it was not light refraction. At one stage I got the driver to stop, got out, and took a couple of pictures on my phone. For some inexplicable reason, Janet was frightened and sank down into the seat. Earlier, at about 6.30 p.m., she had told me that, in the same area of the sky, she could see objects in the clouds which had split into three or four pieces."

They arrived home at 9.45 p.m. (cab docket) and could still see the object, but it had moved further away, and appeared to be over or near Collingsvale, opposite the 'super moon' which was visible that night.

Janet was still scared and went to bed, but Flora stayed up until well after 10 p.m. to get a better view and take some videos and photos – one in particular is a very clear 'zoom'. She said the bright, white ball of light had a phenomenal glowing or 'burning' appearance, and to either side was what looked like wings or a dark saucer shape shadow, which blocked out background stars. She had further sightings of the strange object on the evening of 19 to 20 November, and has better photos. It appears to be egg-shaped with a brightly burning 'yolk' and the previously-described outer shadow.

It was after the initial report we got talking about my previous book *The Gosford Files*. Flora confided: "When I was about 12 or 13 years old I lived on the Central Coast and was in year seven at the North Lakes High School. It was a hot night in the summer of 1988-89 when I was woken by an intense blue light which flooded though my open bedroom window for several minutes.

"The next morning everybody on the bus was talking about it. When I got to school, I discovered all the other students and my science teacher had experienced the unusual event. He seemed really 'spooked' and sat on his desk, telling us he knew of nothing which could explain it. It must have had a big effect on him. He behaved very strangely and resigned his post shortly afterwards."

There was another unusual incident when she was a child. They were visiting family near Yass in New South Wales. They were at a friend's apple orchard one hot sunny day, when an unusual object appeared above them. Flora said military planes often flew the same flight path over the farm, and would always 'dip their wings' as they passed.

"This object, whilst travelling the same course, was different. It was closer and lower – short and stumpy and shaped like an upside-down, silver-pewter christening cup. There was no smoke, noise, or obvious power source, but at times, it looked 'blurry'. It was stationary for some minutes before taking off along the same flight path.

"The locals were not concerned as they had seen something similar before, and us kids were under the trees eating apples. We thought it quite funny that one visitor, a fully-grown man who had been out in the open, dived under a car in fright. The bus driver's brother, Barry, at Reids Flat, had also seen it, but my mother told me not to talk about it.

"Barry himself was a bit of a mystery. He was 60 or 70 then, and not in good health. My mother said she often wondered about Barry. He had always worked on the farm, had no formal education and had never been in the military or worked for the Government. Every so often, mysterious 'men in suits' would pick him up and take him to Canberra. He always came back famished and thirsty. When Flora's mother was a child, he taught her things as she played, and once she saw him with 'black-blue', carbon-type prints of diagrams or intricate specifications."

(I also wondered about Barry, who he really was, and why and what he had been teaching Flora's mother.)

Flora originally lived in Morrisset, on the New South Wales Central Coast, and when a young innocent 17-year-old she joined the Australian Navy. When Flora was about 20-years-old, and on leave, she went to see her mother who had moved to a sparsely-populated area at Lake Llewellyn, near Sisters Beach and Wynyard in North Tasmania.

"One night I had what I thought was a dream of seeing blue lights over the lake. I got up to have a look and get a glass of water, and was chased by 'something' which shaved the side of my head, and left me with the memory of a word something similar to '*Specieology*??', which I found myself writing in unusual script rather than my own handwriting. I had only considered the entire episode just a dream, until I saw the glass of water at the side of my bed."

After this forgotten dream, Flora found a pattern of marks on her body, and much later, experienced flashbacks of undergoing a full medical by what looked like short, slim, grey beings. To her perception they were not young, and had an air of age and authority about them. She felt like she was under some form of sedation or mind control, and they were talking to her in a telepathic manner. They seemed to be working like a team, one near her head, focusing her attention and communicating, whilst the others worked further down. At times, she was watching herself as if in an out-of-the-body experience. Since that time, she often becomes overwhelmed at the whole world situation.

Due to consistencies with other experiencers I asked Flora about her family. "My mother knows and believes in other entities but won't say much. She raised three children alone, and has always had the gift of 'prophecy' – a quality my daughter Janet seems to have inherited. Janet is also an 'empath' which distresses her at times, and I try to help her control it through meditation.

"Janet also told me about a dream she had about four years ago in Tasmania, when she was eight years old. She had three slits cut into her chest, diagonal like gills. They stung and glowed green, but when she woke up there was nothing there."

Flora learned to suppress and control any paranormal abilities during her naval service, and is only now coming to terms with her real self.

Given my interest in genetic manipulation within families I queried Flora and her mother's reproductive histories. Her mother had suffered continual 'miscarriages', eventually having a hysterectomy at an early age. Flora's eldest brother was actually a twin.

Flora herself suffered problems with her menstrual cycle, and following X-rays was diagnosed with polycystic ovaries, just after the 'dream' episode. Doctors informed her she probably wouldn't be able to have children.

"Not long afterwards I was dating a very intelligent fellow naval officer, nothing serious, when suddenly one night we developed the most intense attraction for each other. That one-off encounter left me pregnant with Janet, who was born with bright red hair which neither of us had. Our marriage didn't last for long, and a year after Janet's birth I 'lost' what were apparently twins."

Besides being empathic and close to nature, Janet is extremely intelligent, and at age four was admitted to a child's section of Mensa. Mother and daughter attend Mensa more as a social network, although one of the committee members also runs a psychic group. (I was curious as to the reasons for this group – were intelligent children being monitored for their paranormal abilities as well?)

Flora talked about her ancestors, especially on her mother's side: "My father was born in Glasgow, but my mother is of Irish and New Zealand descent. My Grandfather and Great-Grandfather were in the military during both World Wars. However, despite repeated attempts, I cannot get a copy of their military records. My Great-Grandmother was Irish and had affiliations with the Isle of Man."

Except for any observed or recalled presence of Visitors, this case contains nearly every component of the families I was researching.

Chapter Nineteen

Prophecies, Messages, Lessons to Learn

Prophecies and Predictions

Over the centuries, many predictions and prophecies have been attributed to religious leaders and scriptures, and many psychics, such as Edgar Cayce and Nostradamus. Nearly all foretell wars and natural disasters. Many ancient cultures, such as the indigenous peoples of North and South America (who refer to 'people from the stars'), have also made disturbingly similar predictions involving both a third world war and massive natural disasters. Whether there was any alien influence in their visions is something we may never know.

Some events suggest an element of extraterrestrial or alien contact, not always understood at the time.

Portugal – Fatima

In 1917, three children in the village of Fatima, high in the Siera D'Aire mountains of Central Portugal, met an apparition of the Virgin Mary several times over a six-month period. In 1922, the Catholic Church initiated an eight-year enquiry, eventually pronouncing the visitations as 'worthy of belief'.

During the six months of apparitions, nearby witnesses described globes of light in the sky, self-propelled clouds, buzzing noises and flashes of light. On 13 September thousands of witnesses reported that the sky grew dark at noon, stars could be seen, and they saw a luminous globe in the air, like a great jet of light in the sky. The object came from the east, descended to tree-top level, then rose and travelled back across the sky to the east.

One month later, a miracle described as the 'Dancing Sun of Fatima' was seen over an area of 32 miles by 20 miles, although scientific observatories reported they saw nothing unusual with the sun that day. It was very cloudy and raining, but thousands of people congregated for a promised miracle. Many sceptical media representatives also attended.

Suddenly the rain stopped, and the clouds were 'rent apart'. They could see the 'sun' which looked like a silver disc, the colour of stainless steel' with a clearly identified edge. Witnesses described it as 'revolving on itself and zigzagging in a circle ... spinning and stopping, then spinning around again'. People thought it was the sun, and were terrified when it seemed to be coming towards the earth.

During her visits the Lady imparted several messages, including three 'Secrets'. The first was a vivid and horrific description of Hell. The second was an accurate prophecy of the start of World War 2. The third 'Secret', was for Lucia to keep until 1960, when it was to be given to the Vatican and the Pope would reveal it to the world.

The third prophecy is still controversial. The Vatican is aware of the contents, but in 1967 a spokesman for Pope Paul VI said it was not yet time to reveal the secret. In the 50 years since, the Papacy has not altered this opinion. It was reported that when Pope John XXIII read it, he trembled with fear and almost fainted in horror. It was also suggested that just before his mysterious death on 28-29 September 1978, Pope John Paul I was about to release the third message. It may only be co-incidental, but major UFO activity was witnessed on 14th, 15th and 16th September, when a strange craft was seen hovering over Rome, and a huge object was reported traversing the entire length of Italy. The late Pope John Paul II was reported saying that the prophecy included the massive flooding of large areas of the earth, and the publication of such a message was not something he wanted.

In 1963, a German magazine disclosed what they claim is the Third Secret. The Vatican will neither confirm nor deny the following prediction: "The peace after World War 2 will only be temporary, and during that time the Earth will shake because of many concussions and convulsions. We will endure many continuous wars near the end of this century. The oceans will entirely flood certain parts of the world. From moment to moment millions of men will perish. Only faith, love and hope can bring the reconciliation between people and nations which can save us from war and eternal death."

Many people still believe that the calamity will be a natural one, most probably the passing of a large celestial body, which will severely affect the planet. The chances of our civilisation surviving will be worsened if we are fighting wars and do not work together, as a unified human race. Some people allude to a brown dwarf star being gravitationally 'pulled in' by our sun. There have always been pronouncements and rumour about Nibiru, which according to the ancient Sumerians is a large planet, the home of the Anunnaki, and supposedly in a wide, elliptical orbit around the solar system.

There have been small fragments of evidence surfacing from time to time, but if true it has all been kept exceptionally secret due to the very real possibility of premature world panic. Various observations, mostly by minor astronomers have been quickly explained away, including anomalous sightings, the apparent rise in temperature on neighbouring planets, fluctuations in magnetic fields, and irregular solar flares.

This possibility does have some merit. It accounts for a reason other than genetics when some contactees unexpectedly researched ancient Sumerian history, and why others felt compelled to move to an inland area above sea level. It justifies the reasons for not only the Visitors' appearance at this particular time, but their sense of urgency in relaying their messages. We always think the worst of our world's governments, often with good reason, but could it also be that some of the wars we are fighting now have been prematurely instigated, to get them over and done with, before any perceived natural disaster occurs? And what is the real reason behind the 'chemtrails' – the mass spraying of wide areas of countryside, by unmarked planes – prevalent in *all* major countries but *never explained*?

So many other visionaries and prophets have also predicted massive calamities will affect our Earth. Nostradamus, Edgar Casey, and St. Malachy, are only a few of the many whose predictions, but not always the timing, have so far proven essentially correct. One wonders about the chronological pronouncements of St. Malachy, who said Pope Francis would be the last Pope. He probably didn't help dispel believers' faith in seers when he said he 'wouldn't be here for long'!

There are many problems currently facing mankind, and also many variables in the information received by the experiencers. However, they do seem to reiterate the messages imparted by the benign human-type Visitors.

Several years ago, at the Prophets' Conference in the USA, speakers and delegates seemed, in part, to present a similar view to the early 'Nordic' contactees. The events and future of the 21st Century are dependent upon either the use or misuse of the incredible discoveries of the 20th Century, many of which may have been given to us by the Visitors.

Stephen Greer emphasised that we are running out of time to start using the new physics of which only the secret government, scientists and military are aware. He claims the environment is much worse off than we are being told, and cannot sustain much more abuse without a total ecosystem collapse.

There are already new free energy sources which are non-detrimental to the environment. However, these pose a threat to powerful oil and energy cartels. One must however, in my opinion, recognise the impact on societies whose sole income is derived from fossil fuels. Also, we must carefully consider the new dangers presented by some technologies. Our nuclear power plants are a prime example of the dangers caused by accidents, as experienced in Three Mile Island in the US, Chernobyl in Russia, or by natural disasters as in Fukushima, Japan.

Some experts adopt a more spiritual approach to the Cosmos. In 1973, two years after his historic space flight, Apollo 14 Astronaut Edgar Mitchell, founded the Institute of Noetic Sciences, and stated: "It is becoming increasingly clear that the human mind and physical universe do not exist independently. Something as yet indefinable connects them. This link between mind, matter, intelligence and intuition, is what Noetic Sciences is all about." He continued with the ramifications of recent discoveries, which can play a crucial role in the survival or collapse of our society and the earth itself, it is up to us.

Since ancient times mankind has queried the very nature of life, and new discoveries are rapidly altering the scientific concepts we have held throughout our previous history. Tesla was way ahead of his time, and Einstein was also one of the pioneers in our current knowledge of the nature of energy and matter. While some of his theories are up for debate, they provided the building blocks for further discoveries into quantum physics and mechanics, and the dual nature of matter and energy.

We are now moving beyond these leaps of discovery, but we must adhere to very strict moral protocols if we wish to accumulate knowledge and combine it into beneficial use. Our progress is quite staggering, and penetrates the very nature of matter and energy in both the Cosmos and all living beings. We are now delving into Wave Particle Duality and Zero-point Energy – Quantum Holograms and the concept of 'non-locality'.

Of equal importance are the experiments and discoveries pertaining to human beings themselves, their thoughts, emotions and free will. Already we have digital technology which enables massive surveillance systems and facial recognition technology which monitor our every move and communication.

We tinker with information emissions and recovery, and via MRI machines can access sub-atomic information via the wave form and coherent light phase relationships. We once believed our thoughts were our own, but as we comprehend the transfer of information via particle interaction, and that all conscious living beings and entities can perceive information by recognising the patterns of energy, vibrations and frequency, we tend to become less sceptical of prophecy, prediction, visions and the paranormal in general.

While we can now better understand and appreciate that non-material instantaneous extraterrestrial contact is possible through the propagation of electromagnetic fields, it is also possible for unethical terrestrial powers and interests to deliberately generate and duplicate similar 'experiences' in unsuspecting and vulnerable witnesses.

Planet X or Nibiru

What is the reality of Nibiru, the 9th Planet or 'Planet X' as it is variously called? The truth is we don't really know. We can only speculate while, since the discovery of Uranus, astronomers have been seriously theorising for over 200 years. During their subsequent search they discovered Neptune, Pluto, Eris and many other planetary neighbours, including the unusual Sedna and 2012VP, but not the elusive Planet X.

Linda and Leesa devoted years to their search for the truth of the Anunnaki and the planet Nibiru, a topic upon which Zechariah Sitchin wrote several books.

Many other scholars and researchers have spoken of their belief in the ancient records and legends.

Time and time again, we hear reference to the return of Nibiru, or an unknown planet or astronomical body, with a marathon orbit of our Solar System. Does it even exist? Yes, surprisingly enough our astronomers have suspected its presence for a long time, and are still searching for it in our bright starry skies! We still have much to learn about our own immediate neighbourhood, and our probes are discovering more every year.

Many years ago, Allen Hynek, scientist and astronomer, speculated upon the existence of Planet X, or even a brown dwarf or neutron star. Earlier, gravitational disturbances had been found in the orbits of Neptune and Uranus, which the discovery of Pluto in 1930 did not explain. Hynek hoped the American Space Probes, Pioneers 10 and 11, would provide answers. It was later claimed that '*Voyager*' had negated the previous findings.

In the mid-nineties an elderly gentleman, who had been an astronomer all his life, rang me, concerned that: 'there was something up there that shouldn't be there!' I referred him to one of the large observatories, and after that he went strangely quiet, as had some of my astronomical colleagues.

Nearly 20 years ago, Dr John Murray of the British Royal Astronomical Society, referred to a discovery made three trillion miles away. (Although the latest estimates are just a few billion miles away.) A so-far unseen planet, several times larger than Jupiter, was orbiting the Solar System. Physicists in the US had reached a similar conclusion, had speculated that it could be a 'brown dwarf'. Further, in keeping the ancient texts, apparently it is orbiting in a direction opposite to the known planets.

In 2012, an astronomer at the National Observatory of Brazil reiterated the long-held belief that irregularities in the Kuiper Belt on the fringes of our Solar System, suggested there was a planet four times the size of the Earth 'out there'. It was all down to mathematical calculations. So far, we haven't been able to actually see it. It would be extremely faint, producing no light of its own.

In July 2016, *New Scientist* published an article in which scientists Brown, Batygin and Bailey postulated that the alignment in the sun's spin could support the Planet X(9) hypothesis. Other astronomers had reached a similar conclusion, and suggested it could have a wildly eccentric orbit and elongated trajectory. Over 2,000 exoplanets have been discovered around other stars, it is certainly a possibility in our own Solar System, and probably in an elliptical orbit.

Astronomers suspect Planet X(9) has a very wide elliptical orbit, and does have a gravitational effect on the minor planets Sedna and Biden. It could well be larger than Earth, but would be so frigid that neither the Anunnaki nor anyone else could survive on its surface. Current theoretical estimates, suggest it takes 10,000 to 20,000 years to orbit the Sun.

While its existence has been postulated from gravitational effects on other bodies in the Solar System, experts do not consider it would have any effect on

Earth. Astronomers still disagree on the existence of Planet X, but the search is on, and they do concede that such a body would have gravitational effects on the rest of the Solar System, including our Sun.

Is it a danger to Earth? We don't know. Most probably not, although some people refer to previous Earth cataclysms, and others point to recent changing conditions recorded on the Moon and nearby planets. If the figures are correct, at its closest it would be 200 times the distance as we are from the Sun, at its furthest six times that. The latest discovery, in the far reaches of our Solar System, is called 2012 VP113, and so far referred to as Planet 9. However, this may change, as bodies such as Pluto can suddenly lose their planetary status!

It is unwise to speculate. Some people consider that solar flares, global warming, and increased earthquake activity are being caused by the gravitational pull and magnetic effect on the Solar System by the so far mythical Planet X or Nibiru, which could also affect our magnetic poles and tectonic plates. I have often wondered if Planet X is connected to the third prophecy of Fatima, the sudden arrival of the Visitors, and contactees who move away from coastal areas.

It must be stressed that although the premonitions of the experiencers and prophets relate to some form of cataclysm, perhaps too much emphasis has been placed on a mythical planet, and not enough to another cosmic anomaly.

Russian astrophysicists have been investigating the Sun's cycles and the Solar System, and their relationship to our galaxy. Still controversial is their suggestion that as we move through a local interstellar space in our 25,920 year precessional cycle, we are being bombarded by an abnormal amount of highly-charged plasma and cosmic radiation, which accounts for recent planetary changes on Pluto, Mars, Saturn, Neptune, Uranus, Jupiter and the Moon. They have expressed concern that the combination of these forces, plus man-made technological impacts, could affect the electromagnetic field and geophysical state of the Earth.

Alien Messages and Lessons to be Learned

With regards to the aliens themselves, and their often incomprehensible motives, if some of them show cause for concern, then so should we! It is not just our own behaviour, but that of the different extraterrestrials coming to this planet.

The reason for their sudden incursions onto Earth may be quite simple. Our initial ventures into space could have caused consternation. We certainly maintain militarily strategic bases, away from our home countries on earth. Perhaps our solar system has military significance within this part of the galaxy. There could be outposts, ET bases and facilities on Mars, the moon and other planets or moons.

Many early Nordic contactees were ridiculed because they said the Visitors came from Mars or Venus. We now realise that with the appropriate technology, we could easily maintain communities, in places which would otherwise be uninhabitable. Already our scientists are planning permanent bases and colonies on Mars.

The possibility of alien bases, or even civilisations on the moon or other parts of the solar system has always been controversial. Reports of UFOs being seen by our astronauts, both in space or on the moon, are met with silence or ridicule, as are the descriptions of the remains of massive structures on the far side of the Moon. Some radio hams insist they have picked up communications from Apollo missions which confirm the presence of extra-terrestrial space vehicles.

While attending a meeting over 40 years ago, a teenage girl approached me during a supper break. She showed me a letter she had received from her uncle, who was in the US, working for NASA. He said they were all very excited as they had received photographs from the far side of the moon showing the remains of massive, unnatural structures rising miles into the sky. I checked the correspondence, handwriting, stamp, postage marks, stationery for clues. It all seemed genuine, and was certainly confirmed by later reports.

Rosemary Decker said an astronaut once admitted to her he was not allowed to answer certain questions on what he saw and learned on the moon. Gordon Cooper and Edgar Mitchell both stated that UFOs and alien visitations and technology are a very real occurrence. Scott Carpenter is reported as having confirmed that while in orbit on 24 May 1962, he photographed a UFO and said; "At no time when the astronauts were in space, were they alone. There was constant surveillance by UFOs."

While their Russian contemporaries are equally silent on the matter, cosmonaut Yuri Gagarin was reported as saying: "During my space flights, I saw something that is far beyond any fantasy. If I am ever permitted to tell this publicly, I am sure that the world will be in shock." In 1979 Victor Afanasyev reported being followed by a UFO while on route to the space station *Solyut 6*. "It had an engineered structure, metallic, about 40 metres long with inner hulls, and it followed us during half our orbit." Given our technology at the time, it cannot be fully assumed the craft was extraterrestrial, but this seems likely because of its size.

From information I had access to, I personally believe that, from 1969, we did make several successful Apollo missions to the moon. Pilot-Cosmonaut Leonov has also confirmed that Soviet radars monitored everything, and were able to observe the Americans, with Leonov and his colleagues 'rooting for them.' Why, in all the following decades have we not officially gone back? It has always been of utmost priority to the US, Russia and probably China, to not only to establish a manned, habitable Lunar outpost, but also to mount an expedition to Mars. Some whistle-blowers claim that 'photos of UFOs on the edge of a lunar crater' were genuine, and that aliens there had warned us off.

According to some journalists, NASA has offered several plausible yet questionable explanations for the discontinuing manned journeys beyond our own planet.

1/ They were suddenly concerned about the biological effects of space radiation on astronauts.

2/ There were problems with the 'take–off' of craft returning from the Moon and Mars (despite several successful Apollo missions and the fact that both have a lower gravity than Earth).

3/ There were many technical risks, including vibrations on the craft structure and the inability to recreate material used for the Apollo Thermal Protection System, providing a heat shield for craft re-entering our atmosphere at hypersonic speed.

(One must wonder why we cannot recreate something in use nearly 50 years ago. Also, if our probes travel to the Moon and Mars and reduce speed to land or orbit, why can't our craft use the same procedure when returning to Earth?)

While there could be some truth in the conspiracy theories, it could be something so simple as the more recent realisation that solar flares are far more dangerous and unpredictable than previously thought. If the enormous cost of venturing into space is a factor, then perhaps George Adamski had a point when he noted world economies now rely on wasting vast amounts of money on wars and armaments; money which could be better used for space exploration.

While there have been several NASA task forces to plan our return more permanently to the Moon, I have a feeling they are prevaricating. In the intervening years, space missions have been unmanned ventures to Mars, with robotic technology. Closer to home our manned programs have all been contained to a low earth orbit, and we may reasonably assume some of these projects would contain an element of space control and defence.

It is naive and simplistic to think that all Visitors are benign. Some may wish to conquer and dominate the Earth. If they are essentially like us, they will have various motives and agendas. In the past, when we have colonised new countries, we have given the natives beads to win their trust and friendship. Is this the equivalent of perhaps primitive alien technology we have been given?

Some scientists express concern about a possible alien attack on Earth, and in 2006 collaborated on the book *An Introduction to Planetary Defense – A Study of Warfare Applied to Extra-Terrestrial Invasion*. The authors, Drs. Taylor, Boan, and Powell are all qualified and respected in the field of space science and technologies. X (Why publish this if they did not think there was a possible alien threat?)

When Ronald Reagan was President of the USA, he was sent a letter from Justice for Military Personnel, a group comprised of active and retired military and government officers. They were petitioning for full public disclosure of the reality and existence of UFOs, noting that: "in the interests of national security we all took part in intentionally misleading the nation, manipulating the press, the courts and most politicians." They did not attempt to define the origin or intent of these craft, except to note that we were defenceless against their advanced technology.

Copies of this letter, in its entirety, were sent to major UFO research organisations and included in publications such as *Simply Living* magazine. The letter was comprehensive in both the wrongful acts military personnel had been forced to make, and the dangers to uninformed military and aviation personnel. The authorities did not wish then, or now, to make a public disclosure, although it may have prompted some limited briefing to a privileged few.

Today, in our own societies, peace, love and understanding will not defeat fanatics who are evil, who mistreat their own people, and who are intent on imposing their control and radical beliefs over the rest of us.

I have often considered the tide of human affairs over the past century. Our history is replete with intolerance towards other races and cultures. Two world wars and several revolutions have resulted in mass migrations of peoples to other countries, giving many a more cultural, racial, and religious mix. If our cosmic brothers hoped this would produce a harmonious blending of diverse cultures, it has not been an outstanding success. Some countries have assimilated better than others, but we have entered the 21st^ت century with just as much bigotry and strife as before.

Do we really need to look to extraterrestrials, ancient prophets and modern visionaries to see we are heading into serious problems which could culminate in disaster? I think not. Gene Roddenberry, the creator of *Star Trek, Earth* and other futuristic television and film series, was a genius in his own right with depictions of future technology. He once commented; "Let's say that if we survive into a twenty-third century, ending up with a civilization capable of hurling starships across the galaxy, we will have learned affection for our own planet and the life-forms here as well as in other places."

We have become arrogant in our self-declared domination of this planet. We fail to realise that the ecology is delicate, and nature does not revolve around us. Our thoughtless actions and neglect contribute to the mass extinction of other life forms. About 99% of all species that have ever existed here have gone, and it is predicted by 2100 another third of the remainder will be extinct.

It has been calculated that the rain forests, the lungs of the world, are being destroyed at the rate of 3,000 square miles a month. Think of it – not only slowly decreasing the oxygen output, but also depriving myriad life-forms their means of survival. The continued use of fossil fuels pumps massive amounts of carbon-dioxide into the atmosphere and simultaneously reduces plant life capable of photosynthesis.

We poison the air, land, rivers and sea with our household and industrial waste, and serious mishaps involving chemical, oil and nuclear spills only compound the problem. The Hopi Indians have long predicted this in their legends and lore, noting that only when it did occur would mankind realise we cannot eat money. They believed the only road to survival is a return to spirituality and better care and affinity with Mother Earth.

There is ample evidence and testimonies to suggest that, concerned about our use of nuclear and fossil fuels, some aliens have given us limited information and technology, either directly or by telepathic suggestions to certain scientists. They want us to replace our energy needs with non-damaging alternatives. Certainly, a minority of the population has embraced the more simplistic solar and wind power etc. – but too many world economies and giant corporations depend on coal and oil.

There is obviously a major problem facing the more benign Visitors. Their advanced technology, which could solve all our problems, could also be misused for warlike and other dangerous pursuits. Perhaps the knowledge initially imparted was not only to assist us, but also an assessment period. So far, we have not amended our behaviour to any meaningful extent; in fact while improving slightly in social awareness, we have declined in other areas.

Our civilisation would come to a crashing halt in the event of devastating war or natural disaster. Extensive use of free energy would enable us to recover, to a much better extent. It is more than suspected that, due to self-interest and world politics, all these technologies have been locked-up for possible later use by 'the powers to be'. The problem is if a massive world collapse comes without warning, there will be neither the time nor the ability to manufacture and install the necessary infrastructure, from simple solar-power to the more exotic technologies.

Individuals can do little to prevent ruthless political and corporate power and greed, catastrophic wars, or scientific madness gone wrong. Many threats could be avoided if we each do our part, however small, to help alleviate the damage we are doing to Mother Earth. Humans are systematically destroying this planet, which is not only our home, it also belongs to other forms of life.

We must spend our lives on a living, moving planet, our beautiful world, and we must accept, and indeed plan for, possible extremes of natural occurrences such as earthquake, volcanoes, asteroids, tidal waves, floods, wildfires and other extreme weather events. These are a fact of life which we ignore at our own peril. War, social upheaval, and similar catastrophic events while not a 'given' cannot be dismissed. We are now aware of the potential of super-volcanoes, and while global warming and the apparent increase in large earthquakes are a cause for concern, some panic may be due to 'instant' reporting by the media.

While some talk of Nibiru or Planet X(9) there is a much greater chance of an asteroid or similar-type object striking the Earth. It is believed such an impact ended the reign of the dinosaurs 65 million years ago, and 250 million years ago one caused the biggest mass extinction in history. In most cases, they trigger massive earthquakes and volcanoes, rising sea levels and climate change. Astronomers constantly monitor the skies to identify potential threats, but despite categorizing several hundred asteroids as potentially hazardous, many more have not yet been detected.

That being said, in western society we have compounded our survival problems by becoming totally dependent upon modern and digital technology, ruled by computers and the satellites orbiting our globe. Not only could a natural or man-made disaster disrupt or destroy the entire network, a decent size solar flare could produce the same result, and disrupt our way of life.

We are already aware of the damage more regular solar flares can cause. Years ago, the solar observation satellite recorded how, just after a solar flare, an immense bubble of superheated plasma, rushed outwards at over two million kilometres an hour. More often than not, it speeds harmlessly into space, and when it does come our way, the Earth is mostly protected by its magnetic shield. We do have a couple of monitoring (ACE) satellites, but they only give a few minutes warning for preventative measures to be taken.

In 1989 fallout from a solar flare caused a geomagnetic storm which severely affected power grids in north-eastern US and Canada. (This was only a third of the intensity of one recorded in 1859, which caused the Earth's magnetic field to fluctuate by 4%). In later years, some caused the failure of several communication and weather satellites. Again, in April 2001 and November 2003 there was massive solar activity, but luckily this mainly missed the Earth. In January 2005 a giant sunspot (720) produced four powerful solar flares. A fifth, on 20 January, was much worse than experts expected. Within minutes the most intense proton storm in decades, with high-energy particles, reached the Earth and Moon. Again, in February 2010 another sunspot erupted

These were all considered normal during the Sun's regular solar maximum in its 11 year cycle, but scientists are monitoring events very carefully, concerned that we still don't fully understand the physics of our own Solar System. Nature usually never runs to plan all the time, larger solar events are certainly possible, and could disrupt Earth's magnetic field, causing untold problems.

Severe geomagnetic disturbances occur approximately every 70 years or so, and these super-storms of disruptive magnitude, can wreak a lot more havoc than just a few power-grids failing. There are hundreds of nuclear reactors around the world. They are supposedly designed with fail safe provisions, which provide for generator power to operate the cooling systems for both the core and spent fuel rods. Unfortunately, these safeguards have been calculated to compensate for a blackout lasting a few days, not a few weeks or longer. While it is hoped that most major powers would have already taken steps to remedy this problem, the potential for meltdown, in just a small percentage of reactors world-wide, is almost too horrendous to contemplate.

There are always unforeseen circumstances, such as Fukushima, and one must never forget the development of electromagnetic-pulse weapons. Even the scientists have concerns. I once met with Sir Mark Oliphant when he was still robust but very elderly. He told me that in hindsight he regretted his contribution to nuclear energy research.

In the event of a severe power-grid failure, electricity, water, sanitation and fuel supplies would be affected, as would communications, banking, food and medical supplies and all the necessities of life we take for granted. It could take weeks, months or even longer to manufacture and repair all the damaged infrastructure.

Regardless of the prophecies of doom, it is always wise to have some supplies up your sleeve.

In the latter half of 2015 Elizabeth, Leesa, and one other contactee, all followed an inexplicable compulsion and bought inflatable airbeds, and Vera a collapsible bed. None of them knew why. They were not expecting visitors, and had spare beds if any arrived. All have extra supplies of long-life or non-perishable food, and several the ability to grow their own. They wondered if this was related to their alien connections? Sometime in the future would there be some emergency where they would have to accommodate unexpected friends or refugees?

Lydia had gone one step further, and had bought and kept a caravan she never actually used – she didn't know why. Patty had gone to extremes. She and her mother suddenly purchased a farm and old house west of the mountains behind Sydney. She wasn't even living in it!

As many others did, I spent part of my childhood in rural Europe, with no modern facilities. We lived close to nature, and learned to adapt to her moods and cycles. Often, we were snowed-in for the Winter, and flooded during Spring. We always kept supplies for at least four weeks in advance, and grew much of our own food.

I have the advantage of being involved in Counter Disaster Management for 25 years of my life, and am probably more aware of the potential for unexpected disasters, and the necessity for being prepared in advance. I still keep essential food stocks six weeks in advance, and have a large first aid kit, extra blankets, CB radio, water tank, fire-wood, emergency cooking facilities, candles, wind-up torch/radios and solar lights plus basic tools and seeds, with sufficient garden space to grow my own food. In addition, I have plenty of stationery, writing implements, and 'how to' books and other reading materials.

Very few people live in an environment which is totally risk free. While I live well above sea-level, I always run the risk of forest fires. While I have considered an evacuation plan, I do have the advantage of bore water nearby. People should examine their own environment, and consider the implications of certain, probable and possible disasters. To ensure their property is safe, people should identify and rectify possible hazards, and then devise a plan for foreseeable disasters.

Alternatives should be devised for situations where essential services may break down. Supplies of food, medicine etc. can be stored and kept fresh by regular rotation, and evacuation plans and alternative transport should be considered.

Sensible planning and precautions are no different to any other insurance policy. One hopes it will never happen, but are covered, just in case!

Epilogue

"Any search for knowledge only proves that undiscovered things do exist and that on revealing something new, you only open another hundred questions. In fact, it is an endless pit with no end, therefore why make the assumption that there is a conclusion?" – John Auchettl.

Regardless of whether we ever solve the mystery of aliens and UFOs, they have broadened our horizons and made us 'think outside of the box' on so many levels.

In April 1947, two months *before* the famous Kenneth Arnold sighting, and five years *before* Adamski's meeting and subsequent messages, an article called *Son of the Sun*, submitted under the pen-name 'Alexander Blade', was received by Ray Palmer, then the editor of *Fantastic Adventures* magazine.

Palmer subsequently published it in the November 1947 issue. It was later reprinted in the San Diego BSRA *Round Robin*. When Rosemary and Millen drew Bribsley Le Poer Trench's attention to it, he included it in his book *The Sky People*.

"We are already here, among you. Some of us have always been ... We have been confused with the gods of many world religions, although we are not gods, but your fellow creatures, as you will learn directly before many more years have passed. You will find records of our presence in the mysterious symbols of ancient Egypt, where we made ourselves known ... Our principal symbol appears in the religious art of your present civilization and occupies a position of importance upon the great seal of your country. It has been preserved in certain secret societies founded originally to keep alive the knowledge of our existence and our intentions toward mankind.

"We have left you certain landmarks, placed carefully in different parts of the globe, but most prominently in Egypt ... At that time, the foundations of your present civilisation were 'laid in the earth' and the most ancient of your known landmarks established by means that would appear as miraculous to you now as they did to pre-Egyptians, so many thousands of years ago. Since that time the whole art of building in stone has become symbolic, to many of you, of the work in hand ... the building of the human race towards its perfection.

"You have lately achieved the means of destroying yourselves ... Yours is not the first civilisation to have achieved, and used, such means. Yours will not be the first civilisation to be offered the means of preventing that destruction and proceeding, in the full glory of its accumulated knowledge, to establish an era of enlightenment on Earth.

"However, if you do accept the means offered to you, and if you do establish such a millennium on the basis of your present accomplishments, yours will be the first civilisation to do so ... This time, it is to be hoped that the memory of our spacecraft – passed on to your children and their children, will be clear and precise. That you will not cause them to forget, as your ancestors forgot,

the meaning of the diagrams and instructions we will leave with you. If you do fail, as other civilisations have failed, we will see your descendants wearing wiring-diagrams for simple machines as amulets, expecting the diagrams to do what their forefathers were taught the completed article would accomplish. Then their children, forgetting even that much – or little – would preserve the amulet as a general protective device – or as an intellectual curiosity – or perhaps as a religious symbol. Such is the cycle of forgetfulness."

This message was simple, logical and to the point, and I fear made out of dire necessity. Nobody really knows the true identity of the author, but I can hazard a guess. While mankind paid a fractional amount of attention to these warnings we were being given, we did not really desist our errant and destructive ways.

There is another pertinent quote from the days of ancient Greece, when Solon, the Athenian lawyer visited Egyptian priests over 2,500 years ago:

"There is no old opinion handed down among you by the ancient tradition, and I will tell you why. There have been, and will be again, many destructions of mankind arising out of many causes, the greatest by fire and water."

"Whereas just when you and other nations are beginning to be provided with letters and other requisites of civilised life, the stream from heaven comes pouring down and so you have to begin all over again like children and know nothing of what happened in ancient times."
(Plato *Timaeus* 22)

On examining the experiencers' and other reports over the following 70 years, I have come to the conclusion that the Visitors resorted to their 'Plan C'. They genetically augmented or influenced as many of the world's population as possible, giving them the abilities and awareness to be more in tune with Mother Earth, their fellow beings and animals. It appears, in some cases, they chose particular candidates who already had suitable genes inherited from previous ancestors.

In some respects, this has met with limited success, but I fear, not soon enough. In this book, I mainly concentrate on entities who maybe are, or resemble, their human counterparts. Unfortunately, we cannot analyse the entire scenario in relation to these particular Visitors who may be paternalistic and benign. There are other agencies and/or entities currently creating division, war and barbarity in our society. Once these are factored into the equation the whole situation becomes incredibly complex.

I do have some thoughts regarding the humanoid visitors, and their presence during the 20th century. Reports of their interaction began not long after man mastered flight with the Wright brothers and others. Perhaps this was influential in their urgency to steer us in the right direction with regards to our probable rapid technological advancement.

Maybe, one day, we will know the answers to these and many other questions.

Index

A
Adamski, George, 22, 24–28, 31, 34–36, 47, 248
Akon (entity), 13
Albatross, HMAS, 72, 181
Amicizia (group), 165–166
Amiens (France), 29–30
Anaflow, Anton, 82
Andrews, George, 89–90
animal mutilations, 142
Anjikuni, Lake (Canada), 9
Antarctic, 200, 203–208
Anunnaki, 21, 39, 195–196, 244
APRO (Aerial Phenomena Research Organisation), 201
Arctic, 54, 200–204, 207
Argentina, 24, 201, 206
The Assessment (project), 87–88
Aston, Warren, 11, 30
Atlantis, 21

B
Baez, Robert, 171–172
Bajenov, Major, 61
Barbato, Cristoforo, 27
Barret, Sir Arthur, 16
Bartini, Robert, 55
Baumgartner, Bob, 62
Beckley, Timothy, 88
Bellinghausen, Fabian Gottlieb von, 205
Benitez, Juan, 13–14, 53
Bergier, Jaques, 60
Bhulautsen (researcher), 170
Biefeld-Brown Effect, 78
Bikini Atoll, 77
Bird Tribes, 131
Birdsall, Graham, 90, 126, 141, 202, 208
Birdsall, Mark, 88
Blue Mountains (New South Wales), 99–103, 162, 221, 225
Bologna (Italy), 166–167
Bonham, James, 92
Braun, Wernher von, 56, 84
Brazil, 24–25, 201, 208, 245
Breccia, Stefano, 165–166
Breguet, Louis, 67
Brown, Thomas Townsend, 78
BUFORA (British UFO Research Organisation), 46
Byrd, Admiral Richard, 203–207

C
Cabassi (researcher), 166
Caddy, Peter, 16
Canada, 6, 9, 18, 54, 70, 81, 141, 151, 251
Cape Town (South Africa), 13–14
Carballal, Manuel, 52–53
Carson's Field (Northern Territory), 69
Carter, Jimmy, 74
Casey, Gerry, 59
Catania (Italy), 167–168
'Cave of the Half Moon' (Slovakia), 198
cellular memory, 143
Chodan, Helmut, 12
Clancarty, Earl of (Brinsley Le Poer Trench), 33–47
Claridge, Ronald, 59–60
cloning, 145
Clostermann, Pierre, 67
Coler, Hans, 54
compulsions, 109
Coolamon (New South Wales), 6–7
Cooper, Gordon, 22–23
Cooper, Timothy, 63–64
Cosford RAF (UK), 124
Cramp, Leonard, 37
Creighton, Gordon, 11, 13, 24, 46, 170, 201
CRISPR (gene editing), 145

D

Darwin, Charles, 138
Dean, Bob, 87–88
Decker, Rosemary, 20, 33–47, 48–51, 81, 122, 170, 196, 236–237, 247
Denmark, 10
Diaz, Leopoldo, 30
Dickeson, Bryan, 209, 231, 236
Dims, Derrel, 152–153
DNA (deoxyribonucleic acid), 137–140, 141, 143
Dodd, Tony, 90–91
Dolan, Richard, 54
Donitz, Karl, 200
Dover Beach (UK), 10
Dowding, Lord, 60
Drabier, Jaques, 58
Dragon succession, 140
Drakensberg Mountains (South Africa), 12–13
dreams, 235–237
Dworshak, Leo, 7–8

E

Edwards Air Force Base (US), 47, 89
Einstein, Albert, 68, 85
Eisenhower, Dwight, 34, 47, 81, 89–90
ENCODE (project), 138
entanglement, 79
Erebus, Mt (Antarctica), 208
Essen (Germany), 60

F

Farrell, Mike, 86
Fatima (Portugal), 40, 241–242
Felix, Alidino, 25
Fenton Airfield (Northern Territory), 69
Fenwick, L., 152
Ferrandi, Orlandi, 25
Feuerball (aircraft), 58
Fiorino (researcher),, 166
Fish, Marjorie, 174
fleur-de-lis (bloodline), 104, 108, 116, 122, 139–140, 141, 176, 218
Flying pancake, 57

Flying Saucer Review, 11, 24, 46, 68, 73, 88, 170
foo-fighters, 57–58, 60
Forrestal, James, 67
Fowler, Raymond, 62
France, 59, 59–60, 72, 165, 168
Fry, Dan, 20–22, 36, 38, 147
Fry, Margaret, 9, 23

G

Galli, Luciano, 166
Gardner, Laurence, 140–141
Germany, 11–12, 31, 52–61, 65, 70, 80, 83–84, 87, 91, 150, 165, 198, 200, 203–207, 216
'ghost rockets,' 65–66
Glenn, John, 83
Goddard, Victor, 60
Good, Timothy, 25, 68, 80, 88, 166, 192
Gorbachev, Mikhail, 82
Greer, Stephen, 243
Guimaraes, Professor, 24

H

HAARP, 78, 151
Haigneré, Claudie, 146
Hapgood, Charles, 205
Hellyer, Paul, 80–81
Hill, Betty and Barney, 172–174
Hill-Norton, Lord, 67, 88
Hind, Cynthia, 12–13
Hollis, Freda, 168
Hollow Earth Theory, 204
holograms, 40–41
Holt, Turner, 61–62
Holy Grail, 141
Hoover, J. Edgar, 64
Hopkins, Budd, 154
Horizon (project), 68
Horsley, Sir Peter, 16–17
Howe, Linda Moulton, 208
Huffman, William, 62
Hull, Cordell, 61–62
Hutchinson, John, 78, 92
Hynek, Allen, 245

I

Ilyumzhinov, Kirsan, 82
International Geophysical Year, 207
invisibility, 76, 193
Ireland, 40
Ishiwaka, Kanshi, 82
Isle of Man, 96–97, 110, 116, 120, 122–126, 240
Italy, 53–54, 58, 163, 165–167, 242

J

John Paul II (Pope), 28, 242
John XXIII (Pope), 27, 242
Jones, Cyril, 17–19
Jones, William, 61
Judenwiese (Germany), 12
junk DNA, 137, 143
Jutland (Denmark), 10

K

Kallangur (Queensland), 111
Kangaroo Valley (New South Wales), 178
Kannenberg, Ida, 43
Keyhoe, Donald, 66, 73
Kjellson, Henry, 65, 91
Klarer, Eizabeth, 12–13, 74
Klotzbach, Hans, 11–12
Knights Templar, 141
Knock (Ireland), 40
Komazura, Takashi, 62
Kraspedon, Dino, 25

L

Laithwaite, Eric, 17
Lake Anjikuni (Canada), 9
Latihan, 219
Lazarev, Mikhail, 205
Lear, John, 54
Leedskalnin, Edward, 92
Leir, Roger, 153–154
Lemarckism, 138
Lemuria, 21
levitation, 91–92
Liljegren, Anders, 65
Long Beach (US), 59
Los Angeles (US), 63–64
Lunnisted, Rolf, 66–67

M

MacArthur, General, 64
MacDonald Airfield, 69
McErlain, Kathleen, 146
MacLaughlin, Colonel, 22
Maderno (Italy), 53–54
Magnet (project), 81
Majestic 12 (project), 67
Manchurian Candidates, 151
Mantle, Philip, 135
MasoniChip, 141
Massey, William, 60
Massie, Norman, 6
Medinaceli (Spain), 168–170
Melgar, Mariano, 53
memory, cellular, 143
'Men from the Ministry,' 98–99
'men in black,' 179–182, 190
Menger, Howard, 24–25
Mexico, 30
Michell, John, 135
Missouri (US), 62
Mitchell, Edgar, 243
mitochondrial DNA (mDNA), 139, 141
MKULTRA (project), 151
Moderson, F., 54
Montecalvo, Michael, 88–89
Moon film (1954), 86
Mu (Lemuria), 21
MUFON (Mutual UFO Network), 6, 34, 144, 171
Munico (Spain), 53
Murray, John, 245

N

Nagy, Tibor, 86
NASA, 68
Near Earth Asteroid Tracking (NEAT), 77
Nephilim, 39
Neuschwabenland (Antarctica), 205
'Never Never Land,' 236

New Hampshire, 172–174
New Zealand, 69, 209–229
Nibiru (Planet X), 28–29, 196–197, 244–246, 250
NICAP (National Investigations Committee on Aerial Phenomena), 173
Norcans (species), 6
North West Territories (Canada), 54
Norway, 66
Noury, Leo, 14
Novosibirsk (Russia), 170–171

O

Oberth, Hermann, 55–56, 57, 83–84
obsessions, 109
O'Farrell, James (Shamus), 72
Omega (project), 70
Operation High-Jump, 206–207
Operation Taberlan, 206
Oppenheimer, Robert, 68
Orthon (entity), 25–28, 34–36, 47

P

Palmer, Ray, 250
Pauchet, Victor, 29
Paul VI (Pope), 242
Pauwels, Louis, 60
Peenemunde (Germany), 56
'Peter Pan,' 236
Petersen, Hans, 80
Petit, Jean Pierre, 14
Philips, Ken, 110, 115, 116
Phillips, Ted, 198
Pinkney, John, 8
Piri-Reis map, 204–205
Pius XII (Pope), 27
Planet X/9 (Nibiru), 28–29, 196–197, 244–246, 250
Pointon, David, 124
Polaris, 233–234
Popes, 27–28, 242
Popovich, Marina, 170
Portugal, 40, 241–242
Princess Elisabeth Station (Antarctica), 205
Project Horizon, 68

Project Magnet, 81
Project Omega, 70
Project Silver Bug, 70
Project Winterhaven, 78

Q

Qigong, 218–219
Queen Maud Land (Antarctica), 205
Quiros, Christianne, 144

R

radiation exposure, 183
RAF *Cosford* (UK), 124
Randles, Jenny, 17
Ransome, Valerie, 23
'Red Baron' (Manfred von Richtofen), 52
Redfern, Nick, 70
Reynolds, Rosalind, 135–136
Ribera, Antonio, 168–170
Richtofen, Manfred von, 52
Ringer, John, 58
RNA (ribonucleic acid), 138
Roberts, Andy, 58–59
Roddenberry, Gene, 30, 249
Roerich, Nicholas, 5
Roestenberg, Jennie, 123
Ruser-Larsen, Captain, 205
Russia, 55–56, 60–61, 65–67, 69–70, 80, 82, 87, 138, 170–171, 202, 206–207, 247

S

St Louis (US), 14–15
Sammaciccia, Bruno, 165
'sanctuary,' 223, 226, 228
Santorini, Paul, 67
Sao Paulo (Brazil), 24
Saskatchewan (Canada), 54
Sauder, Richard, 199, 208
Schauberger, Viktor, 56
Schriever, Rudolph, 56–57
Schroeder, John, 14
Schweinfurt (Germany), 60
Scott, Irena, 61
Sesto Canende airfield (Italy), 53
Shambala, 5

Shangri-la, 5
Shuichuan, 218
Sider, Jean, 29
Silver Bug (project), 70
Siragusa, Eugenio, 167–168
Sitchin, Zechariah, 39, 195, 244
Sivier, David, 58
Skunk Works (US), 70, 82
Slovakia, 198
Smith, Wilbur, 77, 81
'Soul Catcher 2025,' 155
South Africa, 12–14
South African Air Force (SAAF), 13
Spain, 53, 168–169
Spanish Civil War, 52–53
Spencer, Stefan, 134
Spighesi, Stephen, 64
Sprinkle, Leo, 34, 51
Steckling, Fred, 26
Steiger, Brad, 174
Stonehill, Paul, 55, 69
Stringfield, Len, 62
Stroganov, Yuri, 69
SUFOI (Skandinavisk UFO Information), 10
Surikov, Boris, 61
Swedish 'ghost rockets,' 65–66
Sydney Harbour, 230–231
synthetic telepathy, 154–155

T

Task Force 68, 206
telepathy, 154–155
Terziski, Vladimir, 53–54
Tesla, Nikola, 84–86
test ban treaties, 77
Thule Society, 203, 205
Timor Sea, 61
Tite family, 23
Tombaugh, Clyde, 22
Tompkins, William, 23, 60
trans-humanism, 155
transient lunar phenomena, 41
treaties, test ban, 77
Trench, Brinsley Le Poer, 45, 46–47
Trench, Millen Le Poer, 33–47
Tsiolkovskiy, Konstantin, 55, 56

Turner, Karla, 109
twinned dreams, 235–237

U

Ummo (movement), 14
United States, 14–15, 20, 22, 59, 62–64, 70, 82, 89, 172–174

V

Vatican, 27, 242
Veri Chip (implant), 150
Vesco, Renato, 58, 59
Villela, Rubens, 208
Visani, Umberto, 54, 165
Voison, Gabriel, 67
Volkenrode (Goering Aeronautical Research Institute), 55

W

Waiheke Island (New Zealand), 209–225
Waitzrik, Peter, 52
Wales, 9
Walsh, Lee, 193
Walton, Travis, 15–16
Warrington, Peter, 17
Wartena, Udo, 11
Wasserbillig (Germany), 11–12
White Sands Missile Proving Grounds (US), 20, 22
Wicklinski, Leo, 171–172
Williamson, George Hunt, 36, 38
The Wingmakers (website), 197
Winterhaven (project), 78
Wood, Robert, 63
Wood, Ryan, 62
The Wrekin (UK), 105, 116, 118, 119, 120, 122–126, 133, 134, 176
Wyllie, Timothy, 192

Y

Yamashita, Tomoyusku, 62

www.ingramcontent.com/pod-product-compliance
Lightning Source LLC
Chambersburg PA
CBHW080246030426
42334CB00023BA/2720